DI**
PARTY

ALSO BY TRACY BLOOM

TRACY BLOOM

DINNER PARTY

bookouture

Published by Bookouture in 2018

An imprint of StoryFire Ltd.
Carmelite House
50 Victoria Embankment
London EC4Y 0DZ

www.bookouture.com

ISBN: 978-1-78681-562-0
eBook ISBN: 978-1-78681-561-3

In loving memory of Hall Farm Kitchen
For the people, the food and the good times

Chapter One

Beth

After she'd changed for dinner, Beth glanced in to the full-length mirror and the awful memory came flooding back to her as it always did. During her nursing training in her early twenties she'd attended a course where everyone was asked to think of a positive word to describe each other. A male colleague wrote CUDDLY in thick green marker pen on her piece of flipchart paper. Beth had laughed and smiled as he jovially put his arm around her but, really, she was devastated. There it was, confirmed in vibrant green ink, what she already knew. She wasn't fat, by any means, but she certainly had curves. She knew she wasn't ugly, but she was also very clear that she was no sex goddess. Her role in life was *not* to attract men. Her role was to comfort, console and support, not entice, allure or dazzle.

She'd never in her life turned a man down. Never needed to. Never had cause to use the words, 'That's very nice that you fancy me, but I'm sorry I just don't fancy you.' She watched people do it on dating shows. Reject someone with such boldness and confidence as though they did it every day. As though it came naturally that they thought they were better than them. She'd liked to have done it, just once maybe. Just to feel what it was like. She felt bad for all the beautiful women who got unwanted attention, she really did, and obviously she would never want a man to force himself on her but… but… she'd liked to have at least been able to say no, just the once.

Maybe she should have said it when Chris asked her to marry him all those years ago.

'No,' she mouthed in to the free-standing mirror from Argos that her work colleagues had given her for a wedding present. 'No, thank you,' she said, aloud this time just to see what it sounded like.

She looked in the mirror again. It took only a moment to confirm that she didn't like what she saw. Her only saving grace was her line-free face, which at forty-five wasn't bad going. However, she suspected it was the one benefit of being a bit overweight. It was the doughnuts that plumped her skin out, not a rigorous and expensive skincare regime.

She'd wanted to wash her hair as it looked limp and lifeless after her eight-hour shift on the ward that day, but she'd run out of time. She'd riffled fruitlessly through her wardrobe praying she'd find her one pair of smart trousers, but she knew they were laughing at her from the bottom of the ironing pile hidden in the cupboard in the utility room. The ironing pile that would fall on her head the minute she opened the door, tumbling over the mountain of shopping bags and the golf clubs that Chris never used but insisted could not be got rid of.

So, there she was in a pair of cream linen trousers that went with a suit she once wore for a wedding even though she knew it was high-risk. Cream linen, cooking and red wine was bound to result in a Jackson Pollock masterpiece down her front at some point. No question. But it was less risky than the jeans that didn't fit and were fond of mysteriously letting the flies down or the black dress that needed scaffolding underwear so tight it would prevent her food intake from dropping anywhere below her belly button.

She would have to do.

Maybe she should have spent time putting some make-up on rather than cleaning the downstairs toilet. No, a clean toilet was more important than how she looked. Of course it was.

She slipped on some sensible shoes and ran downstairs. If she didn't start grating cheese now, she would never be ready on time. She also knew that Chris would be roaming around looking for the obligatory pre-dinner dips and so trouble was looming.

He was going to be really upset that there were no dips.

Her husband loved his dips. Beth suspected if she gave him dips for every meal, then he would be as happy as a pig in taramasalata. It was everything she could do to stop him eating all the dips before their guests arrived when it was their turn to host the monthly dinner party. She'd learnt that the timing of the dips' availability was crucial. She could only place the dip tray on the coffee table seconds before the doorbell rang or else Chris would wolf them down, leaving a few congealed smears of creamy substance along with an abundance of bendy carrot sticks. Chris thought crisps were the only way to scoop up a dip. A carrot spoilt a good dip in his opinion.

'Where are the dips?' shouted Chris from the living room as she ran down the hall and in to the kitchen.

'We're not having dips,' she shouted back.

'What!'

'We're *not* having dips.'

'Why not? We always have dips.'

'Because we're having a fondue.'

Chris didn't reply. Beth wouldn't be surprised if Chris wasn't this very minute searching under cushions to check for hidden dips.

'Fondue?' he questioned, arriving in the kitchen.

Beth looked up at him as she furiously grated cheese and fleetingly wondered if she could trust him to do a last-minute tidy of the hall. She quickly concluded that would be an error. A request like that would be met with as much astonishment and confusion as the lack of dips. Both situations were entirely unnecessary in Chris's mind. A protracted explanation would be required to inform him how to tidy the hall to an acceptable standard and she knew it would be easier and quicker to do it herself. As always. *How would he cope with grating cheese?* she thought. *Badly*, she concluded. She grated even faster. Time was running out.

'Tony rang and asked if I would make a fondue for Sarah's birthday as she enjoyed them so much whilst they were skiing,' Beth told him.

'Was that the skiing trip *with* or *without* children?' asked Chris sarcastically.

Beth glanced up at him. Chris hadn't been impressed that Beth had agreed to look after Tony and Sarah's six-year-old daughter whilst they went off for a much-needed 'minibreak' to the Swiss Alps.

'You know very well they're taking Chloe in half-term.'

'So why can't they have fondue then? And why does a fondue mean we can't have dips?'

'Because,' said Beth, feeling her grating increasing along with her pulse, 'dips wouldn't go with fondue. Too much dipping.'

'Too much dipping?' he asked in wonder.

'Yes. Dipping in *goo*, followed by more dipping in *goo*. Doesn't work does it? Too much *goo*.'

'Sounds bloody marvellous to me. There can never be too much dipping in my opinion. Shall I get out some peanuts?'

'No.'

'Popcorn then. What about popcorn?'

'No! You are not giving them popcorn.'

'But what will we do when they arrive? There'll be nothing to eat,' he said, sounding utterly horrified.

Beth paused the grating. She'd had enough of this.

'Talk, drink, do the Macarena, I don't bloody care. There does not need to be food shoved in their mouths the minute they arrive. You're not a bird swooping back to the nest to feed her hungry chicks. You are, Chris, obsessed with dips, sulking tonight because there will be *no* dips.'

Chris opened his mouth as if he was about to disagree. Beth decided she'd better shut him up quick before she actually throttled him.

'Can you check how many bottles of white are in the fridge?' she asked.

He walked over to the fridge behind her and opened the door.

'None,' she heard him say.

'What!'

'None. There's some milk, some orange juice, some—'

'Do you think Jake and Toby have taken them,' she interrupted. This was entirely feasible. At seventeen and nineteen, Beth's sons were just at the going to 'parties' stage in their adolescence, which meant that prior to them leaving the house a near strip search was required to check what quantities of alcohol were being smuggled out.

'No,' replied Chris. 'I let Jake take two tinnies with him and Toby is out with Poppy, so he's in safe hands.'

'So what did you do with the bottles you bought last night then?' she asked.

'What bottles?'

'You said you were going to buy the wine on the way home from work yesterday.'

'Did I?'

'Yes.'

'I forgot.'

Beth considered using the cheese grater on a part of his anatomy. She turned to him without pausing her destruction of the Parmesan block.

'Why are you still standing there?' she demanded.

He stared back at her, confused. 'Because you told me to check the fridge for wine.'

'But you already knew there was no wine in there.'

'I thought maybe you must have put some in.'

'But then I'd know, wouldn't I, and wouldn't be asking *you* to check!'

She lifted the grater slightly, in preparation for rubbing it against his face.

'Get in to the car and go down to the shop and buy some wine,' she said as calmly as possible.

Chris stared back at her as though he thought this was a suggestion rather than a demand.

'Now!' she bellowed. 'Or... *I will not be responsible for what I do with this grater!*'

'Of course,' he muttered, nodding vigorously before he trotted out of the kitchen.

Grating was now at hyper speed. A bead of sweat dropped off her forehead onto the chopping board, narrowly missing the Parmesan.

'Shit,' she cried as her knuckle scraped one of the sharp edges.

'Have you seen the keys?' asked Chris, poking his head around the kitchen door.

'Blood,' she said, holding her knuckles up to show him. 'I'm literally shedding blood, sweat and tears for this dinner party and you want me to find your keys!'

'No, don't you worry, it's all right. I'll find them. You carry on with what you are doing,' he said, disappearing again.

She could hear him in the hall, opening drawers and rustling coats, as she fought the urge to stop what she was doing, wash her hands and go and end the torture of listening to his version of 'looking' for something.

Ten minutes later, and after much huffing and puffing and running up and down stairs, Chris reappeared at the door. Beth had found a plaster and was hunting in the fridge for the Gruyère.

'It's all right, I've found them,' he informed her. 'In the en-suite!' He laughed.

She didn't look up. If he wasn't out of the house within ten seconds she might actually kill him. She heard him walk to the front door then inexplicably he re-appeared in the kitchen just as she was subjecting the Gruyère to the grater.

'By the way,' he said. 'Forgot to mention it, but I invited Simon to join us tonight. His wife's just left him, so he's a bit down. Needs cheering up. That's all right, isn't it? The more the merrier?'

Beth raised her eyes slowly to look at Chris. He was smiling at her, clearly oblivious to the ramifications of his invite. She'd only bought six steaks (she'd thought steak and a green salad would be a good follow-up to fondue) and made six individual lemon possets (light and refreshing, although now she'd made it she realised that she was dishing up yet more yellow goo. She could open up a great yellow restaurant at this rate!) and... and they only had six wine glasses that matched. What was Chris thinking inviting someone and forgetting to tell her? Who the hell was Simon anyway? She'd never even heard him mention a Simon, never mind his marital woes. Christ, they only had six fondue forks! This dinner party was on the brink of disaster… as usual… and no one had even arrived yet.

'We can stretch the food, can't we,' Chris said. 'Tell you what. I'll buy some crisps and dips whilst I'm down at the Co-op, then we'll be fine. See you later.'

Beth waited to hear the door slam, then threw the cheese grater across the kitchen.

JOURNALIST: So could you start by telling me how long you have been having your monthly dinner parties?

BETH: Well, let's see. Bit of a tricky question that one actually. So, the six of us had been getting together over dinner for a few years. Ever since Sarah moved back to Morbeck really. But that all changed when Chris, that's my husband, invited Simon over randomly one night to join us. None of the rest of us had ever met him before and little did we realise that the arrival of a new guest would ultimately change everything.

Chapter Two

Sarah

Sarah gazed in to her full-length French-reproduction gilt-framed mirror that was artfully leant against a wall in her bedroom.

'Prada sample sale,' she said aloud to herself. 'Got it years ago, when I was head womenswear buyer for Dean & Delphi's in London.'

Wow, that sounded good. Impressive. Wouldn't it be great to be able to say that to someone? How she longed to be asked where she'd picked up this particular gem and for them to be *actually* interested. No chance of that though at tonight's dinner party.

She fleetingly remembered the privileges she'd enjoyed at the peak of her career. Press launches, posh lunches, front rows at fashion shows and previews of designer sample sales, along with much more. There wasn't much opportunity for any of that in Morbeck, a small market town in Leicestershire. It wasn't that kind of place. It wasn't even as good as it was when she was growing up there. Charity shops had replaced the dress shops, betting shops had replaced the gift shops and a Greggs was all you got in terms of cafe culture.

Tony had very kindly made sure when they bought their house together that there would be a dressing room for all of the fantastic clothes she had accumulated throughout her career in fashion. But nothing depressed her more than walking in and trying to decide which particular fabulousness was low-key enough to not stand out like a sore thumb amongst the hoodies and sweatpants of Morbeck.

She watched in the reflection in the mirror as Tony entered the room behind her. Her heart leapt slightly as it always did. He was fourteen years older than her and luckily age suited him. Age often seemed to suit men.

'The babysitter's here,' he announced.

'Great,' she said, walking over to her dressing table so she could put her make-up on.

'Is Chloe in bed?' she asked.

'Yes. Anna's reading to her.'

'Where's Will?'

'In his room.'

'Have you told Anna that Will is here?'

'Yes. She's fine with it.'

She turned to look at him. He shrugged.

'What can I do?' he said. 'I can't *make* him babysit his half-sister, can I?'

Sarah turned back and picked up an eyeliner, lifting it to her left eye. 'It's Anna I'm worried about,' she continued. 'She must think it's weird that your nineteen-year-old son is in the house and not capable of a bit of babysitting.'

She heard Tony walk to the chest of drawers and fish around for something. 'Like I said, I can't make him babysit,' he repeated.

'I just wish he wasn't in the house, making it awkward for Anna,' said Sarah.

'She'll be fine. I bet he won't even come out of his room.'

Sarah sighed and tried to stop the inexplicable tears that had sprung to her eyes. She held her hand up to try to draw an even line along her eyelid and found that it was shaking. She took a deep breath. She'd not bothered with foundation as her skin glowed from the sun and wind of three days spent on the alpine slopes. She could, however, see tiny little lines at the corners of her eyes. She was sure they hadn't been there before… well, before what happened last week.

'This is for you,' said Tony, suddenly appearing at her side. She reached for a tissue and blew her nose. 'Happy birthday, darling.'

'What?' she said, looking up at him. 'But you gave me a present this morning.'

'I know, but I thought maybe you deserved an extra something this year.'

Because of what you did, she instantly thought. She reached out to take the small gift bag dangling on the end of a black velvet ribbon.

Jewellery – had to be.

It was.

A small square black velvet box. Oh God, a ring! She couldn't bear it.

Suddenly Tony was down on one knee right beside her, just as he had been seven years ago in Val d'Isère. He'd taken his skis off at the top of the mountain and proposed there and then. He'd taken her totally by surprise. His divorce had only come through the week before. She thought she had never been so happy.

She looked down at him now as he gently took the box from her and opened it to show her.

'It's an eternity ring,' he said quietly.

She remembered when she'd accepted his proposal that all she could think of was that she had never been so sure about anything in her life.

She had to be, didn't she? After all, such a hefty price had been paid. Tony's previous marriage was the cost of her dream proposal.

She'd never meant to fall in love with a married man. She wasn't that kind of girl. But perhaps nobody thinks they are that kind of girl.

He'd innocently popped up as a suggested friend on Facebook. He was friends with her eldest brother, but she hadn't seen him since she'd escaped the clutches of the small market town at just eighteen to head off to university without a backwards glance. At the time, she wouldn't have cared if she never saw Morbeck again, but somehow when you've lived in London for too long and done the whole amazingly successful career woman thing, followed by the hideously fruitless search for a nice, kind, loving man in the nation's capital thing, there is massive appeal in seeking out your simpler past. And there he was. Tony. Married, settled, stable. What could hurt in sending him a friend request? Nothing. Totally innocent. Well, that was how it started.

It only took one comment, that was all. One connection sparked the entire chain of events.

It was a picture of Tony and his mates on a skiing holiday. She'd hovered. Then thought, *sod it*. She had to say something.

WOW! Looks amazing snow – where are you?

Then came the reply.

Morzine – you still ski? I remember your brother saying you were good!

And that was that. Connection made. Fast-forward through more Comments and Likes of photos, until apparently he had a meeting in

London and would she care for a drink afterwards? Several drinks as it turned out, followed by confessions of an unhappy marriage, followed by an affair, followed by him leaving his wife, followed by a divorce, followed by a proposal on the top of a mountain on the second day of a ski trip.

Fast-forward a further seven years and here she was sitting in front of an antique dressing table in their sympathetically restored and modernised Georgian farmhouse in Morbeck. Married, a child of their own, stepmum to a monosyllabic teenager, a closet full of designer clothes but with absolutely nowhere to wear them. Her career had been left behind in London. Her sacrifice for love.

She looked at her husband, down on one knee, underlining her commitment.

She let the tears flow. At least she hadn't got round to putting any make-up on. She had no idea why she was crying. She figured there were equal measures of joy and sadness. How confusing. How could one's life be so bad and yet so good? How could you have everything and yet feel like you have nothing? There was a massive career-sized hole in her life that she was finding harder and harder to fill.

'There's no need to cry,' said Tony, taking the ring out and slipping it on her finger. It fitted perfectly. Of course it did. Tony would have made sure of that.

'It's just so beautiful,' sniffed Sarah.

'There's a surprise waiting for you at Beth's too,' he added.

'Not another present?' gasped Sarah. *Please no more*, this was only making her feel worse.

'No. I just asked Beth if perhaps she would be able to do a fondue, seeing as we are celebrating your birthday tonight.'

'You did what?'

'Asked Beth if she would do a fondue.'

'Does she even have a fondue set?'

'I don't know. I said if it was too much trouble it wouldn't matter, but she said, no, no, not a problem. She'd be delighted. If it had been Marie's turn tonight, then of course I wouldn't have dreamed of it.'

Sarah snorted. They both knew that if he'd asked Marie, she would have willingly agreed before going totally over the top in a bid to provide the perfect fondue, giving herself a nervous breakdown in the process.

'I knew we were in safe hands with Beth,' said Tony.

'Good old Beth,' sighed Sarah. 'She never says no to anyone.'

JOURNALIST: Can I ask what type of food you normally cook for your dinner parties?

BETH: Oh, just the usual really. My husband isn't that adventurous with food. I did once do a fondue. That's about as adventurous as I get. Perhaps I shouldn't have done it though. If I'm honest, if I hadn't done that fondue then Simon probably wouldn't have tried doing a raclette and then maybe it never would have happened.

Chapter Three

Marie

'Can you call Beth and tell her we are having a no-carbs January?' Marie shouted from the hallway as she surveyed her appearance in the full-length mirror right next to the front door. She couldn't ever leave the house before a full inspection. There was no excuse for an appearance malfunction in this house.

She turned to look at her side view. Christmas didn't seem to have done too much damage. The body-con dress was conscious of her body in all the right places. It's a good job she had carried on going to the gym or else there was no way she would be rocking this look.

She looked down at her legs. Thankfully it was mild outside so no need for the dreaded tights, although that did mean she'd had to organise a quick spray tan to banish the pale glow. She knew Sarah would be turning up with her 'ski-tan', making Marie look even paler if she wasn't careful. She briefly thought about Beth, who always looked pasty. Must be working in a hospital all the time without any natural light. Maybe she should give her a voucher for a spray tan for her next birthday.

'What did you say?' said Duncan, running down the stairs tucking his shirt in as he went.

'Why aren't you wearing the shirt I bought you for Christmas?' she asked, horrified to see that her husband had picked the awful shirt his mother had bought him.

'I… err…' he said, 'I tried it and it's a bit small. It will fit though. After I've lost the Christmas weight.' He slapped his middle-aged spread and dug his hands in his pockets.

'You need to ring Beth and tell her we are having a no-carbs January,' said Marie, turning back to the mirror and tweaking a few strands of her hair.

'Surely it doesn't count if we are out to dinner?' protested Duncan.

'It so does. What did you have for lunch?'

'We had a team-builder over lunch, so it was a buffet.'

'So what did you eat?'

'Just the carrots, you know, and the dips. I didn't go near the sandwiches or the sausage rolls. Honestly.'

Marie knew he was lying. She could practically see breadcrumbs on his top lip. There was no way her husband could be presented with an all-you-can-eat buffet and not partake in all he could eat.

'Well, no carbs tonight. Remember. You need to fit in that shirt and a ski suit. That reminds me, don't let me forget to ask Sarah where they buy their ski clothes.'

'You can ask her,' said Duncan, screwing his face up, 'but we shouldn't be buying designer stuff for our first trip. If we like it, maybe next time. But if we don't then it's just a waste of money, isn't it?'

Marie appeared to ignore Duncan's comment, just checked her legs for telltale orange patches. Her heels were borderline tango, but as long as she kept her skyscraper shoes on then no one would notice. And Beth wasn't the type to make you take your shoes off at the door. And she had sons. There was no way she was putting her bare feet where they might have been. Thank goodness their only child was a girl. Annabelle was so much more hygienic than Beth's two boys.

'Perhaps Sarah could take me shopping for skiwear,' she said to her reflection.

'Is that a good idea, love?' asked Duncan. 'You know Tony's credit card is a lot thicker than mine. Why don't you take Beth?'

'Beth's never been skiing!'

'I know, but Beth's a bargain hunter isn't she. Gets all the deals. That tent she bought last year, my God, we should have had one of those at that price.'

'Like I said at the time, over my dead body,' replied Marie. 'Dead is the only way you would get me in a tent or a sleeping bag or a field for that matter.'

'No. I know. I hear you. I'm just saying, don't go overboard on the skiwear. We'll only be using it for a week after all.'

Marie sighed. Why did she have to marry the tightest man in Morbeck?

She turned back towards the mirror to scrutinise her face. She'd pass for mid-thirties surely? At forty-five, she could keep up with the twenty-something gym bunnies at her aerobics classes. There was no way she was letting them get the better of her.

'Nice dress,' she heard her husband say. 'Is it new?'

'Yes,' she said, doing a twirl to give him the full impact. 'Don't worry, I used my discount,' she added in a singsong voice.

'Good,' he replied before he turned and went out of the hall and in to the kitchen.

Marie sighed again and turned to look back in the mirror. There used to be a time, she remembered, when the word 'discount' had never entered their vocabulary. When the way she looked was admired for purely aesthetic purposes not for how much money she had saved. Duncan really should be very proud that she still cared about her looks; after all, she could be like Beth and have given up. Then he'd be sorry.

JOURNALIST: It's brilliant that your friendship has endured so long. Do you think that has been helped by the fact you make a point of meeting every month to eat dinner together? Do you always get along? Have there ever been any fall-outs over food?

DUNCAN: Normally it's pretty uneventful, to be honest. Very easy-going. I do remember there was an argument over dips once. That must have been the fondue night, I think. Beth threw some dips in the bin at some point. Very dramatic. Not like her. Now, if it had been my wife, it wouldn't have been surprising at all!

Chapter Four

Beth

'Sorry – are we early?' asked Marie when Beth opened the door.

'No, not at all. It's just my make-up artist has not arrived yet, the hairdresser has cancelled and my entire Gucci wardrobe is stuck at the dry-cleaner's, can you believe? It's a tragedy,' replied Beth.

'Very funny,' said Marie, leaning forward to give her a hug. 'You look lovely by the way.'

'We both know that is a lie,' said Beth. 'Oh, and that reminds me, I must get a chicken out of the freezer for Sunday lunch,' she added, staring at Marie's bare legs with goosebumps on their goosebumps.

'Excuse me, I've just had a spray tan,' replied Marie, sticking her leg out to show her.

'Mmm,' said Beth, taking a closer look. 'Bit less basting required, I reckon. You seen Sarah?'

'No, is she really tanned? She always comes back from skiing looking soooo well.'

'She looked great when she came to pick Chloe up. Very healthy. But then, wouldn't you, if you'd been kid-free for three days. Hi, Duncan. Can I take your coat? Chris is down at the shop buying the wine he should have bought last night. If he comes back with dips, I will not be responsible for my actions.'

'I had dips for lunch,' announced Duncan. He glanced at Marie. 'Didn't touch the sandwiches. Definitely didn't have an egg roll. They looked great, but I left them well alone.'

'Oh, we meant to ring you,' chimed Marie. 'We're not doing carbs in January. We are on a strict regime to lose weight before we go skiing?'

'No carbs?' asked Beth. She thought about the mountain of bread she had just cut up ready for the cheese fondue. 'Seriously?'

'Absolutely,' said Marie. 'We'll have whatever you're having but without the potatoes or rice or whatever. No problem. We're being very disciplined.'

'But I've done a cheese fondue with French bread as a starter.'

'Oh,' said Marie.

'It's all right,' said Duncan. 'We'll just have dips. Won't we, love? It's what I had at lunchtime, but that's fine.' He was nodding vigorously.

'As long as you've got carrots or something. Not breadsticks or crisps. We can't have those,' added Marie.

Beth thought she might put the grater in the centre of the table and grate everyone's faces with it.

'Look, we've bought two bottles of wine,' offered Marie.

'So you *are* drinking then?' asked Beth.

'Of course.' Marie shrugged.

'Just no bread.'

'No, definitely not bread.'

'I'll just have dips,' said Duncan again.

'Well that's a real shame,' said Beth, walking past them through to the kitchen. 'I've only done fondue because Tony called and said would I do it as a treat for Sarah's birthday because she loved it so much whilst they were skiing.' She swivelled round in the middle of the kitchen and faced Marie head on, coming in after her. She watched and waited.

'For… for Sarah's birthday,' said Marie, looking back at her wide-eyed.

'Yeees,' said Beth slowly. *Keep quiet; don't say a word*, she thought to herself. *Don't say a word.*

Marie looked awkwardly at Duncan.

She's going to cave, Beth thought. She counted down in her head from five. She could already see Duncan salivating over the mountain of bread chopped up on the breadboard.

'Well, I suppose if it's for Sarah's birthday we can make an exception,' said Marie. Beth saw Duncan do a mini fist pump out the corner of her eye.

'Marvellous,' said Beth, swinging round. 'Try some bread, Duncan,' she instructed. 'Proper stuff from the baker's. Fresh this afternoon.'

Duncan's hand darted out like a snake's tongue. He grabbed at least three pieces and shoved them in his mouth. Beth saw Marie's horrified look.

'Calories in the form of white wine?' Beth asked, getting a bottle out of the bag Marie had handed her.

Marie nodded silently, although Beth could have sworn she heard her stomach rumble.

'Spritzer?' she suggested, reaching up in to the cupboard to pull down some glasses.

'Oh, yes please,' said Marie. 'Of course.'

It was their thing. Spritzers. The three of them – Beth, Sarah and Marie – used to go to the Yew Tree in their mid-teens when under-eighteens were allowed to go in pubs and drink alcohol rather than go down dark alleys and take drugs like many of them seemed to do nowadays. They always used to drink spritzers, thinking it was the height of sophistication despite the fact that lemonade was their mixer of choice. Truth be told, they all still liked Pinot with a dash of lemonade when they were together. Never in sophisticated company, though, of course. In fact, it had taken much persuasion from Beth to get Marie and Sarah back in to their wine and lemonade habit.

When they deserted her to go off to uni after A-levels, she'd been left to drink Blue Nun and Schweppes with all the other apprentices, trainees and YTSs as she commenced her nursing training. When Sarah and Marie came back for their first Christmas holiday, they'd left spritzers behind and progressed to the heady heights of alcopops. They seemed to look down on her still clinking her ice around what looked like a half-pint glass full of piss despite the fact they sucked on a straw out of a bottle like they were six again.

Now Beth always made them drink wine and lemonade at her dinner parties in the hope that they might reclaim some of the camaraderie they used to have back when they were just three mates, messing about. It reminded her of when Sarah, who had always been the beautiful one, chose to reject the call of the cool crowd at secondary school and stayed loyal to Beth, making her feel like she had the best pal on the planet. That was of course before Sarah left Morbeck and became even more beautiful and successful and gathered lots of cool friends throughout the globe until there was such a wedge between their lifestyles that neither seemed to be able to reach across. Despite their best efforts, the fact that life had turned out so differently for them both was the big fat elephant in the room, making their friendship highly convivial but somewhat awkward.

And, of course, wine and lemonade reminded her of the arrival of Marie in their ranks when she moved to the area at sixteen. It was Marie who took Sarah and Beth under her wing, confidence oozing out of her from the day they set eyes on her. She was their leader, forcing the shyer Beth and Sarah to get involved in whatever her latest scheme was. However when Sarah grew in confidence and shined in her career, then to top it all, married a very rich man, Marie struggled to handle it. She wanted what Sarah had, Beth could tell, and dealt with it by throwing herself in to her own career and becoming obsessive about the way she looked. And so whenever they met for dinner there was always a slight air of competition between the two of them that Beth hoped could be thwarted by a few glasses of wine and lemonade.

'Couldn't bloody park,' gasped Chris, bursting through the back door. 'Had to park at the pub, can you believe it? Hello mate,' he said, nodding at Duncan as he dumped several carrier bags on the breakfast bar. 'Did she tell you I screwed up? Should have bought the wine last night?' Chris laughed like it was a funny anecdote not a major screw-up. 'Anyway, not a problem, good old Co-op, eh?' He began pulling bottle after bottle out of the bags. 'Oh, and I got some dips, love. Got one of them four-pack things – thought that would be easier. Thought they might go better with a fondue thing. And four tubes of Pringles! Two for the price of one, so thought I might as well. I'm sure Simon will eat Pringles. Who doesn't like Pringles?'

Beth had put the carving knife out of her reach, in the back of the cupboard, just in case. In plain sight could be too tempting.

'Simon?' asked Marie.

'Yeah,' said Chris. 'My mate Simon is coming tonight. Last-minute thing. His wife's just left him, so he's a bit down, you know, could use some company. He probably won't stay long. Might just have a drink and some dips, to be honest.'

To Beth's horror she watched as Chris pulled out the four-pack of dips, ripped off the plastic cover and put it on top of one of the high stools when he couldn't find anywhere on the breakfast bar. Then he dug out the Pringles, took off the lid, tore off the foil top and shoved the tube under Duncan's nose.

'Have some Pringles and dip,' he said.

Duncan took at least five and helped himself to a generous portion of sour cream and chive, causing it to ooze over the rim and spill onto the leatherette pad.

The doorbell rang then or else something bad might have happened. Beth could feel herself rapidly losing her sense of humour, her usual defence against the daily irritations of married life.

JOURNALIST: So, typically, your dinner parties tend to begin with dips, do they? Have you ever tried anything different?

CHRIS: Like what? Dips are the greatest ever food invented. You always start a good night with dips. It's what marks a party night as different to a normal night. Dips are the ultimate mood setters.

Chapter Five

Sarah

'Happy Birthday,' said Beth, throwing open the door.

Sarah decided not to point out the fact that Beth had spilt something down her trousers. Or perhaps it was an unusual design feature. No, she'd definitely spilt something.

'You look disgustingly gorgeous as ever,' said Beth, pulling her in to the house.

'Prada sample sale,' Sarah started to say. 'I bought it when—'

'Oh, I remember that Prada sale,' interrupted Beth dramatically. 'Wasn't that the one where I bought the maroon trousers without legs and the camel hump holdall?'

'I believe so,' said Sarah, pushing past her to get out of the cold and in to the hall. She was used to Beth taking the mickey out of her ex-career. She took it without complaint. After all, Beth had been the one who had committed her life to the caring profession, so much more worthy than her frivolous aspirations in the fashion world. She so admired Beth for the job she did, but occasionally it would be nice if Beth told her she looked good without a sarcastic back-up line to show that Beth felt clothes were not deserving of any kind of thought and attention. Sarah had offered to take Beth shopping once, but Beth had said it would be a waste of time and money. But it wouldn't have been. Beth actually had a decent figure under all those uninspiring baggy clothes she insisted on covering herself with. Proper curves, unlike the bump-less stick that Sarah was saddled with.

'Happy birthday to you,' cried Marie as they entered the kitchen and engulfed her in a hug.

'Thank you,' responded Sarah.

'Check you out,' said Marie as she pulled back. 'I knew it. I knew you'd look amazing. I can't wait to look like you do when we come back from skiing. Here, look, we bought you champagne. For your birthday.'

Sarah caught her breath. They had. A decent bottle as well. She bit her lip. She remembered how she had said last year when they had celebrated her birthday at Marie and Duncan's house that her favourite birthday ever had been when she drank champagne all night at the top of the Rockefeller Center in New York City with a wealthy knitwear supplier from Pakistan. She couldn't even remember his name and yet it had been right up there as one of the best. She'd offended Beth, she could tell. Beth, who she'd spent countless birthdays with, right from the age of four through to eighteen and then ever since Sarah had returned to live in Morbeck. But the slight had gone right over Marie's head. Marie had wanted every detail of this glamorous evening, clearly wishing that she too had been able to cite this as her favourite ever birthday rather than the ones surrounded by friends and loved ones.

'We couldn't take you to the Rockefeller, but we could bring you the champagne,' said Marie. 'Maybe one day we'll manage both, eh?'

'Thanks, that's so kind,' she replied.

'Do you remember my eighteenth birthday?' said Beth.

'Didn't we go to Pizza Hut?' asked Sarah.

'That's right,' replied Beth. 'Do you remember we were all broke and so we worked out that was the cheapest place to get a decent meal. We all had a salad bar bowl…'

'You must have gone back to that salad bar at least six times,' interrupted Marie.

'I can't help it if I don't like celery and if you don't like celery then you have nothing to build up the walls around the edge of the bowl with so you can get extra in,' replied Beth.

'We nearly got thrown out because you went back to the salad bar so many times,' said Marie.

'I don't think it was that,' replied Beth. 'I reckon it was the fact we made our own spritzers by putting some wine in our glasses and then topping them up when the waiter wasn't looking from the help-yourself soft drinks dispenser.'

'We would have got away with that if you hadn't asked for three straws,' Sarah told Marie.

They all laughed and looked at each other affectionately.

'That was a good night,' Beth told Sarah.

'It was,' she agreed. Probably better than her night at the top of the Rockefeller Centre, she wanted to say but thought no one would believe her.

Beth turned her back to twiddle knobs on the stove.

'Nice dress,' Sarah told Marie. 'One of yours?'

'Yes, it's the new spring collection. It's not even out on the floor yet. Not supposed to be wearing it really, but this is a special occasion. You should come and take a look when it comes in. There are some things that would really suit you.'

Doubt it, thought Sarah. Marie shared Sarah's love of fashion, but her career trajectory had taken her in to retail management. So she hadn't travelled the world, but she had travelled the country, managing various outlets until marriage and family had brought her back to Morbeck to live three doors down from free childcare, i.e. her mum. She now managed several fashion stores in Leicester which were all part of the same group and which, in Sarah's opinion, tended to specialise in clothes for teenagers or women with no taste.

'Well, I'll try and pop in next time I'm up there,' replied Sarah.

'Oh, I have some news,' said Beth, suddenly turning round to face the room again. 'I entered a competition…'

'Not another bloody one,' muttered Chris.

'I didn't see you complaining when the new lawnmower arrived courtesy of a caption competition or when you got a year's free supply of cheese crackers all because I posted a coupon.'

'I miss getting those crackers every month,' said Chris. 'It was like having a little surprise present land at your door every few weeks.'

'So, what is it this time?' asked Sarah.

'A Michelin-starred chef is going to come and cook dinner for us!' announced Beth.

'Wow!' exclaimed Sarah and Marie.

'It was a prize in one of those free food magazines you get at the supermarket. All I had to do was tell them what made my dinner parties so special.'

'What on earth did you tell them?' asked Tony.

Sarah looked at him sharply. Confusion was written all over his face.

'I said,' began Beth, 'that my dinner parties are special because of my special childhood friends who come. We talk, we reminisce and we even drink white wine and lemonade. What could be more special than that?'

'Oh, you didn't really say we drank white wine and lemonade, did you?' said Marie. 'God, I hope they don't print that. How embarrassing.'

'Well they will,' said Beth. 'And they'd like to interview you all and take pictures when the chef comes to cook. Are you all all right with that?'

'Our pictures would be in the magazine?' asked Marie.

'Yes,' replied Beth.

'Fine by me,' she said, automatically producing a pout.

Sarah decided she had better say yes, Beth looked so excited about it.

'Of course.' Sarah nodded.

'Great,' said Beth. 'It won't be for a few months or so, but they might contact you beforehand to ask you some questions. The chef sounds amazing. Can't wait to have someone cook a meal for me in my own house,' she said, looking pointedly at Chris, who was too busy eating dips to notice her dig.

'I'll need a new outfit,' mused Marie.

Chris looked up. 'I think this calls for a celebration, don't you?' he said, pointing at the bottle in Sarah's hand.

It isn't chilled, thought Sarah. *It really should be chilled.*

'Oh yes, let's,' said Marie, 'and we can all pretend we are at the top of the Rockefeller and Sarah can tell us that story again about Alec Baldwin walking in and wishing her a happy birthday before he left.'

'I could pretend to be Alec Baldwin,' said Duncan. 'I could do an Alec Baldwin. Well, I could do an Alec Baldwin doing Donald Trump. How would that be?'

'Might as well just do Donald Trump, mate, cut out the middle man,' said Chris.

'Oh yeah,' laughed Duncan. 'So I'll just pretend to be Donald Trump wishing you happy birthday at the top of the Rockefeller Centre then, shall I?'

'But it wasn't Donald Trump, it was Alec Baldwin,' said Marie. '*The* Alec Baldwin!'

The champagne really needs to be chilled, thought Sarah. And it wasn't Alec Baldwin, it was Gerard Butler, but she didn't have the heart to correct them.

'Shall we have it *after* we have eaten?' asked Sarah, heading towards the fridge to put the bottle in.

'Don't be daft,' said Chris, intercepting her. 'Let's get stuck in, shall we? Not every day you have champagne, is it? I'll get some glasses out. You grab the dips and the crisps, Sarah, and take them through in to the dining room and I'll get this champagne sorted.'

'She'll do nothing of the sort,' said Beth, striding across the kitchen, picking up the dips off the high stool and depositing them unceremoniously in the bin.

The kitchen went quiet.

'I haven't scoured the town for four different types of cheese and grated my bloody, yes bloody, finger off for you to stuff everyone full of sodding sour cream and chive dip and hideous amounts of Pringles.' Beth stood in the middle of the kitchen with one hand on her hip and her other hand raised up with her middle finger encased in a tatty blue plaster, waving at her husband's face in an obscene gesture.

'All right, love, calm down,' said Chris, backing away, looking nervously round at the others.

'I really didn't mean you to go to any trouble,' said Tony.

'I told you not to touch the carbs, Duncan,' said Marie. 'We're not doing carbs in January,' she explained to Tony and Sarah. 'Except tonight, of course. Just for your birthday and because of the fondue and everything.'

Sarah wasn't listening. This wasn't like Beth, not like her at all. Apart from her caustic wit and sarcasm, she was the calm one of the group. The one who organised them all. The engine really behind the prolonging of the lifelong friendship between the three of them. When Sarah and Marie had both left to go to uni, Beth had always been waiting in the holidays with nights out arranged and days out planned. Truth be told, Sarah hadn't gone back to Morbeck to see her parents, she went back to see Beth. She could rely on her. She couldn't rely on her mum and dad. The minute she'd left home they'd split up and gone their separate ways, having successfully put her three older brothers and her through university. She wished they'd done it sooner. Knowing they'd had to wait for her to leave had weighed heavily on her shoulders. She'd known she was an accident, at almost five years between her and her youngest brother, but when they announced their split as they dropped her off at Manchester University, she realised she wasn't just an accident, she had also been a mistake.

And so Beth's house was home to her. She even stayed with her on the occasions she came back to Morbeck rather than in her parents' new homes where every shred of her former family life seemed to have been eradicated. They'd been so close then. They told each other everything, until they began to get pulled in different directions – Sarah up the career tree and Beth on the marriage ladder. As their worlds grew apart, so did they, and even though she had lived back in Morbeck now for seven years, they were still trying to crawl their way back to each other.

'Err right, guys, let's all get out of the kitchen, shall we?' said Sarah, ushering everyone out. 'Let's go in to the dining room and get started on that champagne. You bring some glasses through, Chris,' she said over her shoulder as she steered the two couples away from the domestic that seemed to be about to erupt behind them.

★

JOURNALIST: So when did Beth tell you she had won the competition for a dinner party catered by a Michelin-starred chef?

MARIE: Funnily enough it was at a dinner party at her house. We had fondue and, between you and me, it was pretty terrible and I remember thinking I hope I never have another fondue in my life. Of course, I'll never be able to face a raclette again for obvious reasons. A dinner party that results in the emergency services being called can leave a bad taste in the mouth.

Chapter Six

Beth

'We haven't got any champagne glasses,' hissed Beth.

'Wine glasses will do.' Chris shrugged.

'Marie bought Sarah the champagne to drink at home, not waste it here with us.'

'Rubbish. Marie doesn't buy drink that she doesn't intend to consume immediately. Not a chance. She's wanting to recreate her favourite birthday at…'

'…the Rockefeller Centre when Gerard Butler wished her happy birthday. I *know* the story.'

'I thought it was Donald Trump?'

Beth shook her head.

'Are you feeling all right?' he asked her. 'You're not… you're not…?'

'What?'

'Menopausal?'

Jesus Christ, she was forty-five not… not… Jesus Christ, could you get menopausal at forty-five? Had it crept up on her unexpectedly just like her twentieth wedding anniversary had? She'd known they were both lurking out there somewhere, but she had no idea that they would happen quite so quickly.

'What makes you say that?'

'Erm, there was an article about it in my golf magazine.'

'You don't play golf but you read articles about the menopause in a golfing magazine?'

'It was about the impact of the menopause on female golfers.'

'Why would you read something like that?' asked Beth.

He shrugged. 'Thought I might learn something.'

'Like how to play golf?'

'Nooo. Like what to expect, I guess.' He was studying the floor, but she could see how red his cheeks were from here. Chris so wasn't in touch with his feminine side. So squeamish when it came to anything even slightly concerned with 'women's problems'. This included pregnancy, hence his head injuries sustained as a result of collapsing at both of his sons' births.

'You thought you'd learn what to expect when I go through the menopause from a golfing magazine?' she asked.

'I didn't read it to find out about the menopause, it just happened to be there, so I thought I'd read it.'

'Did it say the menopause would cause me to throw your dips in the bin?'

'No. But it did say that on competition days you should avoid food with added fructose.'

Beth's jaw dropped.

'Just saying,' ventured Chris, 'that maybe this is your equivalent of a competition day, so maybe you should think about avoiding fructose.'

'Having a dinner party is my equivalent of playing competitive golf? Is that what you are saying?'

'I know you like to present this air of calm and control, but this is me you're talking to. I see the behind-the-scenes stress you put yourself under. Just give yourself a break, eh? The fondue is going to be fine.' He put his hand on her arm and leaned in to kiss her.

'Any danger of those champagne glasses?' asked Duncan, poking his head around the door. 'Oops, sorry, sorry,' he exclaimed. 'I'll give you the room.' He disappeared.

'I'll get the glasses,' said Chris, squeezing her arm and turning to reach up to the eye-level cupboard.

She watched as he pulled out a mismatched bunch of glasses and put them on a tray. Some were for red wine, some for white, most really needed a good clean. She closed her eyes and turned back to face the mountain of cheese.

'By the way,' he said as he left the room. 'Simon texted me to say don't wait for him. He's talking to his wife. He'll be round later, depending on how badly it goes.'

Beth could have sworn she heard him chuckle as though he thought he had made a joke.

JOURNALIST: Were all your guests pleased when you told them you had won the competition?

BETH: Mostly, I think. Marie and Sarah were. Not sure about the men. They didn't seem to have much to say about it. Of course, not everyone got to enjoy the prize, not after what happened at the raclette dinner party.

Chapter Seven

Beth

'This is so very kind of you,' Sarah said to Beth when she brought the fondue in to the dining room. 'I'd no idea that Tony had put you to such trouble?'

'No problem,' said Beth. 'Thought I could give it a whirl.'

'So lovely of you,' added Sarah.

Beth could see her beaming round at everyone. Trying to get past the awkward scene in the kitchen earlier. Trying to lighten the mood. Sarah always tried to smooth things over. Despite being an incredibly successful businesswoman in her past, she hated conflict. Always had.

In all honesty Beth didn't know why she had thrown the dips in the bin. Her frustrations were usually unleashed via sarcasm and wit, not the ramming of perfectly good food in to a pedal bin. But words seemed to be failing her tonight. Action seemed necessary to display the brink she appeared to have arrived at. Why she was at a brink now, she had no idea. Was it the cooking of a meal that she suspected no one would enjoy (as if that hadn't happened a thousand times – she had kids after all). Was it Chris's general ineptness that had finally worn so thin that the cracks were showing? Was it that she was sick of having to predict the mini disasters that were constantly headed her way because of his lack of concern over doing the small things that kept life on track? Had she woken up one too many mornings and wondered why she was the only person in the goddamn house who emptied the dishwasher?

She didn't know what it was, but she must try and breathe – oh, and not drink too much. Too much drink would possibly push her over the edge and she wasn't sure she could stop herself.

She carefully placed down the ceramic fondue pot that was borrowed from a nurse on Ward Twelve C. She'd said Beth could keep it. They'd had it ten years and used it twice. Beth had put the box in the utility room knowing she would be happily handing it back to her on Monday morning.

'That will be Simon?' said Chris, diving out of the room as the doorbell chimed the second Beth sat down.

'Who's Simon?' asked Tony.

'Some stray Chris has picked up somewhere,' sighed Beth.

'Really?' asked Sarah.

Beth nodded. 'Sprung this on me about an hour ago. Simon's coming, he said. He's split up with his wife, he said. Needs cheering up, he said. I've no bloody idea who Simon is or why the state of his marriage is suddenly our problem.'

Everyone stared back at her silently.

'This is Simon,' said Chris, standing right behind her.

'Oh my God,' said Beth, whirling round. 'Oh my God,' she said, her hand flying to her mouth.

'Look, I really, I, I, I, err, you're right, this really isn't your problem…' began the stranger who had just arrived in the middle of their dinner party. 'I'm sorry, I, I, I should go…'

'No, goodness no,' said Beth, leaping up feeling mortified. 'Ignore me. Sit down please. I'm not mad at you, I'm mad at my hideous husband for not telling me sooner so I could make you more welcome… Please, please sit down. Chris, take his coat off him, for goodness' sake. Move along, Marie, let Simon sit down.'

'Well, if you're, sure I… I…' began Simon.

Beth wondered if he had a stutter.

'Here, sit next to me,' purred Marie. 'You are very, very welcome. Very welcome to join us. I'm Marie, by the way. I work in fashion and I like going to the gym. Bit addicted, if I'm honest, but you have to keep fit these days, don't you, if you want to keep in shape? Do you go to the gym, Simon?'

Beth stared at Marie. What was she doing? She sounded like she was on a first date not sitting in her dining room with the hideously dated wallpaper, opposite her own husband! She watched as Marie openly ogled Simon, who clearly did go to the gym by the looks of him. Hints of muscly arms strained through his smart shirt. He was probably around mid-thirties, thought Beth. Average to good-looking. A nice smile, when he managed to break one through his miserable face. Ten years ago he would have been right up Marie's street, but judging by her awestruck face she wanted him up her street right now.

'Let me introduce everyone to you,' offered Beth when Chris saw no inclination towards the social decency. 'So, you've met Marie.' *And her tits*, Beth wanted to add as she observed Marie leaning so far towards Simon that there might be a wardrobe malfunction any minute. 'She manages clothes shops as well as going to the gym every five minutes to make sure she can fit in the clothes she sells in her clothes shops.'

'It's important to be healthy at our age, Beth,' bristled Marie.

'Now, Marie is *married* to Duncan sitting over here,' continued Beth. 'Say hello, Duncan.'

'Hello,' said Duncan, standing up and leaning over the table to shake Simon's hand.

'He runs a call centre and likes to test his team-building games on us when he comes round to dinner, so be sure to have your answer ready when he asks you to share a secret that nobody knows about you and if you were an animal, what type of animal you would be and why.'

'Wow,' said Simon, nodding, his eyes wide. 'Sounds like an interesting job.'

'Actually it is,' replied Duncan as Marie yawned.

'And this is the lovely Sarah,' continued Beth. 'Our very glamorous and sophisticated friend. It's her birthday today, which means you will be subject to an impression later of Donald Trump pretending to be Alec Baldwin but who really should be Gerard Butler.'

'It's a very long story,' Sarah told him, leaning over to shake his hand.

'Sarah met Alec Baldwin on her birthday once,' said Marie proudly.

'No she didn't,' said Beth.

'She did,' said Marie.

'It was actually Gerard Butler,' Sarah told her. 'Not Alec Baldwin.'

'But you said it was Alec Baldwin.'

'I didn't—'

'And this is Tony,' interrupted Beth. 'Sarah's husband. The Godfather of Morbeck. Tall, dark, handsome, loaded and *ruthless*!'

'Beth!' exclaimed Sarah and Tony simultaneously.

'What?' replied Beth. 'It's true.'

'I know but…' said Tony, looking uncomfortable. A rare occurrence. He stood up and shook Simon's hand. 'Glad you could join us.'

'Thank you,' said Simon, looking nervously at Tony.

'Don't believe a word she says,' he replied. 'She's making it all up.'

'I'm not,' said Beth. 'Especially the loaded and ruthless bit. He's an architect, you see,' she told Simon conspiratorially. 'He can charge what he likes per hour for drawing lines on a piece of paper and he has a wealth of building sites at his fingertips to bury the bodies in.'

'Ignore her,' said Tony. 'Overactive imagination.'

'And Chris, of course you know Chris,' continued Beth. 'Wait. How do you know Chris exactly? As mentioned before, the timing of my husband's announcement didn't allow for any sharing of useful information. Are you a postman, like Chris?'

'No, no,' said Simon. 'Your husband – well, your husband has been a bit of a knight in shining armour really.'

'Bloody hell,' said Beth, aghast. 'Seriously?'

'Yes, well you see, err… well, it's a bit unusual, I guess, how we met really, isn't it, and embarrassing, to be honest.'

'You don't have to tell them,' said Chris, putting his hand on Simon's shoulder.

'I think you do,' interrupted Beth. Her mind was currently in overdrive whilst worrying that the fondue really needed to be started. It was bubbling furiously. Too furiously!

No, she needed to know how Simon and Chris met first, then they could start eating.

'Well, my wife,' started Simon. Beth noticed he couldn't even say her name. 'She buys a lot of stuff online, you see, and because I work shifts, I was always the one at home to receive the parcels. So, as Chris is our postman I'd end up seeing him nearly every other day and we kind of got to know each other. We'd have a little chat and stuff and then Chris happened to be the first person I spoke to the day she left me. He knocked on the door and I was in a state. A real state, and your husband was really kind. He made me a cup of tea and helped me pull myself together a bit. Made me go to work as normal.'

'I said he couldn't stay at home like that on his own. He needed distracting,' Chris said earnestly.

Christ, thought Beth. *Since when was Chris so in tune to another human being's feelings?*

'I don't know what I would have done without him that day,' admitted Simon. Beth could see that there were tears in his eyes.

'When was this?' asked Beth.

'Last week sometime,' replied Chris with a shrug.

'It was Tuesday,' said Simon. 'I got home from my shift and she was gone. She'd left me a Dear John letter on the kitchen table.'

'I thought his name was Simon,' Duncan whispered to Marie. 'Who's John?'

'Oh, for fuck's sake, Duncan,' Marie hissed back.

'Wow,' said Beth. 'Who would have thought it? Chris being a knight in shining armour.' She was struggling to get her head around that one. She dreamed of a knight in shining armour but never once had she pictured her own husband.

'I can't believe he invited me over for dinner,' continued Simon in amazement.

Neither can I, thought Beth.

'I mean, we hardly know each other, but he said that none of you would mind and that you all have such a good laugh and it would do me good to get out, you know, and socialise rather than mope at home.'

'Of course.' Beth nodded. 'Like I said, you are very welcome. I really didn't mean what I said earlier.'

Simon looked up at her as she hovered, wondering if now was the right time to demand they start eating the bubbling fondue. Enough of the polite introductions.

'He said that you were a good woman,' Simon said to her. 'He said that you were a fantastic wife. I can *see* that he wasn't wrong.'

Beth felt herself gasp ever so slightly and heat instantly rise to her cheeks. Partly because Simon was looking at her so intently and partly because he appeared to be complimenting her so sincerely. But mostly it was because of his choice of words. He said he could *see* she was a fantastic wife. He thought she *looked* like a fantastic wife.

The words and the unexpected intensity of them gave her jolt. She felt something go through her veins that she hadn't felt in a very long time. She dragged her eyes away to see Sarah staring at her with a weird expression on her face.

'We'd better start this fondue before it's ruined,' Beth said briskly, sitting down and grabbing a fork. 'Dig in, everyone.'

JOURNALIST: So you mentioned that in the past a random guest has been invited to join your close-knit group. How did that change the dynamic, I wonder?

DUNCAN: Well, it's only happened once. When Simon came along. His wife had just left him, so Chris took pity on him. How did it change the dynamic? Well, it didn't take long, of course, for the girls to start pecking round him. I remember he was wearing a tight shirt, just like me, but it wasn't because he was a bit chubby, it was so you could see his muscles.

Chapter Eight

Sarah

Sarah stabbed a piece of bread with her fork and fished around in the pot for some lip-scalding cheese.

She didn't really like fondue, to be honest. Too greasy. But Tony had made such a big deal whilst they were skiing of taking her to a restaurant he used to go to with his mates. He said they did the best fondue in Europe, never mind Switzerland. She hadn't had the heart to tell him she wasn't keen on it. Still, the waiter had been very attentive and attractive and wore his clothes so well. So effortlessly stylish, in that way continental men are and British men aren't. She'd admired him to the extent that she'd asked to go back again despite her indifference to fondue. Just to look at him and feel him look at her. In that knowing way. In that 'if things were different' way. To her surprise, her skin had prickled when he leant over to remove the fondue pot from between her and Tony.

She shouldn't have been surprised that Tony had spotted it. Of course he had. He was forensic in his work, obsessive about detail, unwilling even to let the smallest misalignment go. It was unsurprising too that he'd spotted the look the waiter had given her. A look of appreciation. Lust, even. What she was surprised about was what he did about it.

Afterwards she'd felt dreadful, of course. Had she encouraged the waiter? Was it all her fault? She'd enjoyed his admiring glances, but that wasn't a crime, was it? It wasn't like she would have ever done anything about it. She loved Tony. But she was just bored. So bloody bored, so bloody tired of being so bloody bored. Now that the house had been completely refurbished and that Chloe was at school, the monotony of her life was killing her to the extent that the sight of an attractive man could excite her, not because of a potential relationship but because it was something less painful for her brain to think about than the utter boredom present in her life.

'Is it as good as the fondue you had on holiday?' she suddenly heard Chris ask her.

The cheese had started to boil over the flaming methylated spirit because they had been so busy discovering Simon. So much so that much of the cheese had become chewy and stringy rather than smooth and gloopy. It really wasn't very nice.

'It's great,' replied Sarah. 'Just like it. If I closed my eyes I could be in Switzerland right now.'

'Sarah and Tony have just been skiing,' Chris told Simon.

'We're going at Easter,' Marie added. 'Do you ski at all? You look like you would be a skier.'

Sarah watched as Marie cast her eyes along his muscled left arm. Marie really was the most unsubtle person she had ever met.

'I used to, but it wasn't my wife's thing. She liked her beach holidays, to be honest, so I haven't been skiing in years.'

'Well, you can go on holiday wherever you like now, mate,' said Chris, grinning. 'This is really good, love,' he said to Beth as he drew out a piece of bread, dragging a yard of stringy cheese behind it.

'I guess,' replied Simon, not looking like this was remotely an upside of his wife leaving him.

'So, err, was there someone else?' Marie asked Simon.

'*Marie!*' exclaimed Sarah and Beth simultaneously.

'What?' she replied. 'I was just asking.'

'You don't have to answer that question,' said Beth. Sarah watched her put her hand over Simon's, then withdraw it quickly as though she'd caught herself doing something she shouldn't. She blushed again. That was the second time she'd blushed that night, thought Sarah. What was with Beth tonight?

'Leave the poor man alone,' Sarah told Marie. She smiled warmly at Simon. 'He's traumatised enough without you interrogating him.'

'It's okay,' said Simon. 'I think you have a right to know, seeing as I have gatecrashed your dinner party.' He put his fondue fork down and dabbed his mouth with his napkin. 'She's been sleeping with one of my neighbours. Right under my nose.'

The entire table gasped.

'That's terrible,' said Marie, grasping Simon's forearm and not letting go.

'Is that the chap at number forty-six?' asked Chris. 'He gets a lot of letters from the tax office and he has a subscription to *Vending Times*.'

Simon nodded sadly. 'He's a salesman for chocolate vending machines.'

'She's left you for a man who sells vending machines!' said Marie, aghast.

'And guess what Simon does?' Chris said to Marie. 'Much more impressive than selling vending machines.'

'Well, clearly, he's something in the fitness industry,' said Marie. 'Got to be with that body.'

'You said you worked shifts?' asked Duncan, ignoring Marie's obvious flirtation.

'That's right,' Simon replied. 'Nights mostly.'

'Supermarket shelf stacker?' said Tony.

'Security guard?' suggested Duncan.

'No, neither of those,' said Simon. 'I'm actually a paramedic.'

'Wow, seriously impressive,' announced Sarah.

'Oh my God,' said Marie, fanning her face with her hand. 'You are a hero. A real-life hero.'

'It's just a job.' Simon shrugged.

'How could anyone have an affair when they are married to someone who save lives every single day?' announced Marie. 'Insane, don't you think?' She was asking the table, but no one seemed to want to answer.

Sarah glanced over at Tony. He was studying Simon closely. Weighing him up. They were opposites entirely. Tony was cool, calm and collected. Tall and handsome, intelligent, controlled. Whereas Simon wore his heart on his sleeve. His muscle-bulging sleeve.

'I don't know how anyone could have an affair full stop,' said Simon. 'I just… I just couldn't deceive someone like that. I couldn't lie to them, day in, day out. How do people do that?' he asked the attentive faces around him. 'I just don't get it.'

'You'd better ask Sarah and Tony,' replied Marie. 'They managed it.'

JOURNALIST: So can you remind me exactly how long you have all been friends?

SARAH: Well, Beth and I have been friends since primary school. Marie came along after we started secondary school. It's Beth really who's made sure we all kept in touch. She was the one who suggested we have a monthly dinner party. If it wasn't for Beth that Marie and I would still be in touch.

Chapter Nine

Marie

Marie had stopped eating the fondue after two pieces of bread. She'd gingerly dipped the pieces in to the vat of near lard bubbling away, hoping to minimise the contamination of her body with saturated fats. She reckoned Duncan had greedily drenched at least thirteen pieces of bread in the cauldron and she was desperately trying to increase the ferocity of her stares in his direction to indicate that no-carbs January was back on. His frolics with dough had to stop.

As she dropped the bombshell of Sarah and Tony's adultery in to the middle of the conversation, she leaned over and extracted the fondue fork from Duncan's hand and placed it on his plate. As though he were a toddler who had been happily indulging in banging his spoon on the table much to his own delight but now the fun was over and it was time to be sensible again.

'Well,' spluttered Sarah in response to Marie's exposé. 'We didn't mean to have an affair. I don't think anyone *wants* to have an affair.'

'Of course not,' said Tony, putting a calming hand over Sarah's whilst looking Simon steadily in the eye. 'Who wants the love story of their life to begin that way? No one. But we can't help who we fall in love with, can we?' Marie watched as he glanced over at Sarah in the adoring way he always looked at her, then turned back to look at Simon. 'I do think it is naive to say you would never have an affair, because you just don't know what or who is round the corner and you can't pass judgement on people who have affairs because you have no idea what their circumstances are.'

'Of course.' Simon nodded, looking mortified. 'I didn't mean to offend, I really didn't. I guess what I meant was I personally have never been in a situation where I have felt like I would be tempted. So I guess I've never fully understood what that must feel like.'

'What? You have never been tempted?' Marie asked Simon incredulously. Too incredulously. Like you would react to someone who didn't like salted caramel. She saw Duncan look at her sharply. 'Well, he is a man,' remarked Marie quickly. 'All men are capable of being tempted, aren't they? Surely? That's the default mode, isn't it?'

'No,' said Chris and Duncan in unison.

'I wouldn't ever, couldn't ever,' spluttered Chris, reaching over to grasp Beth's hand.

'I think your opinion of men is pretty low if you think we are not capable of saying no,' said Duncan.

Marie looked away for fear that guilt would be written all over her face. She'd failed to say no once. Just once, a very long time ago, but that was no excuse. As Tony said, it was circumstances, that was all. Circumstances drove her to it. It was eighteen months after she'd had their daughter Annabelle. She'd gone back to work after a year, but working full-time and raising a child who didn't like sleep had taken its toll. She was exhausted.

And then an oasis had appeared on the horizon. A conference in London. All the store managers were invited down to view the following season's range and stay the night at a swanky hotel. Marie had installed her mother at home and had actually cried when she collapsed on the pristine double bed in the silent hotel room. She'd lain there just listening to the silence. She would have happily lain there all afternoon and listened but she had to go and watch the catwalk show arranged to motivate the sales staff and then go out to dinner, in a restaurant without high chairs and with free wine. It was the free wine that did it. Free wine and sitting next to Jason Cuncliffe, Area Manager for Scotland and the North West. He was charming, he was single, he was flirtatious, he was tactile, and he was complimentary. She was twenty-five again, when in her normal life she felt fifty-five.

Then, after dinner and after more wine and after they'd all gone back to the hotel bar and had more wine and after everyone else had gone to bed, he was direct and he was honest. He made it absolutely clear he fancied her, he wanted to have sex with her and then that would be that. He didn't want anything more. 'Tomorrow it will be as if it never happened, I promise you,' were his words. 'I'm sure that would suit you too,' he'd said, eyeing her wedding ring.

And it did. It had suited her very much. Too much. A night of glorious sex without the dreaded interruption from the baby monitor nor the lethargy of two parents battling to look after their first child, shoving intimacy well to the bottom of the pile.

He was gone before she woke up the next day. She didn't even have to face an awkward goodbye. She sat in the chair in her hotel room drinking a peaceful cup of coffee, thinking. Thinking that she didn't feel bad. Thinking that she felt so much better than the person who had collapsed on the bed less than twenty-four hours earlier. She felt alive, something that she hadn't felt in a long time, and yet she felt nothing for Jason. Nothing at all. He could have been anybody;

it was as though she just needed a tonic, a boost, someone to lift her back in the saddle.

By the time she arrived home that night to Duncan, though, the guilt had hit her. She'd cheated on her husband. She knew that if he ever found out it would crush him. So she took him to bed, switched off the baby monitor and shagged him for Britain. She recognised the expression on his face the next day. *She* had been his tonic, his boost; *she* had got him back in the saddle. They had a marriage again outside of the baby. All because of Jason Cuncliffe, Area Manager for Scotland and the North West. All because she committed adultery.

'Men are capable of saying no. You can *always* say no,' said Tony. 'Just depends if you want to.'

'So who asked, then?' Marie asked Tony.

'Excuse me?'

'Who did the asking? Did you ask Sarah to have an affair or did Sarah ask you?'

'Marie!' complained Sarah.

'I'm so sorry I raised this subject,' said Simon, shaking his head. 'Really I didn't mean to… God, I am the worst dinner party gatecrasher ever. What must you think of me?'

'It's okay,' said Tony, giving Marie his steady gaze now. 'If you really want to know, there was no asking. It just happened. We kept looking at each other and we both knew. We both knew we wanted to take things further. There were no words. No questions. It was entirely mutual.'

'I bet your neighbour did the chasing,' Chris suddenly said to Simon. 'I bet your wife didn't go looking for it. He looks the type. Arrogant, you know. He never even looks at me if he has to sign for a parcel. No smile, nothing. I'd bet my life he chased her.'

'Maybe you're right,' said Simon. 'He always has been a cocky bastard.' He grimaced.

Everyone muttered and nodded in agreement despite the fact they had never met the egomaniac chocolate vending machine salesman who lived near Simon.

'But she could have said no,' muttered Beth. 'You can always say no… given the chance.'

JOURNALIST: So what do you normally talk about over dinner? Are there any go-to topics? Is there anything you have learned to avoid?

SARAH: Oh, you know, family stuff, kids stuff. There's not much chat about work because, for one, I don't work so I have nothing to say on that score and everyone does such different jobs. I guess there's not a lot of common ground actually – apart from family and kids. Oh, and the past of course. We can always dredge up the past if we are stuck for conversation.

Chapter Ten

Beth

Damn, thought Beth. She'd forgot to buy salad servers.

Salad servers – discuss.

Beth had grown up in a working-class household where the requirement for salad servers was about as remote as a bowl to put olives in. She'd first met salad servers at Sarah's house when she had been invited around for tea and they'd had pasta followed by salad, in the true continental way (Sarah's mum was a French teacher). As if an entire course designated to salad wasn't enough of a novelty for Beth at the age of eight, the handling of the supersized wooden spoon and fork contraption that apparently should be used in the movement of lettuce from bowl to plate just blew her mind. Suffice to say, she dropped her iceberg on the white tablecloth and after several attempts to reclaim it with the aforementioned salad servers, Sarah's mum told Beth to use her fingers, much to her mortification.

It is true to say that this experience had tainted Beth's relationship with salad servers and indeed also salad when in public. Subsequently, salad was not high on her list of dinner party specialties, preferring to stick to the safer staples of a tried-and-tested curry or perhaps a casserole, which seemed to pass the dinner party test as long as it contained lots of wine and at least one unusual ingredient such as fennel or celeriac.

Beth riffled through her drawer to see what she could find to approximate salad severs. Would she get away with a serving spoon and a carving fork? Probably not. Tony would sniff out her shortfall immediately, she knew. As an architect, he liked order and for everything to be in the right place. She could already imagine him studying the carving fork suspiciously as he delved in to the leaves, and as for the serving spoon complete with Mickey Mouse ears on the handle (a gift from a friend who had been to Disney World), well, that would completely throw out the aesthetic of the salad bowl and ruin Tony's enjoyment of the food.

She sighed and stuck a normal fork and spoon in the salad and then poured a highly priced passion fruit salad dressing from its Waitrose bottle in to a jug. Beth was never comfortable shopping in the high-end supermarket that hovered not far from where she worked. She felt like an imposter and as though at any moment a security guard might throw her out for not wearing the right brand of wellies. Still, she knew that this dressing was Sarah's favourite, so she had been willing to make the sacrifice of suffering the suspicious looks from her fellow shoppers.

She walked back in to the dining room and put the salad and the dressing down in the middle of the table. The fondue had been cleared away and was sitting in the sink. Beth was praying that the concrete cheese block that was now steadfast in the bottom of the pot would somehow chisel off.

The rest of the guests didn't even look up when she entered. She noticed that Sarah and Marie were deep in conversation with Simon. Of course they were. That's how it always was. Whenever a new man came in to contact with the three of them, Sarah and Marie would pull him in like magnets, leaving Beth on the sidelines. However, she noticed that despite the fact that the three men were also chatting, both Tony and Duncan were watching their wives' interaction with Simon suspiciously.

'They're all medium,' said Beth, when she arrived back in the room with three plates of steak. 'Sorry – there was no way I could remember individual preferences. She placed the steaks in front of Sarah, Marie and Tony, then left to collect the rest.

She had just sat down again, having delivered the rest of the steaks to their owners, when, predictably, Chris piped up.

'We on rations, love?' he said, poking his steak with his knife.

She wanted to kick him really hard under the table. Or else stab him with his steak knife. All hell was about to break loose. She could see it coming.

'No,' she said. How could she put this? 'Because you invited a guest, a very welcome guest, and failed to give me any notice whatsoever, it means that we have had to share six steaks between seven, hence you and I are sharing a steak.'

'No,' said Tony.

'Oh no,' protested Marie.

'No, that's not right,' added Sarah.

'No way, I can't have that,' said Simon, shaking his head vigorously. 'I shouldn't even be here. You have my steak. I insist,' he said, lifting his plate up and offering it to Chris.

'No, mate, no,' replied Chris. 'Anyway, you should let Beth have it. It's my fault, not hers. And she really loves her steak, don't you, love?'

Beth didn't think she had ever been so mortified. What must they all be thinking? That of course she loves her steak, just look at her.

'Yes, Beth,' said Simon. 'Please have it. I insist. I can't sit here and eat your steak. You have it.'

'Look, I'll have a small one,' piped up Marie. 'I'm on a diet anyway, carbs not protein, but it still helps.' Marie lifted her plate and offered it to Beth to swap. There were now two plates of steak hovering in front of her nose demanding to be eaten.

'And I'll have a small one too,' said Sarah. 'I'm not a big red meat eater at the best of times, so it's fine.' Up came Sarah's plate from its setting, waiting to be swapped out with one containing half a steak.

'There we go,' said Chris, handing his plate over to Sarah before reaching up and swapping Beth's and Marie's plates for them. 'You put your plate down and tuck in, Simon. See, everyone's happy.'

Beth's mouth was hanging open. She wasn't happy. Everyone had made her look like a greedy pig. She looked over at Simon. He gave her a weak smile back in sympathy. Yes, sympathy. The stranger in her house understood. He got that she'd been made to feel uncomfortable and his mere presence was partly to blame.

No one had asked her what she wanted. She only wanted half a steak. A full steak was the worst possible answer. She couldn't even pretend to be full and leave half on her plate. How rude would that be when they had all insisted that she have the whole steak and then not have the decency to gobble it all up like the greedy pig she obviously was.

She picked up her steak knife and cut down the centre of the meat and then laid half on her side plate.

'I really only want half,' she said, putting it in the middle of the table. 'I had too much fondue. If anyone wants the other half, help yourself.'

There was a pause. Beth could have predicted who would end up with the now homeless half of sirloin.

'Not for me.'

'No – I'm fine with this.'

'Couldn't possibly eat any more.'

'I'll be lucky to finish this.'

'No, really, someone else have it.'

'Well, if it's going begging,' said Chris, leaning over and spearing it with his fork. 'Can't let it go to waste now, can we?' Beth watched as he laid it alongside his other steak, then started to get out of his chair. 'I forgot to get the ketchup out,' he said. 'I'll go and get it. Does anyone else need any sauces? Mayonnaise? Salad cream? Anyone?'

No one replied. Beth stabbed her half-steak hard with her steak knife.

JOURNALIST: I'm interested to know if what you cook has evolved over the years that you have been having dinner parties?

BETH: I guess we've got a bit fancier over time. What with all these cookery programmes and competitions on the TV, perhaps we have felt like we've got to keep up. Tony was always the most competitive though. Always tried to show the rest of us up, to be honest. Not that he'll be doing that any more.

Chapter Eleven

Beth

'Please will you allow me to help with the clearing up?' Simon asked Beth after dessert had been served. She had decided she couldn't face the debacle that would no doubt erupt as she attempted to share six lemon possets between seven and so she had tipped them in to one bowl and dug out an emergency shop-bought Swiss roll. She divided it in to seven and then doused it with the lemon goo. She thought she had got away with it until Marie reminded her of their no-carbs January pledge and she had watched as both Marie and Duncan had scraped the posset off the cake, although Duncan had managed to scrape a fair bit of sponge up along the way.

Everyone looked at Simon in awe at his genuine request. The clearing-up protocol was pretty clear for their dinner parties. It was left until after all guests had left and therefore completed by the hosting couple. Well, in the case of Beth and Chris, Beth did the majority whilst Chris faffed around with recycling and reorganising the wine rack. Tony would bear the brunt at their house, whilst Sarah went to check on Chloe, and Duncan was in charge at theirs as Marie thought it only fair that he clear up as she did most of the cooking. He was, however, normally too drunk to finish the job that night and so had to face it the next morning, by which time stains and grease were twice as stubborn to remove.

'You're all right, mate,' said Chris, putting a hand on Simon's arm as he got up and started collecting plates. 'Me and Beth will do it later.'

'No, I insist,' said Simon firmly. 'I feel bad enough as it is, ruining your evening. I need to contribute. It's the least I can do.'

'Honestly, Simon, there is no need,' said Beth, thinking of the disaster zone that was currently residing in her kitchen.

'I must,' he insisted. 'Really, I don't mind.' He walked off out of the dining room with a stack of plates before anyone could stop him.

'I'll give him a hand,' said Marie, getting up.

The rest of the group turned to look at her in shock. Marie rarely volunteered help for anything, in particular menial help.

'Are you feeling all right?' asked Beth in wonder.

'Yes, why?' asked Marie.

'It's just so not like you… to offer help,' said Beth.

'I do, I like being helpful.'

Duncan was the one that laughed.

'It suits you,' said Beth.

'What does – being helpful?'

'Yes, makes you look younger.'

'Does it?' exclaimed Marie, her hand flying up to her face. 'Does it really?'

'Of course it bloody doesn't,' said Beth, pulling herself out of her chair. 'You sit down. I'll help Simon with the washing-up.'

'I offered first!' exclaimed Marie.

Beth was speechless. She daren't look at Duncan. How Marie could have so little self-awareness, Beth had no idea.

'Sit down, Marie,' said Duncan firmly.

'But I offered first…'

'*Sit down,*' he repeated, before going slightly pink. 'It's Beth's house. Just sit down and let Simon and Beth get on with it.'

Beth found Simon leaning over the sink. *Oh God, the cheese-welded fondue pot*, she thought. *He can't actually be trying to clean that?*

'Chisel?' she asked as she bent to open the dishwasher.

'JCB might be more effective,' he said, throwing her a grin.

'Can I get you gloves or a pinny or anything?' she asked.

'God no,' he replied. 'Would ruin my hero image if I were caught wearing Marigolds. Not a signature item of superhero clothing, is it, rubber gloves?'

'You're right. Underpants over your trousers has superhero written all over it, but rubber gloves – maybe not.'

'Look, Beth, I'm so sorry if I have ruined your evening. I really am. I'll do this and then go and you can get your night back on track.'

'No,' she said so firmly that it surprised her. 'You haven't ruined it at all. It's been good to have someone different round. Given us something else to talk about.'

'Well, that's very kind of you to lie so well,' he said, looking over to her.

'I can be very good at lying,' she replied. 'When I need to be.'

'Well, thank you for being good enough at it to stop me wanting to kill myself for ruining your night.'

'You're welcome,' she replied.

They fell in to silence and Beth crammed as much in to the dishwasher as she dared, whilst Simon continued his wrestle with the fondue pot.

'You're lucky to have such a close group of friends,' Simon said as he finally upended the fondue pot on the draining board.

'Do you think?' replied Beth, failing to veil her astonishment.

They exchanged a glance and Beth tried to imagine seeing the group through his eyes. What would Simon write on their flipcharts, she wondered, post this initial meeting?

Chris – clueless

Marie – self-obsessed

Sarah – beautiful

Tony – controlling

Duncan – unappreciated

Beth – what would she be… cuddly, of course… always cuddly.

A gale of laughter suddenly came from the dining room. Beth tried to shut the door on the overfilled dishwasher.

'Duncan's probably just doing his Donald Trump impression,' said Beth. 'You know, for Sarah's birthday.'

'Is it any good?' asked Simon.

'Oh, it's a showstopper,' replied Beth. 'Literally, I'd walk out of a show if someone did that impression.'

She looked up to find Simon laughing. She noticed the lines at the corners of his eyes when he smiled. They suited him. She couldn't help but start laughing too.

'I'm sorry about your wife, by the way,' she said.

He stopped smiling and looked down at the tea towel in his hands.

'Thank you,' he said, then looked back up at her. 'She called me tonight to tell me I wasn't exciting enough. That we never did anything together.'

'Sounds pretty normal to me,' muttered Beth.

'She told me that he's invited her to go to Amsterdam for the weekend to a conference. What am I supposed to make of that?'

'A vending machine conference?' asked Beth.

'I suppose.' Simon shrugged.

'She'll be back with you within the week,' said Beth.

JOURNALIST: So was it a success, the dinner party with the 'mystery guest'? Did you invite him again?

SARAH: To be honest, we never expected to see him again, but then of course Marie had to invite him to our next dinner party. But she certainly didn't expect him to come with his wife!

Chapter Twelve

Three Weeks Later

Chris

He was just about to post the parcel delivery slip through the door when it was flung open.

'Sorry, mate,' gasped Simon, looking as though he had just got out of bed.

'Oh, I thought you must be out. I was just leaving you a slip, but I can give you the parcel now. Save you a trip to the sorting office, hey?'

Simon rubbed his eyes and took the black plastic bag with a label from Chris.

'How are you anyway? Not seen you in ages. Been hoping you'd get a delivery to give me an excuse to knock on the door.'

'I'm all right,' said Simon, still looking a little dazed. 'You?'

'Oh, you know, same old, same old.'

'Right, good.' Simon nodded. 'Cuppa?'

Chris looked at his watch although he didn't need to. He could always squeeze in a quick cup of tea.

'So how come I haven't had cause to deliver you any parcels in the last three weeks then, mate?' Chris asked a few minutes later as he sat at the breakfast bar in Simon's kitchen. He wanted to add that he'd missed his near-daily chats with Simon, but he thought that might be coming on a bit too strong.

'Well,' said Simon, turning round and putting a mug in front of him. 'Candice was the online shopper.'

'Oh God, sorry, mate,' replied Chris. 'What was I thinking? Of course you wouldn't be getting any parcels.'

'But I am now!' exclaimed Simon with a big grin.

'What? What do you mean?'

'Parcel deliveries have resumed and so…'

Chris shook his head, feeling under the spotlight. He had no idea at what Simon was hinting at. 'You've got in to sex toys?'

'No!'

'You'd be amazed at how much of that stuff I deliver in this area. They try and disguise it with plain packaging, but you can't fool a postie.'

'Please, I really don't want to know.'

'So, what you been buying then?'

'I haven't been buying anything.'

'Someone falsely using your address? That happens a lot too, you know.'

'No! Candice has been ordering stuff!'

'Why is she getting it delivered here?'

'Because she's moved back in. She's back, Chris. She's come back.'

Chris leant back on his stool. He hadn't been expecting that.

'Wow – since when? What happened.'

'She called me last week and asked if she could come round, so I said yes. To be honest, I thought she was going to ask me for a divorce. Anyway, she came round to tell me she wanted to come home. That she thought she had made the biggest mistake of her life and that she wanted to try and make another go of our marriage.'

'What did you say?' asked Chris. 'And what about the vending man at number forty-six?'

'I didn't know what to say, to be honest. I was so happy to see her back but… but, well, she'd been very hurtful.'

'And had sex with a vending machine salesman,' added Chris.

'Yeah, yeah, I know. But she said she only did it because I was never here. Because I cared too much about my job and not about her. That me being on nights did her head in. Made her so lonely.'

'Right.' Chris nodded. He didn't know what to say. He wished Beth were here; she'd know what to say.

'So, anyway, we talked all night. It felt good actually. I think we'd been drifting since, well, before she went off, I'd just not seen it. She was right. We barely saw each other. Something was bound to happen.'

Chris said nothing. He wanted to say that Candice telling him she was lonely would have been a much better thing to happen than her having an affair in order to show him she was lonely. But then again Chris didn't understand affairs. You had to sleep with someone to have an affair, and as he had only ever slept with Beth, the thought terrified him. These people who could just drop their pants for anyone were like aliens to him. How could they do that? He'd only ever had Beth and he only wanted Beth, end of.

'So, err, you let her come home then?'

'Yeah,' said Simon, nodding resolutely. 'I had to give it another chance. I couldn't walk away without us trying to fix it. Not when I know Candice wants it to work as well.' Simon gave a strange laugh. 'No one ever said marriage was easy, did they?'

Chris found himself agreeing, but he didn't really. Marriage wasn't difficult when you found the right person, he was convinced. He had just been very lucky to find the right person from the start. He'd been just fourteen when he'd first asked Beth out. Yes, Chris counted himself as very lucky indeed.

'Well,' said Chris, knocking back the dregs of his tea. 'I'm really pleased for you. And I'm delighted that Candice has started ordering online again. Means I get to call in for a cuppa now and then, if that's all right?'

'Of course. Although she won't be ordering much as we're having to tighten our belts, you see. I said I'd go off nights, as that was part of the problem. We need to make sure we spend more time together. The only thing is that the money isn't as good, so less online shopping. In fact, we agreed no online shopping, so I'm not sure what this is?' Simon picked up the parcel and scrutinised it.

'Oh,' said Chris. 'So you might not be in when I call anyway.'

'I'm still doing the odd weekend so I will be in sometimes during the week. Oh, and I'll see you at Marie's.'

'What?'

'Hasn't she told you? She invited me to your next dinner party.'

'Did she? When?'

'Oh, I don't know, a couple of weeks ago. Turns out she goes to the same gym as me and she's started doing a spinning class that I do. Small world, eh?'

'Yeah,' said Chris slowly. 'Small world.'

'So she asked me. I assumed she'd checked with the rest of you. I said yes because she was very persuasive and I thought at least I could contribute this time. You know, bring wine to make up for me turning up empty-handed last time.'

'No, it's great that you're coming. Really great.'

'Actually, can I ask you something?'

'Yeah.'

'Do you think it would be okay to ask Marie if I can bring Candice along? Only, she asked me before Candice came back, but it feels odd going off to dinner on my own. I've been meaning to catch Marie and ask her, but I haven't managed to get to spinning class since my shifts changed.'

'I'm sure she won't mind,' said Chris. 'Tell you what, I'll ask her. Just in case you don't see her. If it's a problem, I'll leave a note through your door. But I'm sure it will be fine. Everyone would love to meet your wife. Especially as we have heard so much about her.'

JOURNALIST: So you had yet another surprise guest at the next dinner party? I have to say I really admire the way you react so well to unexpected guests. It can really throw an evening, something like that.

MARIE: Well, at the time it was pretty inexcusable. Simon didn't bother to tell me beforehand. The first I knew of it was when she was standing at my front door, looking like a man in drag.

Chapter Thirteen

Duncan

'Louder!' Duncan screamed at the top of his voice. 'Come on, Team Ken Dodd Stole My Underpants, I can barely hear you. Are you going to let Team Gary Barlow is a Spanner get the better of you? Come on, show me what YOU HAVE GOT!!'

He looked down from where he was standing on an office desk at his latest band of new recruits. Twelve upturned faces to his right shouted the lyrics to 'Greatest Day' by Take That, finally outsinging another twelve faces who were channelling 'We are the Champions' by Queen. Oh, how he loved new intake day. It was the performance of it; it really got his adrenaline going. His favourite trick was to pretend to be just like them. Arriving in the plush reception of Vitaline just as they did, winking at Jean the receptionist as he gave his name. He would take a seat alongside them, waiting to be called in to start their first day's training at the biggest call centre in the East Midlands. He'd mingle, chat and ask questions. He'd find out a lot in those fifteen minutes whilst they all waited nervously for their new careers to begin.

Eventually Issy would appear and collect them and take them up to the training room. Duncan would fall to the back of the group, still pretending he was as green and new as the rest of them. Chatting, talking, gathering vital information. Issy would ask them to take a seat and then welcome them all before inviting the Operations Director of Vitaline to introduce the agenda for the day.

There would be a few gasps as he took centre stage. Usually from the ones who had already told him they were only there because their Jobseeker's Allowance was about to be cut off or that this was just a stopgap before they got a *real* job.

And so the stage was set for him to be able to deliver his rallying speech. One honed over many years. The speech that said Duncan Mottershall prided himself on turning everyone who arrived at Vitaline in to winners, achievers, champions.

They had not come to Vitaline to *work,* they had come to Vitaline to *succeed.*

He wouldn't get to them all. He knew that. Some had already positioned themselves out of reach through cynicism or hopelessness. But the ones who wanted to, he would. The ones who needed the lifeline he was throwing them, he would get to them. The chance to be a champion in life when they thought that they would never feel success at anything, those were the ones he wanted to capture, and capture them he always did.

The singing before lunchtime was the test. If after just three hours of brainwashing and motivational speaking they were prepared to sing their hearts out in the type of abandonment usually reserved for late-night karaoke after several pints, then he had them in the palm of his hand. They would be his star sellers of electricity or gas or double-glazing or PPI claims, or whatever came their way. If you could sing 'We are the Champions' at the top of your voice in public at noon on a dreary wet Monday, well, you could do anything.

'Splendid,' announced Duncan, leaping off his table as the songs came to a rousing end. 'Splendid. But I have to say I think Team Ken Dodd Stole My Underpants just got it at the end after a shaky start. They saw their competition rising, regrouped and smashed it. That's what I like to see. You got knocked down and you got back up again. True fighting spirit, that. Now, you go off for your lunch and Team Gary Barlow is a Spanner will clear up the mess you've all created this morning,' he said, waving his hand around the army of flipchart sheets hanging from every available wall space and Post-it notes littering the floor. 'This afternoon you will be building towers out of pasta, so get your thinking caps on. Tallest tower gets put in the weekly internal newsletter. Last month's winners based theirs on the Taj Mahal!'

He watched as Team Ken Dodd Stole My Underpants filed out already discussing ideas for what epic structure to make out of pasta. That was what he loved about his job. Watching people flourish. It truly gave him joy. And he was proud. Proud that he did a job that actually could make a difference to people's lives. But he knew that Marie wasn't proud. Despite his comfortable salary, medium-sized company car and private healthcare, it wasn't enough for Marie. She constantly pushed him to apply for more lucrative roles with flashier sounding titles. She clearly didn't want to be married to an Operations Director for a call centre. She wanted more... much more. She hadn't always been like that. His status hadn't been an issue until Sarah married Tony.

Duncan suddenly felt his stomach rumble. God, he had to eat. And eat soon. He couldn't survive a new recruit day on a breakfast of low-fat yoghurt and fruit. How could he be expected to? He put so much energy in to it. Surely no-carbs January could be paused for new recruit days?

He walked back to his office and sat down heavily on his chair, leaning down to pluck a Tupperware box out of a carrier bag at his side. He was already filled with a sense of dread. He peeled back the lid to reveal lots of green, probably lettuce, maybe even spinach, tomato, cucumber, peppers – red and orange – and one, two, three, four pieces of chicken. He groaned in dismay, putting his head in his hands, dreaming of a slice of white bread, or even a cracker, anything that stood a chance of quelling the hunger boiling in his belly.

'Cake?' said a voice.

He thought he must be dreaming, hallucinating. He looked up.

'Cake?' said Issy, walking towards him with a cardboard tray in her hand, loaded with all types of delicious confectionary. Doughnuts, eclairs, scones, meringues.

Duncan blinked. He *must* be dreaming.

'It's Stella's birthday. I made sure they didn't start them before you had finished.'

Duncan wanted to fall on them and gather several up and stuff them in his mouth. Instead, he said, 'No thank you.'

'What?'

'No thank you.' He stared at his computer. He couldn't bear to look at the delights any longer.

'Why?'

'I'm having salad.'

'Bollocks are you,' said Issy.

'I am. We are doing no-carbs January,' he informed her.

'Who says?'

'Marie. Need to lose weight before we go skiing.'

'Oh for fuck's sake,' said Issy, picking up a chocolate eclair and handing it to him. 'Eat it, will you? Before you pass out. You're not a salad man; you're a cake man. Go on. I won't tell anyone.'

The eclair was so close to his face, he could smell it. The irresistible aroma of sticky chocolate, choux pastry and cream. Could he say no? Could he deprive his stomach?

No, it turned out.

Before he could stop himself, his hand reached out and took the sweet sticky cake. Half of it was already in his mouth and being chewed to a soundtrack of satisfied moaning within seconds.

'That's better, eh?' asked Issy.

Duncan nodded. He had his eyes closed, such was the satisfaction of cake during no-carbs January. 'Thank you,' he mumbled.

'So, why do you need to lose weight before you go skiing then?' asked Issy. 'You too fat to go on the ski lift or something?'

Duncan felt too happy to be offended. He held his finger up to indicate he would answer after he had finished chewing. She knew the sign. She could read him like a book by now. He had no idea what he would do without Issy. She had arrived for a training day less than a year ago, a ball of energy but prone to shooting her mouth off. She rarely thought before she spoke, which turned out to be quite a drawback when trying to cold-call and persuade people to buy something they didn't know they even wanted. On her first day on the phones, Duncan could hear her effing and blinding from his office as she dealt with customer after customer who were upset by her abrupt tone and intrusive nature.

He'd immediately called her in to his office, where she had burst in to tears, already knowing what was coming. She spilled out a tale of four disastrous jobs in two months, her bluntness upsetting the most accommodating of employers.

'Mum's sick and Dad buggered off years ago. I need to work, but I'm just not very good at it.'

'Whoa, hold up. What do you mean your mum's sick?'

'Multiple sclerosis. So she can't work, can she? Look, I'll go. Would you do me a favour though? Just don't say you had to sack me. Doesn't go down well, you see. At the job centre.'

'But I haven't sacked you.'

'But you're going to.'

Duncan looked at her. He had never met anyone like her. In her late twenties, she had numerous piercings, a tattoo of a spider's web over her left elbow and was wearing a purple fur coat. She looked like a Muppet that had gone off the rails.

'Can you type?' he asked her.

'Course,' she said. 'Can't everyone?'

'Can you answer the phone politely?'

'Of course. It was just when those fuckers were swearing at me down the phone, that's what I couldn't handle.'

'I'll ask you again. Can you answer the phone politely?'

She paused, staring at him.

'Yes, Mr Mottershall,' she said, a bemused smile creeping onto her lips.

'And this is the most important question. Can you give someone a good bollocking when they need it?'

'Shit yes!' exclaimed Issy. 'You should see me with our Kady and our Callum. They don't know what's hit them when I lay in to them.'

'Who are Kady and Callum?'

'My sister's kids.'

'Do they live with you?'

Issy nodded.

'You've got a week's trial as my new PA,' he told her. 'Mine left last week. Went on honeymoon and never came back. Now, listen to me,' he said firmly, pointing at her. She had already jumped out of her chair and looked as though she was dangerously close to hugging him. He waggled his finger at her to prevent her from getting overly tactile. 'You arrive on time. You are never late. You do not swear at clients or customers. You come smartly dressed and, most of all, you don't let me down.

'Oh I won't,' she gasped. 'I promise I won't.'

'One-week trial, got it?'

'Got it. And then do I get to give people bollockings?'

He couldn't help but smile at her. She had so much spirit. This could either be a massive mistake or a genius move.

'You prove to me in the next week that you are up to the job, then I'll let you do some bollocking.'

'You are the best,' she told him, leaning forward to give him a peck on the cheek. 'You will so not regret this.'

'Hope not,' he muttered as she walked out of his office, fist raised in the air in victory.

It turned out it had been a genius move. All Issy needed was for someone to believe in her and give her clear instructions on how to behave and she proved to be an utterly brilliant PA. Not afraid to ask questions, ruthless in her protection of her boss's time and, best of all, ruthless in her taking down of anyone who was not toeing the line. Duncan soon found that he no longer had to take errant employees to one side to get them back on track. All he had to do was point Issy in their general direction and she took great pride and enjoyment in reminding them of the key values of Vitaline and exactly how they were flaunting them. She was his wingman... or wingwoman. He was left to focus on what he loved most, the motivation of his team members, whilst Issy was blessed with the ability to give a kick up the arse in such a way that created no bad feeling. She was without a doubt his most important member of staff. And she brought him cake!

He had finished his eclair and got a handkerchief out of his pocket to wipe his lips.

'Apparently a middle-aged pot belly on the slopes is not the thing,' he told Issy, sticking his stomach out and slapping it.

She grinned back at him, causing him to stop abruptly. He'd been to a seminar the previous week on sexual harassment in the workplace, which had made him so self-conscious that sometimes he barely dared speak to the female workers now. He had no idea where the line was to be drawn these days, particularly in the female-dominated workspace that he operated in. What exactly was he supposed to do when a table full of middle-aged women wolf-whistled and catcalled Geoff from Finance whenever he walked past their desk? The fact he was gay and insisted on playing to the crowd by executing a perfect top model catwalk strut didn't help at all in deciphering how one should treat such an occurrence in a world where sexual politics were as baffling as what the hell was going to happen after Brexit.

'Nothing wrong with that belly,' said Issy. 'I dream of a belly like that,' she continued, thrusting her own non-existent stomach forward. 'Doesn't matter what I eat, I can't put weight on. I could do with some tits as well, not these pathetic excuses for breasts. How am I supposed to pull a nice man with these?' Issy cupped her near non-existent breasts.

Duncan looked nervously through his office window in to the open-plan operating area. Christ, if anyone caught a young woman standing in front of him cupping her breasts, God knows what might happen.

'There's nothing wrong with your…' began Duncan, getting up to indicate that it was time for Issy to get back to work. Shit, he couldn't say 'tits' or indicate that he had observed there was nothing wrong with them. What was he supposed to do now? 'Look, I have a really important phone call to make,' he said, holding the door for her. 'Can you make sure I'm not disturbed?'

'Obviously,' she told him, making her way out. 'Another cake? Strictly one each, but I won't tell if you won't?' she said, giving him a wink.

'I'm good,' he said, hastily shutting the door behind her, well aware his stomach didn't agree with him.

He sat down at his desk, got his phone out and began scrolling through his numbers. He thought he must have Tony's somewhere, but he wasn't sure. They weren't that close. Duncan had tried. He'd invited him out for a beer, invited him on a charity golf day, even asked if he wanted him to get Tony's firm shortlisted to design Vitaline's latest call centre, but all his requests were politely declined, leaving Duncan in no doubt that Tony tolerated Duncan for the sake of their wives' friendship and nothing else.

But at the fondue dinner party, Duncan had sensed a connection, a moment of rare camaraderie that had previously never occurred. They had shared a fleeting look of sympathy, empathy even, and Duncan realised that this might be his in. His moment to finally connect with the elusive Tony in a way he had never managed before.

'Err, hello,' said Tony when he answered the call.

'Hi, mate, it's Duncan,' said Duncan jovially. He could already sense the hesitation in Tony's voice. 'You got a minute?' Duncan hadn't wanted to call him at work but neither did he want to call him from home when Marie might overhear.

'Well, I have a lunch meeting with a client starting in ten minutes, so if you are quick, yes.'

Duncan instantly could picture the standard of the lunch one would eat in an architect's practice when meeting a client. A whole different level of carbs to the ones shipped in whenever they had a working lunch at Vitaline. Duncan imagined focaccia with pesto and roasted vegetable or ciabatta and olive oil and balsamic vinegar. Not the standard cheese, ham or egg on sliced white that he was used to. Still, during no-carbs January, he would take whatever he could get.

'Well, err,' he faltered, suddenly feeling like he was telling tales out of school. 'Well, I just wanted to let you know that Marie has invited Simon over for dinner with us at ours next week.'

'Oh,' was the reply.

'She, err… she happened to bump in to him at the gym. Pure coincidence. She asked him then.'

'Right.'

There was an awkward pause that clearly Tony wasn't going to fill.

'So I thought I should just warn you, you know. So you're not surprised.'

'Why?' asked Tony.

Shit, thought Duncan. He'd read it all wrong. They hadn't shared a moment of frustration that both of their wives appeared to be fixated by the unexpected guest at the last dinner party. They hadn't raised eyebrows at each other when their flirtations got too loud and giggly.

'Well, Marie and Sarah were kind of impressed by him, weren't they?'

'Not really,' replied Tony. 'I know my wife. And I know his type.'

Yet another awkward pause.

'What do you mean, his type?' asked Duncan.

'Pretending to be vulnerable.'

'You think he was pretending?'

'Of course,' said Tony sternly. 'No one who cares that much about how big their biceps are is that vulnerable. He was playing a part. The poor deserted husband.'

'Blimey,' said Duncan, his mind blown. He so couldn't read signals. 'So you don't think he's upset about his wife leaving him?'

'No. He just likes female attention and he knows how to get it.'

'Blimey,' Duncan said again. Maybe he should try it with Marie. Maybe that was why she wasn't giving him too much attention lately. He needed to show his weaker side. Shed a few tears. Was that what she wanted to see? 'Okay,' said Duncan, unsure of how to sign off and conscious that Tony had fancy bread waiting for him. 'Well, anyway – thought I'd let you know. So we'll see you next week then?'

'Absolutely. And don't worry, mate. We won't be seeing Simon again after the next dinner party. Bye.'

Duncan stared at his phone. He didn't know whether to feel thrilled at Tony calling him 'mate', something that had never happened before, or acknowledge the slight chill running down his spine at the menacing tone Tony had used to accompany his statement that Simon would not be enjoying their company for very much longer.

JOURNALIST: So I understand that it's the wives who have known each other for a long time. It's lucky that the husbands get on so well.

TONY: Yes, we have so much in common. You wouldn't believe how much I've learnt about architecture from a call centre manager and a postman!

Chapter Fourteen

Beth

'Have you got your glasses with you?' Beth asked Marie. She'd spotted her down the wine aisle at the Co-op and she needed someone to read the cooking instructions on the back of a ready meal as she'd left her own glasses at home.

Marie looked round, indignant. 'I don't wear glasses!' she said.

'Seriously,' said Beth, looking at her in wonder. 'But I told you last Christmas to go and get your eyes tested because you couldn't read the joke out of your cracker.'

'My eyesight is perfectly fine,' replied Marie.

'All right then, can you read this for me,' said Beth, thrusting the packet under her nose. 'Can I cook it from frozen or not? I haven't got the time or inclination to let it defrost.'

'No problem,' she replied, taking the packet from her.

Beth was utterly shattered and she had a headache. She'd been on her feet all day at work and all she wanted to do was get home, shove some food in the oven and collapse.

'So what does it say?' she asked Marie.

'I think it says…' Marie squinted, pulling the packet forwards and backwards in front of her face. '…well, I think it says…'

'Oh, for goodness' sake,' cried Beth, taking the packet off her. 'I'm so sorry,' she said to a passing blonde teenage girl. 'But could you possibly read this and just tell me if I can cook it from frozen?' She stabbed her finger at where she thought the instructions were.

The girl looked at her in confusion.

'Old, tired eyes,' Beth explained, pointing to both herself and Marie.

The girl nodded and looked at the box. 'It says microwave from frozen on full power for nine minutes.'

'Thank you,' said Beth, taking the ready-meal back from her so she could escape.

'I was just about to tell you that,' said Marie huffily.

'Really,' said Beth. 'So what time do you want us to come over on Friday?'

'Oh, let's see. Shall we say seven-thirty?' Marie suggested.

'What particular diet book will you be cooking from this month?' asked Beth. 'Or are we still on no carbs?'

'That was January and it's done us both the world of good actually.'

'Mmmm,' said Beth. 'So what's the reject this time? Sugar, fat, food in general? Are we having the first non-food dinner party ever?'

'Oh no. I think I'm going to do fish. Oh, I must ask Simon if he's allergic to anything.'

'Simon?'

'Yeah.'

'What do you mean, Simon?'

'Simon. You know, Chris's friend, Simon.'

Beth looked at Marie in astonishment. 'Has Chris had the audacity to invite Simon to your dinner party?' she asked, aghast.

'No. I invited him.'

'How?'

'Oh, didn't I tell you?' said Marie. 'Funny story, but I decided to change the gym I went to. I never liked the Pilates instructor at mine and the hairdryers never worked properly. Anyway, I joined a new one and guess who I bumped in to?'

'The green goddess?'

'No, Simon, silly. He was doing weights, obviously – did you see his biceps?'

Beth continued to stare at Marie.

'No, I did not see his biceps,' she lied. 'So you just bumped in to him, did you?' she asked.

'Yes. Literally. He was on his way to hot yoga and insisted that I join him. Well, I couldn't not invite him over then, could I? He's still very distressed over his wife, you know. I really think he needs someone to talk to. He was telling me all sorts of stuff you wouldn't believe!'

Beth felt herself gulp. She actually felt tears spring to her eyes. Simon confided in Marie? She felt betrayed. It was her that Simon confided in. Not Marie. Hadn't they shared a moment in the kitchen after the fondue? A connection? Or was she just being ridiculous?

'I must have that type of face that people feel they can open up to,' continued Marie, oblivious to Beth's discomfort. 'But then again, I suppose he's hardly likely to talk to Sarah, is he? Not now he knows she had an affair. And you and Chris are so… so… joined at the hip, he won't think you can relate to his situation at all.'

Beth was sure her mouth had dropped open. Was that how Marie saw her and Chris. Really?

She found herself thinking about a patient who had died on her ward that day. A woman of approximately their age. A mum with two teenage kids. She'd taken an overdose of Superdrug paracetamol. *I guess if you are going to kill yourself why waste money on the expensive branded drugs,* she thought. She'd arrived semi-conscious with a hysterical husband stumbling along next to the gurney. They thought they had managed to stabilise her, but she wasn't having any of it. Two hours later and she got what she wanted. She was dead. Released from whatever hell she must have thought she was in.

Beth could still hear his wails now. The husband hollering, 'why, why why!' as he was led down the corridor to the grieving relatives' area. He clearly had no idea what she thought was so terrible about her life that she decided it wasn't worth living. That anything was better than existing. Her husband had no clue, none, as to what had made her feel so dire. He clearly knew nothing of her inner turmoil. She'd kept it all hidden inside, refusing to share, until she decided to let go of life instead.

It had unsettled her. Seeing what could happen to someone who keeps it all on the inside. A solid wall of 'coping' stopping any true emotions ever coming in to contact with another human being.

Sometimes Beth felt like she was two people. There was the outside Beth who was capable, reliable, down-to-earth, productive, ready with a laugh and, of course, *cuddly*. Then there was the inside Beth. She had a constant monologue whispering in her ear: *This isn't enough, you're not happy, there must be more to life than this, you're taken for granted, you look hideous, you must make people laugh so that they don't notice that you look hideous, you must look happy and content because why shouldn't you be, you are Beth, capable, reliable, down-to-earth and, of course, cuddly.*

Beth knew that no one else could hear the painful whispers in her ear. No one else knew the inner Beth.

No one else knew the person inside the woman lying in the mortuary and now it was too late. Too late for anyone to help her.

Her and Chris joined at the hip! Was that how everyone saw them? Not the voice inside her head. That voice declared, *He takes you for granted. Does he really love you? He never tells you, never says. He's just happy that you are there to cook and clean and bottle-wash. He doesn't even fancy you. Of course he doesn't – how could he, you're cuddly!* Is that what the woman in the morgue really thought about her husband but failed to tell him? That gibbering wreck knee-deep in his own tears.

It was no surprise really that Marie had concluded that she would automatically be the one that Simon was drawn to. As always, either Marie or Sarah were on lead vocals and she was the backing singer. Outer Beth pretended this was all right. Coped with a laugh and a joke. Inner Beth cried a silent tear in frustration that she would never be the most exciting one. No one would ever introduce her with pride. In life she was an also-ran, somewhere in the middle of the pack, never the star of the show.

'So you offered him a shoulder to cry on then, did you?' Beth asked Marie in an attempt to show interest.

'Well no. He didn't cry as such.'

'Didn't you try pinching him then or something? Maiming him in some way. *Really* force those tears out.'

'No!' exclaimed Marie. 'I didn't do anything. He was just really down… I'm not sure he has any other friends to turn to.'

'What on earth makes you say that?'

'Well, he was on his own at the gym.'

'So? Loads of people go to the gym on their own, don't they?'

'Not the muscle guys,' said Marie seriously, shaking her head. 'You normally see them in packs.'

'You watch them, do you?' asked Beth.

'No. It's just a little observation I've made, that's all. You just tend to see the bodybuilder types in groups. You'd know if you went.'

'When have I got time to go to the gym?'

'It's your health, Beth. You should make time.'

'I'm too busy trying to stop other people from dying,' bit back Beth.

'Well, I really think you need to spend more time thinking about Beth, and less time thinking of others,' replied Marie. 'You're not getting any younger, so you really need to start looking after yourself.'

JOURNALIST: It must be lovely when you go to someone else's house. Not having to do all the preparation. Getting to eat someone else's food?

CHRIS: I guess so. But I like Beth's food best. I mean, she always does dips for a start – apart from the fondue night of course. And Marie… well, she goes a bit too healthy. Everything she cooks seems to have to be bright green and with kale! I mean, who the hell likes kale? And as for Tony – well he goes too fancy for my taste, like barely any food. I'd come home and have to dive in to the nachos and any leftover dips I can find in the back of the fridge.

Chapter Fifteen

Sarah

Sarah hated to go in to shops where you were hit with loud music and the pungent smell of piped-in aftershave the minute you crossed the threshold. It was like a barrier to deter anyone above the age of twenty-one from entering. She watched the three boys with barely-there bum fluff and tattoos creeping out from underneath their shirtsleeves clock her arrival then turn their backs in dismissal, automatically assuming she had mistaken their youthful territory as her middle-aged territory. This was *her* territory, she wanted to shout at them. Fashion was *her* territory. She wanted to go up to them and ask them, 'Do you know who I am? I used to control a budget of millions back in the day, bringing fashion to a much more discerning clientele than you. Do not tell me this is not my territory.' But of course she didn't say any of that, just walked on with her head held high.

She gasped for breath as she passed through the cologne cloud in the menswear section and in to womenswear to the relatively fresh aroma of overused deodorant and celebrity perfume.

Marie was towards the back of the store, an armful of hangers over her arm. She was talking to a younger woman wearing a black T-shirt and jeans. She waved and Marie waved back in delight.

'How lovely to see you,' gasped Marie, putting her free arm around her. 'You come to check out the new range?'

'No, err, yes, err…'

'This is my oldest friend, Sarah,' Marie was telling the woman she was with. 'She used to be a buyer for Dean & Delphi's.'

'Oh,' the woman said. 'Who's that, then?'

Sarah stared at her, aghast.

'A high-fashion chain based mainly in the south-east and Europe,' said Sarah.

'Right.' She nodded. 'Cool. I don't get to the south-east much or Europe… ever in fact.'

'Sarah has met Alec Baldwin,' added Marie. 'In New York. He said happy birthday to her.'

'It wasn't—' started Sarah.

'Who's that, then?' asked the woman

Sarah stared at her.

'Anyway, do you want to make a start on the window, Megan? I'll come and join you in a minute.'

'Right.' She nodded without a glance at Sarah.

'Can't get the staff,' said Marie. 'So, do you want to take a look round?'

'No,' said Sarah, trying to stop herself from sounding too negative. She'd already clocked the rows of dresses that were glued together due to their lack of fabric. Peepholes here, short skirts there, off-the-shoulder here. Everywhere she looked there were clothes only an inch from looking like something from Ann Summers, and that definitely wasn't her style. She didn't really do overtly sexy. She did sophisticated, stylish, individual. Not slutty. 'No, I just popped in to say hello really and see what time you are expecting us on Friday,' she lied.

'Oh, the usual – seven-thirty okay?'

'Yeah, sure.' Sarah left an awkward pause hanging that she didn't know how to fill.

'By the way, Simon's coming,' said Marie.

'Oh, is he? Well, actually I did hear. Duncan told Tony that he was.'

'Did he? Where did Duncan see Tony?'

'I've no idea. Maybe they bumped in to each other or he phoned him or something.'

'He never said,' said Marie, looking puzzled.

'Must have slipped his mind. So how come Simon's coming?'

'Well, total coincidence really. I moved gyms and, would you believe, I bumped in to him and, well, it seemed rude not to invite him really.'

'Are you sure it's a good idea?'

'What do you mean?'

'Well, it's just that it's comfortable, isn't it, the six of us. We can just relax. Don't you think it's a bit weird with an outsider?'

'No! I just felt sorry for him. His wife has just left him after all. I think he needs us, I really do.'

'He must have other friends. Why would he want to hang around with our bunch of happily marrieds?'

'All I know is that when I asked him he seemed very eager, so I think he would be grateful for our company again whilst he's going through this difficult time. We can be generous, can't we?'

'Well, I suppose, when you put it like that,' said Sarah. 'Tony didn't really take to him, that's all.'

'Didn't he? I never noticed. Why on earth not?'

Sarah shrugged. 'He didn't buy the sob story. Thought he was putting it on a bit.'

'Why would he do that?'

'I don't know. For attention?'

'Why would he want attention from us?'

'I don't know! I'm just telling you that Tony was a bit suspicious, that's all.'

'He never said.'

'Well, you know Tony. Always the gentleman. He didn't want to appear unwelcoming.'

'But he was so nice to him. He even hugged him as he left.'

Sarah looked away. Of course he'd been nice to him. It had been just the same in Switzerland when the waiter had given her that look. Tony had said nothing at the time. Just carried on eating the fondue. Maybe he was a little quiet. A little brooding perhaps, but nothing that would have predicted how she would find him half an hour later.

He'd said he needed the bathroom after the fondue was finished but when he failed to return for fifteen minutes she wondered where on earth he had got to. Perhaps he was caught up on a phone call, she thought. The office had been calling him every day with an update on various building projects. He didn't like to be out of touch, but he was also a stickler for protocol and good manners. It was unlike him to allow a phone call to interrupt dinner. And so, after another ten minutes, she went to look for him. She found him. Flat on his back in the hotel lobby. Out cold. She also found the attractive waiter holding an icepack against his own chin.

Luckily the receptionist was fluent in English and on hearing Sarah crying out, dashing towards her husband, she explained quickly that an ambulance was on its way. That Tony had approached the waiter and, it would seem, had struck out at him. The waiter had struck back, knocking him out.

'The police will come too,' the receptionist added.

Sarah looked to the waiter to explain, but clearly he was in no mood to talk and turned his back on her.

It was lucky for Tony that he didn't get charged, just a caution.

Apparently he'd gone out to find the waiter to tell him to stay away from his wife. When the waiter had reacted by swearing back at him in French, Tony had lashed out, punching him on the chin, causing the waiter to punch him back.

Sarah suspected that, for once, his age was on his side. The twenty-something waiter took no pride in knocking out a fifty-eight-year-old. It didn't make him look good and so he didn't press charges.

Sarah and Tony spent the last night of their minibreak in separate beds, Tony being monitored in hospital and Sarah back at the hotel. Not the ideal ending to their holiday at all.

Sarah had sat chewing her nails as a doctor told her that her husband should not be getting himself in to these kinds of situations. That his blood pressure was too high. That he needed to look after himself. That he was too old for this type of thing.

Which was why she was here, talking to Marie, trying to dissuade her from encouraging Simon.

She feared he could be bad for Tony's health.

'Well, I thought Simon was perfectly lovely,' announced Marie. 'A breath of fresh air in fact. I for one enjoyed talking about his marital woes and he wasn't too shabby to look at either.' She smirked.

Sarah couldn't argue with this, but that was the point. He wasn't too shabby to look at, which was why Tony had taken an instant dislike to him.

'Bloody Marie!' he'd exclaimed when he'd come home to share the news that Simon would be joining them again for dinner.

'What do you mean?' she'd asked. She'd been looking at fashion-buying jobs advertised online but quickly closed the page down on her iPad.

'She only invited that Simon over for dinner again.'

'Oh. Have you seen her then?'

'No. Duncan called to tell me.'

'Did he? Just to tell you that?'

'Oh, I can't remember exactly why he called, but he happened to mention it.'

Sarah shrugged. 'He was all right. I quite liked him. It would be nice to see him again.'

Tony had looked at her in silence, then walked out of the room without saying another word. In fact, he hardly spoke for the rest of the night. Deep in thought, brooding. She didn't like it. She didn't like it at all. Perhaps it would be better for everyone if they got Simon out of their lives. She didn't want a repeat of the incident with the waiter.

Sarah looked back at Marie, who had been distracted by a customer wanting to know if a crop top in bright yellow with the word WHAMBAM emblazoned on it, came in a size 18. Marie was doing a great job of gently guiding the her towards a more 'flattering and sophisticated' style. She watched her work. Admiring her ability to make the customer feel special and want to part with much more cash than she had intended to when she first walked in as she headed towards the changing room with some tailored trousers, a fitted shirt and a denim jacket.

Marie walked back towards her, beaming.

'Another satisfied customer,' she said. 'Now, we'll see you at seven-thirty, shall we?'

Sarah looked at her. She'd tried her best but it was clear that Marie was determined to invite Simon. She would just have to hope that Tony's blood pressure could handle one more dinner party with him.

'Of course.' She nodded. 'We'll see you then.'

'I promise not to mention your affair this time,' Marie continued.

'So good of you,' sighed Sarah wearily, turning away.

JOURNALIST: So how would you say catering for eight differs to catering for six? What extra challenges does it represent?

DUNCAN: Well, we didn't know it was eight until the last minute as we didn't know Simon was bringing an extra guest. On that particular night, eight instead of six made all the difference. I guess if there hadn't been eight then Candice would never have met Tony and then things might have turned out very differently.

Chapter Sixteen

February – Dinner at Duncan and Marie's

Marie

Marie heard the front door open just as she was putting the peas on to boil, ready to make the dip. She hoped it was going to work. She'd never made a dip before. She always bought whatever the exotic-looking ones were at Marks & Spencer or Waitrose, but she thought she'd make the effort tonight. Try something a bit different. Especially as they had a special guest coming who clearly knew how to look after his body.

'Hi, love,' said Duncan, coming in to the kitchen. He squeezed her waist from behind as he did every day when he came in. She hated it when he did that. Made her feel all funny. 'Good day?' he asked.

'Not bad. Well, I finished at lunchtime, so I thought I might as well get my hair done and grab a manicure before I took Annabelle to Katy's for the sleepover.'

'Good idea,' said Duncan, peering over her shoulder. 'What are you making? Smells great.'

'A dip.'

'A dip?'

'Yes.' She was barely listening as she was reading the recipe off the iPad and annoyingly it kept shutting down before she had time to complete a step.

'Oh. You don't normally do that, do you?'

'No. But I thought I would tonight. They must have so much rubbish in those shop-bought dips. I thought I'd do a healthy version.'

'Can I do anything to help?'

'You can chop some carrots and celery and peppers, if you like.'

Marie took the peas off the boil and strained them before dropping them in to an ice bath.

'Are they for the dip?' asked Duncan.

'Uh-huh.'

'A *pea* dip?'

'Uh-huh.' She added lemon juice and zest, mint, olive oil, a spoonful of tahini and finally the peas to the food processor before turning it on to full blast, hoping to drown out any more of Duncan's interrogation of her home-made dip.

A chopping board and a bag of carrots arrived next to her as she switched off the machine and peered inside.

'Great colour,' commented Duncan.

She got out a teaspoon and dipped it in to the vibrant green mush so she could taste it. It tasted good. Healthy good. Fresh, light, zingy. The exact opposite to most shop-bought dips.

'Can I try some?' asked Duncan.

'Sure,' she said, rinsing the spoon and offering it to him.

'That's really good.' He nodded vigorously.

She knew he was lying. Good would have been a thick, gloopy sour cream and chive. Good wasn't crushed peas and mint, delicious though it was.

'Are we having any other dips?' he asked.

'No,' she said, shaking her head. 'Thought we'd stick to one.'

'It would taste lovely with those crackers we have left over from Christmas,' he added hopefully.

'I gave them to my mum,' she replied. 'Didn't think we'd ever eat them.'

'Oh, right.'

She reached inside the cupboard for two Middle-Eastern-looking dishes bought from Ikea on a whim maybe five years ago. She knew they would come in useful one day.

'One of my new recruits won employee of the month today,' announced Duncan as he washed some celery under the tap. 'He only started last November and he's already beating some of our best performers. He was really chuffed. He'd been out of work for three months and he came in to my office to thank me in person. Said he used to get told off for talking too much when he worked in a packing factory. He can't believe he gets paid to talk all the time now.' Duncan laughed. 'He reckons it's easy money. I guess it is to him. He's got it. It just comes naturally to him. He could charm anyone, that lad – anyone.'

Marie didn't hear any of Duncan's thoughts on his day. She was busy running through her preparations list in her head. *So if I put these in the fridge and then check the tagine in the oven, then I've just got to lay the table and I can go and get dressed*, she thought. She had an hour before anyone was due to arrive so just enough time to get changed and put her make-up on.

'…Apparently Issy told him to stick his business card up his backside and said he had as much chance of getting an appointment with me as he had of having a Porn Star Martini with the Queen.'

'Mmmmm,' replied Marie as she peered at the chicken inside the tagine. It smelt good and the apricots weren't too mushy. It should be safe for the next hour or so.

'...So I told Geoff that we couldn't possibly take on any more contracts. We are at total capacity. Can you imagine if I told Barbara her team was going to have to deal with enquiries about the free gift inside Sugar Puffs as well as selling alternative electricity? She'd do her nut, wouldn't she, and I can't afford to have her walk out, it would be...'

Table, thought Marie. *I'll just check that*. She walked out on Duncan mid-sentence.

'Wow,' said Duncan, coming up behind her. 'Looks amazing.'

Marie had taken the candlesticks off the mantelpiece in the lounge and bought turquoise candles to match the napkins that were poked, bishop's hat style, in to the top of each of the seven wine glasses placed around the table. Marie was pleased. It did look good. Especially on the new round table they had bought to fit in to the extension.

She looked around her, satisfied. It had been the right choice, extending the kitchen to make a kitchen diner. No one had a separate dining room any more. No one except Beth, or someone of her parents' generation, or someone minted like Tony and Sarah, who had more rooms in their house than they knew what to do with. It just didn't suit modern living. This was so much better. And the bifold doors? Well, it was all about getting the outside in, wasn't it? The fact it had only been warm enough to open them fully for two days the previous summer was immaterial. It was the fact that you could, that's what mattered.

'Good job we bought the eight matching dining chairs,' she said to Duncan, 'now we have an extra guest. I hate to see odd chairs round a dinner table.'

'I guess so. Be a tight squeeze to fit eight round though, wouldn't it, if we ever had eight,' he replied. 'Still not convinced we needed eight.'

Marie turned to look at him. 'Well, we will have to keep all our dinner parties to seven then, won't we,' she replied. 'Now, I'm just going to pop upstairs and get changed. Are you going to wear that shirt I bought you for Christmas? You must fit in it by now? Although I have to say I can't see much progress. Maybe we will have to try something new this month.'

She was literally just adding her final layer of mascara whilst looking in the downstairs mirror when she heard giggling outside the front door. She'd decided to dress down but kind of up this evening. Choosing to go with a designer pair of jeans, which made her bum look the business, and heels. The cashmere jumper clung in all the right places and she thought she looked sophisticated and sexy, without looking old or the dreaded mumsy. She nodded at her reflection. She was happy.

She turned sharply as she heard another giggle and then the doorbell rang. It fleetingly crossed her mind that it was an unfamiliar female voice that she had heard but it had no time to register before she flung the door open with a big smile on her face.

'Hello. Oh!' she gasped as she clocked what greeted her on her doorstep.

'Hi, Marie,' gushed Simon, stepping over the threshold and engulfing her in his arms. 'Good to see you. Look. I didn't come empty-handed this time. Wine *and* chocolates!'

'Oh,' Marie gasped again, unable to take her eyes off the blonde standing in the doorway behind Simon.

'And this is Candice,' he continued merrily, oblivious to Marie's look of astonishment. 'So good of you to invite us along. Really. I told Candice all about you and she's so looking forward to getting to know you all.'

'Hi,' said the blonde, sticking her hand out to Marie. 'It's good to meet you.'

'Yes, err right,' said Marie, gulping. Her mind was racing. Simon had a new girlfriend already! What had happened to the sad, lonely and frankly quite pathetic person she'd seen at the gym? He'd not mentioned another woman, had he? Not mentioned a new girlfriend? Where on earth had she come from? Clearly not the gym. Not with those thighs. 'Err, do come in, both of you. Duncan will be down any minute. Let me have your coats and then I'll take you through to the kitchen.'

Marie watched as Candice checked out her surroundings whilst she poured them each a glass of wine. She waited for Candice to compliment her on her choice of designer wallpaper on the far side of the room or the portraits of her family lining the other wall. But Candice said nothing as she finished her appraisal and walked back to Simon and took his hand in hers, making Marie feel like a gooseberry in her own kitchen/diner. Simon had been chattering away happily as Marie automatically followed the key steps required of being a gracious host. The greeting, the coat taking, the escorting to the entertaining space, the wine opening and the wine pouring. But she hadn't really been listening. As Candice silently assessed her home, she silently assessed Candice. White skinny jeans… in February? Not cool. Dusky pink Lycra top, a size too small and revealing a shade too much cleavage. Large hoop earrings that admittedly were currently in fashion, but some people could not wear fashion. Jimmy Tarbuck, for example, or Piers Morgan. Candice too was clearly the type who didn't wear fashion well. Where had Simon dragged this woman from? Simon clearly needed to understand that he was worth so much more than this. Just because his wife had left him he didn't need to go trailing in the gutter for a replacement. Oh no, far from it.

'I'll just go and see where Duncan has got to,' she said, handing them each a glass of white wine. 'Won't be a sec.'

She walked out of the room in to the hall and then ran up the stairs.

'You are not going to believe it,' she said, bursting in to their bedroom.

'What?' asked Duncan, desperately trying to button up his Christmas shirt.

'He's brought a woman with him.'

'Who has?'

'Simon.'

'A woman?'

'Yes – well, more of a girl actually.'

'Did he tell you he was bringing a guest?'

'No,' she hissed.

'Wow,' said Duncan. 'What did you say?' he asked.

'Nothing! What could I say? He must have assumed I meant for him to bring someone. Maybe? Would you assume that if you were invited to a dinner party that you should take a partner?'

'Erm, I don't know. Maybe. Whatever. She's here now isn't she, so we'll just have to get on with it. Is there enough food?'

'Yes I think so. But I've only set seven places.'

'Don't worry,' reassured Duncan. 'I'll squeeze another one in whilst we are having drinks. Put that eighth chair to good use after all, eh?' He grinned. Marie did not grin back, just turned on her heel and walked out the room, back downstairs.

★

'I'm so sorry about that,' said Duncan, dashing in to the kitchen moments later. 'I had leaving drinks after work for a team member and, well, it dragged on a bit and oh… hello, Candice.'

Marie watched as he pulled up short, a look of surprise on his face. She also watched as Candice's jaw dropped slightly in shock. It was not a reaction she generally saw to the arrival of her husband.

'Hello,' Candice said eventually. 'Fancy meeting you here.'

Now everyone looked confused.

'You know each other?' asked Marie. Could this evening get any weirder?

'Good to see you,' said Duncan, lunging forward and holding out his hand, which Candice looked at with even more surprise. 'You are very welcome here,' he continued formally. 'And you, Simon,' he continued, turning to him. 'Good to see you again. So happy to welcome you in to our home. I'm sure it's going to be a very successful evening.'

What is he doing? thought Marie. He sounded like he was in work mode. Introducing one of his sales development workshops that he banged on about all the time.

'Thanks, boss,' said Candice, a smile appearing at the corners of her mouth. 'I'm sure it will, as long as you don't get us to sing "We are the Champions" at the end of the night!'

'Boss!' exclaimed Simon. 'You mean you work together?'

'Oh yes,' replied Candice, now grinning at Duncan. 'Well, when you say together, actually he's the boss and I'm just a lowly telephone operator.'

'No, no,' sputtered Duncan. 'No one who works for Vitaline is just a lowly telephone operator, they are all…'

'Champions,' said Candice, holding her hands up in an ironic cheer. 'Is he like this at home too? Must send you mental,' Candice said to Marie.

Marie was standing with her mouth open. How could this be happening? She had been so looking forward to this evening. She'd even made the dip from scratch, for goodness' sake. She'd thought Simon needed her. She'd been really looking forward to a deep and meaningful chat with him over a few glasses of tongue-loosening wine. But that wasn't going to happen, was it? Not now he'd brought along his new girlfriend and there was a strange woman in their midst with whom her husband was overly familiar. This wasn't the evening she had been expecting at all.

JOURNALIST: I'm sure our readers would love to know what to do in the event of an unexpected guest at a dinner party. Do you have any top tips for them?

BETH: I am the last person to ask for advice on this score. I have succeeded in offending every unexpected dinner party guest I have ever come across.

Chapter Seventeen

Beth

Chris hadn't commented that she was wearing the dress she usually wore on New Year's Eve. Her best dress. She was relieved. She didn't want any tricky questions. Not that she ever got any tricky questions from Chris. Maybe occasionally she would like one. A very minute display of noticing would be welcome. Noticing something about her appearance unprompted by herself would be nice. Maybe even a compliment wouldn't go amiss.

They'd walked. Usually she would offer to drive as she wasn't a big drinker, but she felt like a drink tonight. She was looking forward to a few glasses of Prosecco and living on the edge of slight oblivion.

'Watch your step, love,' said Chris. 'It's a bit icy there.'

'Thanks,' she replied, tiptoeing past in her medium-height black patent court shoes. Maybe they hadn't been such a good idea.

'So what do you reckon will be on the menu this evening?' Chris enquired.

'Cauliflower,' replied Beth.

'What? Just cauliflower?'

'Marie apparently has discovered during no-carbs January that cauliflower rice is the new rice. Swears by it. So don't go getting your hopes up for bread or pasta or even real rice. Your main satisfaction this evening will be from cauliflower, mark my words.'

'But I don't even like cauliflower.'

'I know.'

'Can't stand it raw, you know when they sometimes give you raw cauliflower with dips. What's that all about?'

'I don't know,' sighed Beth.

'Ruins a good dip, does raw cauliflower. I think I'd rather not have dip at all. And that's saying something.'

Thankfully they had arrived at Marie's doorstep before Chris could enlighten her further with his opinion on the relative merits of dip accompaniments.

'Hi,' said Marie, opening the door. 'Come in quick, it's freezing outside.'

'Are we having cauliflower?' asked Chris, taking his coat off and putting it on a hook.

'Yes,' said Marie. 'Instead of couscous. Why do you ask?'

Beth looked at Chris. 'At least she didn't say instead of chocolate or wine or beer. You can sacrifice couscous, can't you, for cauliflower?' she asked him.

'Lesser of two evils, I suppose,' he replied.

'Well, there you go then. The night has started well,' said Beth, grinning at Marie.

Beth was suddenly aware that Marie was staring at her with her eyebrows raised. Beth raised her own back, but that only caused Marie to raise hers further without any explanation as to why they were in this fascinating eyebrow-height competition.

'Why don't you come through?' Marie said, her eyebrows now virtually touching her hairline.

'We most certainly will,' replied Beth. It had been such a good decision not to drive.

'Ah, here they are,' said Duncan, turning to greet his guests as they walked in to the spotlessly clean kitchen/diner. Every time Beth had dinner at Marie's she got the urge to go home to her cluttered, dated, bashed kitchen and rip it all out and give it a good scrub. The reality was she perhaps got round to cleaning out the cutlery drawer and that would be the extent of her de-cluttering.

Beth then experienced to her surprise the decidedly teenage sensation of her heart suddenly beating faster at the anticipation of seeing Simon again. This really had to stop. She was a grown woman, a married woman, long past crushes. But it felt good to feel her blood rush through her veins slightly quicker in her rapidly ageing body. Like it was actually rejuvenating her. She allowed it to flow before looking round to see how her heart would react when she actually laid eyes on him.

'Hi,' said Simon, grinning at her. 'Can I introduce you both to Candice.'

Beth was moving forward on autopilot to embrace the woman standing next to Simon with her arm draped proprietarily around his shoulder. *Candice*, she thought, *who the hell is Candice?*

'Good to meet you,' she said as they embraced, trying not to let Candice's perfume tickle her throat. She drew back again. This was a surprise. This was a shock. She needed to react and react quickly. 'Blimey, you don't mess about do you?' she said to Simon.

He screwed up his face. 'What do you mean?' he asked.

'Well,' she said. *Sod it*, she thought, *just say what everyone must be thinking.* 'I thought, given the state you were in last time, that it was going to take you a long time to get over your wife sleeping with the chocolate vending machine salesman, but I'm so happy to see you have put that cheat behind you and found someone new. Good for you,' she said, giving him a slight punch on the arm.

Time stood still as everyone stared at Beth and her boldness.

'Candice *is* my wife,' said Simon quietly.

'What!' Beth heard Marie exclaim behind her as she felt all the blood drain from her heart to her cheeks.

'Oh my God,' she said, hiding her eyes. 'Oh my God, what have I done? I'm so sorry.'

'Chris, didn't you… I thought…' she heard Simon say.

'Oh bollocks,' exclaimed Chris. 'Oh, mate, I'm so sorry,' he said, raising his hands in submission. 'I'm such an idiot. Marie, I'm so sorry. I saw Simon and I was meant to ask you if it was okay if Simon could bring his wife tonight. But I clean forgot. We've had a new shift pattern introduced and it's thrown me, to be honest, not that it's any excuse. I… I… meant to call as soon as I got home that night. Look, I'm so sorry.'

Beth was now peering through her fingers at Simon and Candice. Simon looked supremely awkward as he rubbed his wife's shoulder in reassurance. She was staring down in to her Prosecco glass.

'I… I didn't mean what I said,' she said, pulling her hand away from her face. 'I'm always putting my foot in it, ask anyone. I'm so sorry. I just didn't expect… I just never thought…'

'We've had a chance to talk,' said Simon surprisingly calmly. 'A lot. Like I told Chris last week, we were having problems and we've talked it all through and we are trying to make another go of it, aren't we.' He squeezed Candice's shoulder and she raised her head. Beth held her breath.

'We all make mistakes,' Candice said to her.

Beth nodded. 'Of course,' she said. 'I married the idiot who forgot to tell everyone Simon was bringing you. I am very familiar with mistakes, believe me.' She smiled at Candice. Hoping she was forgiven. She needed to be or the night was going to be absolute torture that no amount of Prosecco was going to improve.

JOURNALIST: I hear there was a case of mistaken identity at one of your dinner parties. Some crossed wires?

DUNCAN: Yes, well, Beth proper put her foot in it, I can tell you. Of course, I had met Simon's wife before. She worked for me, but I didn't know who she was married to. It was a real shock to see her in our kitchen. But I might have known that she was going to cause chaos from the minute she walked in.

Chapter Eighteen

Sarah

'I've got a six o'clock meeting on site in the morning,' Tony told her as they drew up outside Marie and Duncan's house. 'Up in Sheffield. So, if you don't mind, we need to leave early tonight.'

'But won't it be dark at that time in the morning?' questioned Sarah.

'Yes – but that's the only time the client could meet us.'

'On a Saturday?'

'Yep.'

'Shall Chloe and I come with you? Then we could go down Abbeydale Road. See if we can purchase some vintage finds.'

'It's too early to get Chloe up, isn't it? I should be home by ten and then I thought we could perhaps go to Oakham. Get a decent lunch.'

'Okay,' replied Sarah. 'Yes, that sounds nice. There's a couple of shops I wouldn't mind seeing that way actually.'

'Great, come on then. Let's get this over with.' He got out of the car and slammed the door. He was tetchy, she could tell. She didn't really believe he had a six o'clock meeting on a Saturday; he just wanted to make sure they didn't stay long, that's all. Why couldn't he just say that?

'Come in, come in,' said Duncan cheerfully when he opened the door.

'Sorry we're late,' said Sarah. 'Chloe didn't want us to leave and it took a while to settle her down.'

'No problem at all,' replied Duncan. 'We have been busy getting to know Simon's *wife.*'

Why is he looking at Tony like that? thought Sarah. *Hang on a minute. What did he say?*

'Did you say Simon's *wife?*' she asked.

'Yes,' replied Duncan, looking over his shoulder to check he had pulled the kitchen door shut behind him.

'Wife?' echoed Tony.

'Yes,' whispered Duncan. 'They are back together. Isn't that good news?'

'But what about the chocolate vending machine salesman?' asked Sarah.

Duncan shrugged. 'No idea, but he must have forgiven her because they are *all* over each other in there.'

'Seriously,' said Sarah, feeling herself recoil.

'Oh yes,' said Duncan. 'And the really funny thing is that I know her. Candice works for me. Small world, hey?'

Tony looked at him in confusion. 'You know Simon's wife?'

'Yeah.' Duncan nodded, clapping his hands together. 'Weird, eh? Come through and I'll introduce you.'

Candice clearly shopped in the stores that Marie ran, thought Sarah when she walked in to the kitchen, but Marie didn't look too impressed by her presence or her display of their wares. She was staring at her as though she had just crawled out of a particularly shitty hole. They were all sitting round the table and Simon leapt up straight away to give the introductions.

'Hello, Tony, hello, Sarah,' he said. 'This is Candice.'

'It's his wife,' added Beth helpfully.

'We've heard,' said Tony. 'Delighted to meet you and to see Simon looking more himself.'

'Oh yes,' said Beth. 'Because we all really know what Simon's self is having only met him once before.'

Sarah thought Beth was slightly slurring her words. Surely she wasn't drunk, was she? Already? Beth rarely drank much anyway.

'Good to meet you,' Sarah said, extending a beautifully manicured hand, which was met by a spiky clutch of false nails.

'You too,' Candice replied, looking her up and down. 'Wow! Simon never said you were a model. You must be a model, right? You look amazing. Who does your hair? Are they extensions? I've always wanted extensions, but my friend Cat said that you have to have the expensive ones or it looks like you're wearing a wig. And you certainly don't look like you're wearing a wig.'

Wow, thought Sarah. This wasn't who she expected Simon to be married to. Despite the muscles, he came across as rather sensitive, perhaps even a little shy. A thinker who took things to heart. She'd imagined him with someone similar, attractive but with hidden depths. First impressions of Candice did not conform to this view. She was mile a minute, out there, in your face, *HELLO – look at me, my name is Candice. Look at me, everyone. I am totally up for a good time.* Tonight could be very interesting indeed.

'No, I'm not a model,' Sarah pointed out to her.

'Really!' exclaimed Candice. 'Well, you could be. You should look in to it.'

'Well, yes maybe,' replied Sarah, quite taken aback.

'Simon was just telling us how he and Candice got together,' said Chris.

'Oh great,' Sarah countered through gritted teeth as she took a seat. She never really enjoyed hearing how couples got together as her own story was not one to be proud of.

'So, as I was saying, I was on a stag do and Candice was on a hen do…' said Simon.

'Pre-hen do,' interrupted Candice. 'Well, actually it was a pre-pre hen do. I think Louisa had four in the end.'

'Anyway, so we were all stood at the bar and you all had challenges, didn't you,' Simon said to Candice.

'Yeah – you know the sort of thing, a shot in every bar, get all your drinks bought for you, convince a stranger you are foreign and can't speak English, convince a stranger you are famous, all the usual stuff.'

'I could so do that. I could do my Alec Baldwin impression,' said Duncan excitedly.

Sarah and Tony exchanged glances. Sarah had persuaded Tony to invite Duncan to his stag do when they got married. Duncan had insisted that karaoke had to be part of the evening forcing Tony to sing 'Up Where We Belong' with his best man. Sarah suspected that Tony had never really forgiven her.

'Anyway,' continued Simon. 'You had to get hold of a pair of man's underpants, didn't you, and, well… the rest is history.' He beamed at Candice.

'Wow,' said Marie. 'What a story. Did they tell that one at your wedding?'

'Yeah.' Simon nodded, chuckling. 'Well, it had to be done, didn't it? So I'd love to hear how you two met?' Simon asked Marie. 'I don't think I've heard your story.'

This will be interesting, thought Sarah. She wondered if Marie's and Duncan's versions of their road to marriage would match.

'She was a waitress in a cocktail bar…' said Duncan, smiling at his wife.

'Not really, was I?' interrupted Marie sharply.

'I was trying to make it sound romantic,' replied Duncan. 'Sounds better than saying our eyes met across a crowded room in a late-night curry house.'

'I was a penniless student,' Marie explained to Simon and Candice. 'Drunk men in curry houses tip very well, especially if you are nice to them.'

'Only you got in to a bit of bother that night, didn't you, love?' said Duncan.

'Well, I was used to it then, to be honest. Men thinking they can take advantage just because you've got a pretty face. It was part of the job.'

'This wanker on the next table was giving her a load of grief,' said Duncan. 'Then he grabbed at her and I couldn't bear it any longer. I got up and punched him. I have never punched a man before or since.'

'Wow!' exclaimed Candice. 'I never would picture you hitting someone. Wait till I tell the girls at work.'

'I don't know where it came from really. I just saw red,' said Duncan. 'Didn't even think about it. The owner came rushing over and chucked the man out. Best night of my life really,' sighed Duncan. 'I got a free curry and I met my future wife. I gave her a lift home in my MR2 and invited her out the following week.'

'He had a car and could afford to take me out to dinner,' added Marie. 'I'd been used to dating students who could barely buy me a packet of Rolos.'

'I took her to the best restaurant in Newcastle.'

'First time I had scallops,' said Marie.

'First time *we* had scallops,' added Duncan. 'I didn't even know what they were. Thought I was going to gag, to be honest. So slippery. But Marie, I remember, ate them like she'd been eating them all her life. I think I would have asked her to marry me there and then.'

The room went quiet for a moment before Chris decided to chip in.

'You got a free curry!' he exclaimed. 'You never told me that. How lucky is that. Which curry house? I need to know where you can go and punch someone and get a free curry.'

'It's gone now, mate, I'm afraid,' said Duncan. 'But Spicy Nights on Cocklington Road will always hold a special place in my heart. I took Marie back there as a surprise for our tenth wedding anniversary.'

'It's now a dry-cleaner's,' said Marie. 'We had to have greasy fried chicken next door. Gave me food poisoning.'

'I think that was the two bottles of wine you drank afterwards in the Wetherspoons down the road,' offered Duncan.

'What do you expect when my husband takes me to a dry-cleaner's for our wedding anniversary? You drive me to drink, you really do,' said Marie in exasperation.

'Err, so how did you two meet?' Simon asked Beth, diplomatically moving the conversation away from Duncan and Marie.

'McDonald's,' said Beth. Sarah noticed she took yet another swig of wine.

'What, you both worked there?' asked Simon.

'No, it was our first date,' said Chris. 'We were at school together but we barely spoke until I invited her for a happy meal. Happiest meal of my life. We were just fourteen.'

'Fourteen!' exclaimed Candice.

Chris nodded enthusiastically. 'Yep. Fourteen,' he said.

'Are you serious?' asked Candice.

'Very serious,' said Beth.

'So… are you like… did you ever… have you ever with, you know, someone else…' stuttered Candice, looking utterly flabbergasted.

'No,' said Chris and Beth in unison. Chris with a smile on his face, Beth with a grimace.

A heavy silence fell round the table. Sarah could tell that Candice would have liked to pursue her line of questioning, but Simon yet again stepped in to save any further embarrassment. Or so Sarah thought.

'And so you, then?' he said, turning to Sarah. 'How did you two meet?'

Sarah stared back at him. He couldn't have forgotten their conversation at the last dinner party. The one about adultery.

Simon must have recognised her confusion and dredged out of his memory the cause.

'Of course, you told me last time,' he said, going red. 'I forgot, no need to go over that again. Can I have another drink, Marie?' he asked quickly.

'No, tell me,' said Candice. 'I don't know. I've not heard the story.'

A heavy silence fell yet again.

Eventually Beth piped up. 'Their story is the opposite of ours. Lots of sex with other people before they finally found the one they wanted to have sex with for the rest of their lives.'

'Oh right,' said Candice, staring at Sarah and then at Tony. 'Very sensible. Always pays to be sure.' Sarah couldn't be certain but she thought she saw Candice raise her eyebrows at Tony.

'Right,' said Marie, suddenly leaping up out of her chair. 'I think we should eat, don't you? I've made some dip.'

'Great, dip,' Sarah heard Chris mutter. 'I could eat a whole dip, just like that.'

Marie placed the Moroccan-style bowl full of bright green pea and mint dip surrounded by sticks of carrot and celery and red peppers down on the middle of the table with a flourish, where it was greeted with a moment's silence.

'Seaweed?' asked Beth, looking up at Marie with a pained expression on her face.

'No,' replied Marie. 'Actually, it's pea and mint with tahini.'

'Tahini?' said Chris, screwing his face up as though he were about to take part in a Bushtucker Trial and was being asked to eat a hippo's bottom.

'Have you not had tahini?' asked Marie.

Chris shook his head silently.

'It's basically crushed sesame seeds and gives a creamy texture without the need for cream.'

'Ahhh,' said Beth, raising her glass as if she were about to toast the hostess. 'So you've given up fat this month.'

'No,' denied Marie. 'Just thought I'd try something different, that's all.'

Sarah knew this was a lie. She strongly suspected that Marie was trying to impress Simon with her home cooking. They never usually got dips at Marie's, maybe a few olives if they were lucky.

'It's really tasty,' said Duncan, leaning forward, grabbing a celery stick and plunging it in the radioactive-looking mass. He stuffed it in his mouth, nodding vigorously in an attempt to convince the onlookers.

Chris was the first to cave. He picked up a carrot stick and took the plunge, then everyone else followed his lead.

'This is delicious,' announced Candice. Everyone turned to smile at her warmly. 'Nearly as good as loaded nachos,' she said to Marie. 'I absolutely love nachos. Really I do. I could live on nachos.'

'I bet Marie has some nachos somewhere, don't you, Marie?' said Chris, grinning massively a Candice. 'I tell you what, nachos would go great with this dip.'

'Yes, we've got nachos,' said Duncan, leaping up out of his chair.

'No we haven't!' exclaimed Marie.

'We have, I've seen them,' he said, disappearing behind the kitchen island.

'They're Annabelle's nachos,' replied Marie.

'So!' he said, reappearing triumphantly with a large bag of Doritos. 'We can buy her some more.'

'But they're the really cheesy ones.'

'Brilliant,' said Chris. 'My favourite,' he announced just as Duncan banged a bowl full of cheesy nachos in the middle of the table and Marie looked at them as if she was in the Bushtucker Trial and had just been asked to eat hippo's bottom.

Sarah had listened to the entire conversation without really taking any of it in. She'd just watched as Tony had made a beeline for Candice, turning on his salt-and-pepper charm at full throttle. As the cheesy nacho debacle was about to reach its crescendo, a catastrophe that Candice herself had set in motion, Tony had taken the opportunity to start a conversation with Candice and now he was looking completely fascinated by her description of how she happened to work at the call centre with Duncan. He was totally engaged and already at the bottom end of his first glass of wine.

'Shall I drive then?' she asked when Candice drew breath from the detailed description of how she'd smashed her call time target that day.

'Oh, let's get a taxi,' said Tony. 'Why not?'

'I thought you had to get up early?'

'Oh, err, I'll be fine. Don't worry about that.' He turned back to Candice, asking her whether or not she had always worked in the communications industry, whilst Duncan joined in, happy to have the opportunity to talk about his managerial role in communications in front of Tony. Something he'd never shown the slightest bit of interest in before.

'Candice has been with us for two years, haven't you?' Sarah heard Duncan say.

'About that,' she replied.

'I remember your first day,' he said proudly as though she were his daughter. 'You really stood out. I told you, you had the gift of the gab, didn't I?'

'He did actually,' said Candice. 'Has he told you that he pretends to be a new starter himself? Sits in reception just like everyone else and gets talking to you as if he's the same as you. Then you go in this room and suddenly he stands up and it turns out he's the boss. He's been checking you out all along.'

Duncan nodded proudly. 'By the time they start at nine in that training room I already know who are going to be the stars and who will have left by the end of the week.'

'Wow,' said Tony, leaning over to grab the wine and top everyone's glasses up as well as his own. 'Sounds unconventional but effective.'

'Oh it is.' Duncan beamed. 'Seriously. I could come and talk to your HR person about it if you want. You have to know the right questions to ask obviously, but it saves so much time.'

'Well, I'll mention it to them,' said Tony, turning back to Candice. 'I am a partner in an architect's practice,' he told her. 'We built the…'

Sarah turned away. She'd heard Tony's CV speech many times before. She didn't need to hear it again, especially if it was only for the benefit of Candice.

She saw that Beth and Marie had left the table and were standing in the kitchen area having a hushed conversation. She glanced back at her fellow diners who were now all totally enrapt in Tony's description of the challenges facing the design of his latest project, then silently left the table to join her friends.

'I was just apologising again to Marie for Chris's utter failure to warn us about the extra guest tonight,' Beth told Sarah. 'I will actually kill him when we get home. The local news tomorrow will have the headline running of "Wife drowns husband in dips after multiple forgotten-dinner-guest blunders".'

'I blame Simon,' said Marie. 'He shouldn't have left it to Chris to let me know. He should have had the decency to find a way to tell me himself. You don't just turn up at a dinner party with you wife, do you? I mean, so rude.'

'It is his wife,' added Beth. 'Not so unusual really, is it?'

'His wife who has been sleeping with a chocolate vending machine salesman down the road, for goodness' sake. I mean, what is he thinking, taking her back,' hissed Marie.

'Sshhhh!' gasped Beth. 'Keep your voice down. They might hear.'

'Alexa – turn the sound up,' Marie suddenly shouted. The background music went up a notch, which meant they couldn't hear the conversation at the table and hopefully those at the table couldn't hear them. 'We got one of these voice-activated speaker things at Christmas,' explained Marie. 'It's brilliant. You can ask it anything. Seriously.'

'Like what is the best way to poison your husband following a major dinner party faux pas?' said Beth.

'Like how do we stop Duncan boring the pants off everyone about work during the dinner party?' sighed Marie.

'Like who's driving now that Tony has decided to neck his wine despite the fact he said he wasn't drinking because he has to be in Sheffield for six tomorrow morning,' said Sarah.

'If only Alexa could solve all our dinner party problems,' said Marie.

'I'm sorry, I do not understand the question,' said the voice from the speaker after a moment's pause.

They all collapsed in to giggles.

'That reminds me,' said Beth, gathering herself. 'Did the journalist get in touch with you about the dinner party I won with the Michelin-starred chef?'

'Oh yes,' said Marie. 'She did. She was ever so nice. We had a really good chat and she talked to Duncan, though what he could tell her about dinner parties I have no idea.'

'She called me too,' said Sarah. 'Not sure I said the right things. I think I made us sound pretty dull actually. She said she would call us all again before the chef comes to cook our dinner with more questions. Perhaps I will have something interesting to say by then.'

They all took a glug of wine as they observed the group happily chatting at the table.

'Do you know what?' said Beth eventually. 'I can see her nipples from here. What's she so excited about, do you think? Your dip, Marie?'

'It was good,' said Sarah. 'But not that good.'

'Perhaps it's the nachos then. Or having four men hanging off your every word…' added Beth.

Candice was clearly deep in to a story and the rest of the men were enrapt whilst Simon had his arm draped over the back of her chair, occasionally stroking her bare shoulder.

'It's never going to last, is it?' muttered Sarah, shaking her head.

'Yeah, poor Simon,' agreed Marie.

'He looks like the cat that got the cream,' said Beth.

'I strongly suspect the cream might be about to turn sour,' replied Sarah.

JOURNALIST: Perhaps we should do a feature on home-made dips in the magazine.

CHRIS: Perhaps not.

Chapter Nineteen

Beth

'You said she'd come back,' Beth heard a voice say behind her as she made her way along the hall to the downstairs cloakroom. She'd banged in to the wall twice, but she assumed that might be because of the shoes she was wearing and not the amount of Prosecco she had drunk.

'Did I?' Beth asked, swinging round to find that Simon had followed her.

'You did. Don't you remember? I told you she was going to Amsterdam with him and you said she'd be back within the week.'

Beth shook her head quickly, but she had to stop because it made her feel a bit sick. 'You told me she was going to a vending machine conference. That's why I said she'd be back within the week.'

'Well, you were right.'

'It was meant to be a joke,' she replied.

'Oh,' he said. 'Well, it gave me hope anyway, even if it was a joke, and do you know the first thing I thought when I found Candice on the doorstep?'

'"She's run out of knickers"?' asked Beth.

'No,' said Simon, grinning. Beth fleetingly thought how good-looking he was when he smiled. 'No, I thought about you.' Beth's heart stopped for a moment. 'I thought, wow, Beth, she was right. She knew that Candice would come back. She's so smart.'

Beth was tempted to point out that making a joke that a vending machine conference would be so boring as to kill an affair was not that smart really, but Simon was looking at her as though she had been the one to save his marriage and perhaps she shouldn't shatter the poor boy's delusions.

'So you're happy then?' she asked him bluntly.

'Of course,' he replied. 'Of course I am.'

'Good, good.' She nodded, thinking she really had to pee soon. Her bladder was not what it used to be.

'I mean, I'm just glad we got a second chance, that's all. This is going to sound really weird, but her having the affair has brought us closer together. We've talked about stuff over the past few days that we have never talked about before. I never knew she resented my hours so much and that I was never there. It's made us talk, it really has, Beth, and we're better for it.'

'So, you'd recommend it then?' asked Beth. 'Having an affair.' She'd better hold off the Prosecco now. Her mouth was engaging before her brain.

'No… God no. I'm not saying that. And I know that Chris would never… never, he's just not that kind of guy… You should never worry about him… No, no, that's not what I meant, I just meant in our situation it has helped us.'

No comment on my potential to have an affair, thought Beth, an irritation building up inside her. Of course he would never consider her adultery material. She was cuddly, after all.

She'd had enough of this ridiculous conversation.

'So what you are saying is that your wife having sex with another man has had a positive impact on your marriage,' she confirmed. 'Well, I'm delighted for you, Simon. I really am. Such a positive attitude. So highly commendable. I'm so glad I was right. Now, I must go to the loo before I burst. If you would just excuse me.'

I'll give their relationship until the end of the week, thought Beth to herself as she gratefully sat down on the seat.

Chapter Twenty

Beth

Beth sat there for a good five minutes mulling over what Simon had said. He was ridiculous to think that Beth had predicted their future. Predicted what might happen to these two relative strangers and their marriage.

If only we could see. If only we could see the end at the beginning. How would that make us feel? As we utter the words, 'Till death do us part', do any of us actually imagine what our parting will be like?

What if we were given the truth on our wedding day? What if we were told exactly how we would part during our vows? How might that change the dynamic of the celebration and the view on our future happiness together?

'Till a chocolate machine vending salesman do us part.'

'Till a promotion to area sales manager causing prolonged periods away from home do us part.'

'Till making friends with my high-school sweetheart on Facebook do us part.'

'Till finally having the guts to reveal I am gay do us part.'

'Till discovering I am infertile do us part.'

'Till gaining twenty pounds in weight do us part.'

'Till you losing your job and failing to get off your backside do us part.'

'Till roadworks on the M62 causing a diversion straight in to the path of a lorry do us part.'

'Till discovering you in bed with my best friend do us part.'

'Till watching you battle breast cancer for two years until it attacked every part of your body so I no longer recognise you do us part.'

'Till you forgetting me because of Alzheimer's do us part.'

'Till I bought you your last cup of tea in bed, at the age of ninety-two, only to discover you went to sleep and you were never going to wake up ever again do us part.'

Beth couldn't get this thought out of her head. If you knew how you would part right from the beginning, would you change your mind?

Beth found herself thinking back to her own wedding day. She married Chris at the age of twenty-three, so over twenty years ago. She'd not slept the night before because she'd convinced herself that Sarah wasn't going to make it. There had been threats of rail strikes and Sarah had been unable to get up from London the night before. She'd camped at the rail station all day, but all her trains had been cancelled. She'd rung and assured Beth the strike was off the following day and she would be on the first train out of London, but Beth had an impending sense of doom. That the strike was going to carry on and she would be minus a bridesmaid at the top of the aisle. She had tossed and turned all night.

She realised pretty soon that worrying about Sarah turning up was merely a displacement activity. She'd needed to find something. Anything to worry about other than the thing she should be really worrying about. Was she making the right decision marrying Chris? The only man she had ever been out with. The only man she had ever had sex with. Should she have tried some others out first, just to check what she was feeling was the best she was going to get? The trouble was, she didn't know if there were others out there that would want to try her out. What if there weren't and she had passed up on the one man who would fall in love with her?

So of course it was the right decision. Of course it was the right choice. He adored her. He was a good, solid, sensible, reliable man who adored her. What more could she ask for? What more indeed. She didn't think she could ask for more. After all, she was cuddly.

No one could ask for more once they had been branded cuddly, could they? There wasn't more for someone like Beth. She couldn't expect more.

And so she had floated down the aisle in her beautiful gown that she knew would look beautiful on someone two sizes smaller than her, with her two impossibly glamorous bridesmaids Marie and Sarah floating down behind her as Chris stood waiting for her, a big grin on his face, nervously pushing his side parting to one side.

I, Elizabeth Mary Cavendish, take you, Christopher Malcom Greening

To be my husband

To have and to hold

From this day forward

For better, for worse

For richer, for poorer

In sickness and in health

To love and to cherish

Till death do us part…

Would they get to the death bit, she and Chris? Would they make it all the way? Would death be the conclusion of their marriage? She found herself wondering if she could wait for death. She wasn't sure.

Chapter Twenty-One

Tony

It had actually turned out to be an okay evening up until that point, thought Tony. Considering he had been dreading it. Actually, dare he say, it had been fun. He'd expected to be a bystander as he watched Simon entice the women of the group in to his conceit of the lonely and betrayed. Instead, the presence of Candice had proved to be exactly the tonic that the evening needed. Simon had a smile on his face and she was actually very good company. She was blunt and confident in a way that led to some highly amusing truths about her fellow dinner party guests coming out totally unselfconsciously.

On Duncan as a boss:

'He's all right really. He wants to be the boss of you, but he wants to be your mate more. Once you've worked that out you can pretty much get away with murder.'

On Marie's Middle-Eastern-inspired menu for the evening:

'It was good to try it, but it doesn't really make me want to go there.'

On Chris forgetting to tell Marie that she was coming:

'Perhaps it's early-onset Alzheimer's?'

Beth's reply: 'That's very kind, but I think it's just sheer stupidity.'

Candice's response: 'Well, that's something.'

On learning Tony ran an architect's practice:

'Minted. I could tell.'

Tony found he actually quite liked her very straightforward view on the world. He dealt in bullshit every day of his life. He dealt with people who were telling him one thing and then thinking the other or, even worse, doing something completely different. The world of architecture could do with a few more Candices, he thought. The ability to call a spade a spade or even a brick a brick had somehow disappeared from the entire industry.

'Shall we show them how we do it at Vitaline?' Tony heard Duncan say to Candice. Tony froze as he anticipated the dreaded words he always hated to hear at Duncan's...

'I've got a karaoke machine.'

Tony's heart sank as he prayed that Candice wouldn't take the bait.

'Go on then,' he heard her reply. 'Then I can tell the girls I've done my quota of singing with the boss for the week.'

'I think we should do our specialty, don't you, Duncan,' interrupted Marie, looking daggers at Candice.

'You're right, love.' Duncan beamed. 'Simon and Candice need to see our rendition of "Islands in the Stream". It's our party piece.' He moved over to Marie and put his arm around her.

Normally Tony would have put his head in his hands. He had seen it so many times he thought his eyes might bleed if he had to be subjected to it again, but he was distracted by the look on Marie's face. A look of triumph that she had managed to snatch her husband back out of the clutches of karaoke with another woman. Such a contrast to the last dinner party when she had fawned all over Simon, leaving poor Duncan a little bereft.

'Everyone through to the lounge,' announced Duncan. 'It's already set up. I was hoping someone would want to step up to the mike tonight.'

Tony blew his cheeks out and glanced at his watch. It was just after eleven. He should really book a cab and then they could leave. It had been a good evening, but he was tired. He didn't seem to be able to stay up as late as he used to. He grabbed at his glass and drained it before standing up and reaching in his pocket to pull out his phone.

'Here, I'll put in my number,' Candice said as she took the phone out of his hand.

He looked up. Everyone else had already left the room to join the sing fest. It was just him and Candice.

He looked down again and watched as her fingernails clacked on the screen, working at a highly practised speed.

'Nice phone,' she said, handing it back to him.

'Thanks,' he replied, his brain struggling to catch up with what was happening.

'Call me,' she said, looking him square in the face.

He looked at her quizzically. What was she doing? Why was she doing it?

'Are you two coming or do we have to suffer this torture on our own?' a female voice could suddenly be heard from the doorway.

Tony's head flew up, as did Candice's.

There was Beth standing in the doorway. How long had she been there?

'Err yeah. Coming now,' he replied, moving fast towards her. 'I was just calling a cab.'

'Sure,' said Beth, as he brushed past her. 'Simon's picking a song for you,' she told Candice. 'I think he'd like to sing one together.'

★

JOURNALIST: Do you think I could speak to Simon and Candice for the feature? I think it would make a great side thread about the positives and negatives of being invited to a dinner party where the rest of the group know each other well and you don't know anyone.

BETH: Are you serious? After what happened? No way.

Chapter Twenty-Two

One Week Later

Beth

This really wasn't like her. She really shouldn't be doing this. It was none of her business, was it?

She stood at the heavy oak door of the converted chapel that housed Tony's architectural practice.

She'd never been to Tony's place of work before. Never had any need to. It was not like they were ever going to be asking for his services. He'd probably laugh at them if they did.

'Hello, Tony. We've suddenly found ourselves with a spare half mil floating around and we want you to build one of those super modern glass houses that look really cool and you can see in to them so everyone can see how utterly loaded you are.'

No, never going to happen. Beth was as likely to be able to afford the services of an architect as she was the services of a plastic surgeon.

She pressed hard on the buzzer located next to the door and waited for a no doubt perky and uber-cool young person to answer.

'Can I help you,' came the voice out of the box.

'Err, yes, I was wondering if I could come in and see Tony for a minute.'

'Do you have an appointment?' the female voice barked.

'No, I'm just a friend, well, a friend of his wife's really. Just tell him Beth needs five minutes, will you?'

'Give me one second,' the voice came back.

It wasn't one second. More like at least two minutes. She could picture Tony in his glass office, his face screwed up as the receptionist apologised profusely for interrupting him but some mad old bat was at the door wanting to see him.

'I'll let you in,' came the reluctant voice.

She heard the buzz of the door unlocking. She didn't like the feeling of letting herself in to a strange unknown building. You let yourself in to your own house, period. Not a commercial establishment such as this one.

She hovered, not knowing what to do. She felt disorientated. She was in a place of worship, coming to see Tony? No wonder she felt weird.

'Hi, Beth,' said Tony, appearing on a balcony just above her. 'Do you want to come up?'

They exchanged a look. He knew why she was here. She was sure of it. He was no fool. He knew why she was here, but he didn't know what she was going to do about it.

She followed him through an open-plan office buzzing with slim, busy, cool people. She had possibly never felt so out of place. *Surely there must be one fat person who works here*, she thought, looking desperately around. Or was it part of the recruitment criteria? 'All candidates must reflect the values of the company, which include integrity, excellence and a build no bigger than Joanna Lumley'.

'Nice office,' she said as Tony guided her in to a glass-walled workspace at the far end of the chapel built probably about where the altar would have been. 'Which god gets worshipped here now, then?' she asked.

'The client of course,' he said without even a flicker. He'd used that line before. He must have done. 'Can I get you a coffee?' he asked.

'Tea,' she said. Not particularly because she wanted one but because she liked the idea of Tony making her a drink.

He picked up the phone and moments later requested a minion to bring a tea and a black coffee, no sugar.

'So, to what do I owe this pleasure?' he asked, leaning back in his ergonomically designed chair.

'Well,' she said. She wanted to take her coat off but she'd sat down now and she'd have to get up. Should she take her coat off? she thought. No, she was just trying to put off what she had to say. *Keep your coat on and spit it out.* That is what she should do.

'I wanted to ask you why you took Candice's number the other night?'

'I didn't,' he fired back.

'You did. I saw you.'

'No, Beth,' said Tony, leaning forward in his chair. 'You saw Candice giving me her number. I did not ask for it. I did not take it. She took my phone out of my hand and put in her number.'

'Oh,' said Beth. She scratched her cheek and cast her mind back to the moment she had stuck her head round the door to tell Candice to come and pick a song. What Tony said was entirely plausible and actually logical. As she had turned the incident over in her head, whilst she tried to block out the pain of Duncan's and Marie's singing, what she couldn't fathom was why Tony would chase after someone like Candice. But she could totally understand why Candice would chase after the millionaire architect, Tony. (She didn't know if Tony was a millionaire but she suspected that he was. He smelt like a millionaire.) So Tony actually hadn't done anything wrong, which was good – really good – but Candice had. 'So what do we do?' asked Beth, looking up at Tony.

'Nothing,' said Tony, standing up to open the door so the minion could bring in the tea tray.

'Thank you,' Beth said to the girl before she disappeared.

'Biscuit,' said Tony, putting a plate of chocolate digestives under her nose.

She could smell the chocolate.

'No thank you,' she said. She was trying to cut down. She was always trying to cut down.

'But we have to do something,' Beth said to him.

'Why?' asked Tony, taking a seat and dunking his biscuit in his coffee.

'Because… because… of Simon. He thinks she's back with him. He thinks his marriage has been saved now she has got over the chocolate vending machine salesman. Turns out one sniff of a loaded architect and she's off again.'

'I so wish you wouldn't go on about how loaded I am,' he said.

'Because you hide it so well,' she argued, casting her eye around the swish office.

'Look,' he said. 'We don't owe Simon anything. We hardly know him and I don't think he would thank us for meddling in his marriage.'

'So if Sarah gave her phone number to someone, you wouldn't want to know about it?'

'That's different,' he snapped.

'Why is it?'

'Sarah wouldn't do that.'

'Simon thinks Candice wouldn't.'

'Are you comparing me to Simon?'

'No. I'm just saying that… that…' She suddenly felt slightly scared. Tony looked cross. 'I'm just saying that we perhaps all like to believe things about people and sometimes they can prove us wrong.'

'Is Sarah messing me around?'

'No, no of course not!' said Beth. What had she started? 'I'm just saying that if I was Simon I would want to know. Wouldn't you?'

Tony took a sip of his coffee, never taking his eyes off Beth.

'You would want to know, wouldn't you,' she pressed.

'Yes,' he hissed, putting his mug down.

'So you need to tell him,' Beth said.

'What!' exclaimed Tony, running his hand through his hair. 'I'm not telling him.'

'Why not?'

'Because I don't want to. Because he might blame me. I don't want to be involved. Really I don't. Christ, I wish Chris had never met this guy.'

'It's not Chris's fault Candice is… well… a bit on the loose side,' said Beth.

Tony raised his eyebrows at Beth.

'Harsh,' he said.

'But fair,' replied Beth. 'So shall I get Chris to tell him?' she asked.

'Oh yeah, great idea. Like he's going to get that right. If we trust Chris to tell him I could end up in casualty having been assaulted by a jealous Simon.'

'Fair point,' agreed Beth. She knew that the chances of Chris communicating the issue correctly and empathically were zero. 'So I'll have to tell him then,' she said, getting up. She'd had enough now.

'You?'

'Yes.'

Tony looked at her in astonishment. Then said, 'Okay then, if it means that much to you. You do it. But tell him exactly what happened, won't you. That I didn't encourage her at all.'

'Of course,' replied Beth. 'Can I ask you one thing though?'

'Okay.'

'Did you tell Sarah?'

Tony paused before he answered. 'No.'

'Oh.'

'There was nothing to tell.'

Beth wasn't sure that Sarah would see it that way.

JOURNALIST: Do you all feel at home in each other's houses? I imagine that after all these years your gathering is quite informal?

BETH: We are only capable of informal at our house. Tony's, however – well let's just say that even the dog has a napkin.

Chapter Twenty-Three

Chris

'You seen Simon lately?' Beth asked Chris.

He glanced up at her. She'd set up the ironing board in the front room and so had commandeered the TV to watch some drama about a woman whose husband had been murdered. Chris did not understand why anyone would want to watch such a programme for 'entertainment' especially when there was a perfectly decent football match on the other channel but he knew better than to watch sport when Beth was ironing. He'd tried it once and she had said that was perfectly acceptable as long as he did the ironing whilst watching the football! Apparently there was a rule that if you have an iron in your hand you can watch whatever you want on the TV.

'Not since Marie's,' he replied. 'He's changed his shifts though, so he's not in during the day as much as he was. Apparently that was a condition of Candice coming back.'

'She's still there then?' asked Beth.

Chris shrugged. 'I assume so. Why, do you think she'd go off again?'

'Maybe,' replied Beth, holding a shirt up to scrutinise a mark on the collar.

'Naaa,' replied Chris. 'She's learnt her lesson, I reckon. She's realised how lucky she is with Simon. I mean, don't get me wrong, she's a very attractive girl and could probably have who she wants, but she went back, didn't she. She went back to him. That's got to mean something.'

'Mmmm,' said Beth. 'If you say so.'

'Not convinced then?'

'No. She's gone off once. She could quite easily do it again.'

'Do you think that's how it works?' asked Chris. 'Once an adulterer, always an adulterer?'

It was Beth's turn to shrug as she turned her attention to the sleeves of a blouse. 'Maybe,' she said again. 'It's got to make it easier, hasn't it?'

'Like you've broken a seal?'

'Yes.'

'Like when you go for your first wee on a night out and then you can't stop going even if you wanted to.'

Beth turned to look at him. Her eyebrows raised. He was trying to make her laugh. She looked so serious.

'If you say so,' she replied.

'So do you think that about Tony then?' asked Chris.

'What? That he's capable of doing it again?'

'Yeah.'

'No,' replied Beth. 'I think he's devoted to Sarah. His mistake wasn't adultery with Sarah, his mistake was he should never have married his first wife. Perhaps there should be a different word for those people who stray from their marriages just because they like having sex with other people and those who stray because they fall in love. Perhaps it isn't fair to lump them all in to the same category.'

Chris looked up at Beth. He hadn't really listened to any of that as he'd been distracted by the discovery of the husband's remains on screen.

'Mmmm.' He nodded in what he thought was an interested type fashion.

'I mean, if you marry but then fall in love with someone else, then that's just kind of unlucky, isn't it. It's not like you went looking for it. It just happened. And yet you are tarred with the same brush as someone who just likes to sleep around.'

Chris was too busy staring at the wife of the murdered husband attacking a chief constable outside his house.

'Don't you think, Chris?' he heard from somewhere. Oh, Beth was talking to him.

'What? Yes. Yes of course you are right,' he spluttered, hoping that was the right answer.

He looked at his watch. If this programme finished at ten, then maybe he would get away with turning over to watch *The Premier League Show.* He glanced over to check out the ironing basket. Maybe four items left. Brilliant. Five minutes and she would be collapsing the ironing board and taking it out of the room, at which point he could casually ask if it was all right to switch over now that her programme had finished.

'So you've no idea if Simon and Candice are still together then?' Beth asked.

'What? No. Not seen him.' The woman was now in custody and being grilled by a man in uniform. This wasn't going to end well.

'Where does he live again?' he heard Beth ask.

'On Cresswell Road,' he replied. The woman on the TV was sobbing. Desperate. He couldn't watch. To his horror, he felt tears spring to his eyes. This woman had lost the love of her life and no one could help her. He could literally feel her pain.

'Oh, which one?' he heard Beth ask as he hastily tried to brush away the tears at the corners of his eyes without Beth seeing. He feared she would laugh at him if she caught him crying at a TV programme. She saw this sort of thing every day in her job. He had no idea how she dealt with it, but she did. He couldn't let her see him affected by a piece of fiction when she dealt with life and death in the real world every day. He was in awe of his wife, to be honest. She was just so capable. Put him to shame really. He did his best to be a good husband, look after them all, be in charge. But she was just so much better at it than him. Seemed a good idea to let her get on with it.

'Is it one of the new builds at the end?' she continued.

'Yeah.' Chris nodded. 'It's the first one. The biggest.' He sniffed. 'I tell you what, you would die for his kitchen.'

'Right,' said Beth.

He nodded vigorously and looked away from the TV. 'It's got a sofa in it. In a big bay window. Lovely spot.'

'Right. But you hardly see him now, you say?'

'That's right. I think he said he's only at home on Mondays now he's changed his shifts.'

'I see,' replied Beth.

'Oh, it's finished,' said Chris, glancing back at the screen with relief. 'You done, love?' he asked. 'Mind if I switch over for a sec?'

'Go ahead,' replied Beth, already collapsing her ironing board before walking right in front of the TV. Fortunately it was just the ads so he didn't miss anything.

JOURNALIST: So did you invite Simon and Candice to your next dinner party?

MARIE: God no. Well, actually, Simon came to the next one. But, of course, Beth had split them up again before that.

Chapter Twenty-Four

Marie

Marie had checked online before she'd arrived. She'd chosen Starbucks because at least they published the calorie content of all their food and drinks, albeit on a chart so minutely typed that she could barely read it. She'd scanned down the list, attempting to find an item that would fit in to her strict calorie-control regime. Not long to go now until they went skiing and she still looked like the Michelin Man when she put all her ski gear on. She settled on a fruit pot despite the fact that she could see pomegranate seeds in it, which were very high in sugar. Perhaps she would leave the pomegranate seeds. Then she would have a fruit tea. No need for milk, so extremely healthy.

She was already settled at a sofa in a cosy corner by the time Beth and Sarah arrived. She waved, then waited patiently for them to get their drinks and sit down.

She noticed Sarah didn't have anything to eat. She was so blessed with no appetite. Sarah clearly didn't enjoy food. God, how she dreamed of that. And surprisingly Beth didn't appear to have any food either. Marie thought she could have relied on Beth to have something to eat. She usually did.

But this was new. She was the only one eating, albeit just a pot of fruit minus the pomegranate seeds. Now she was going to have to suffer the embarrassment of eating when no one else was. Perhaps she would take the fruit home and eat it there.

'Is everything okay?' asked Sarah, sitting down with a concerned look on her face.

'Everything's fine, I just fancied some fruit,' she replied.

Sarah gave her a strange look. 'It sounded like you needed to see us urgently – I thought something must be up.'

'Oh no, no,' said Marie. 'I just thought that I hadn't seen you since our dinner party and, well, I thought we could do with a download that's all.'

'Do you want to gossip about Candice?' asked Beth.

'Well no… I… well, yes, of course I do,' she finally admitted.

'Cheese and ham toastie!' shouted a man from behind the counter.

'That's me.' Beth waved whilst getting up.

Marie felt a wave of relief. She'd be able to eat her fruit pot after all.

'We do actually have some proper gossip,' Sarah told Marie as they waited for Beth to sit back down.

'What do you mean, proper gossip?'

'Wait for Beth,' Sarah replied, patting her arm.

Wait for Beth! You can't say a thing like that and expect me to wait for Beth. Marie tapped her foot vigorously in frustration.

'How's the new stock going?' Sarah asked her.

'Fine,' replied Marie, unable to take her eyes off Beth's slow progress across the cafe.

'Have you told her?' Beth asked Sarah as she sat down.

'No, she bloody hasn't,' cried Marie. This was almost as bad as the time she was last to find out that Sarah was having an affair with Tony. Apparently Sarah had confided in Beth weeks before they shared the news with Marie. She'd been devastated that she wasn't in on it. Many times she'd wanted to ask Sarah why she felt she couldn't tell her, but she'd bottled it. It was all coming back to her now. Feeling like an outsider amongst her closest friends. She didn't like that at all.

'Do you want to tell her?' Beth said to Sarah.

'Okay,' replied Sarah. She took an agonisingly long breath. 'So, at your dinner party something happened.'

'Right,' replied Marie. She was confounded. She'd been there the whole time. Apart from Candice turning up uninvited, there hadn't seemed to be any other event of note. She hoped that this wasn't just something stupid. What a crushing disappointment that would be.

'Candice tried to come on to Tony,' declared Sarah.

Marie gasped first, then her hand flew to her mouth as she tried to process what Sarah was telling her.

'What? How?' she spluttered. 'When! I was watching her the whole time. Believe me. I knew we couldn't trust her.'

'It was when everyone went through to do karaoke,' added Beth. 'Candice gave Tony her number.'

'What!' exclaimed Marie. 'In my new kitchen/diner!'

Sarah and Beth stared at her.

'The cheek of it!' she said, reeling. 'I welcomed her in to my home with open arms…'

'Hardly,' interrupted Beth. 'You were giving her daggers all night.'

'Well, she was an uninvited guest.'

'Thanks to my clueless husband,' said Beth. 'I'm really sorry about that.'

'I know. But still, she ate my pea and mint dip… with nachos… and then has the audacity to proposition one of our husbands?'

'Tony said he couldn't believe it. He was in shock,' said Sarah.

'When did he tell you?' asked Beth.

'The other day. He said it had been preying on his mind but he didn't want to make a big deal out of it and then he suddenly thought that actually Simon had a right to know.'

'Oh my goodness,' said Marie, her hand flying up to her face for the second time. 'The poor man. And he thought it was all going to be all right. Poor Simon. But we predicted it, didn't we? So is Tony going to tell Simon then?'

'Well, understandably, he's not sure if that's a good idea,' said Sarah. 'He's not sure if it would be best coming from him. He thought actually Chris should be the one to tell him, but we know his track record, don't we?'

'Sadly yes,' agreed Beth.

'So Tony suggested that Beth should tell him. He might take it best from her.'

'Oh,' said Marie, taken aback. She hadn't been expecting that. 'Oh,' she said again, staring at Beth. 'Or I could do it. I could try and catch up with him at the gym.'

Beth stared back at her for a moment.

'No, it's fine,' she replied. 'I don't mind.'

'Really it's no trouble,' said Marie. 'I'll probably bump in to him anyway. Save you the bother.'

'No, I'm happy to do it,' replied Beth. 'You might not catch up with him at the gym for days.'

'Where are you going to find him?' Marie asked Beth.

'Oh. I know where he lives,' said Beth. 'Chris told me. Because that's how they met, of course. Chris delivering mail to him.'

'Right.' Marie nodded, her brain doing overtime. 'So you are going to go to his house.'

'Yes,' said Beth, taking a big bite out of her cheese toastie.

'Alone?'

Beth nodded whilst chewing vigorously.

'Is that wise? I mean, we hardly know him. We've only met him twice after all.'

Beth shrugged, still chewing.

The three of them sat in silence, all deep within their own thoughts.

'Perhaps we should all go?' Sarah said suddenly.

'Yes!' said Marie, as though she had just discovered she had got a surprise A in GCSE physics. 'Exactly what I was going to say. We should all go, shouldn't we? Safety in numbers and all that. We couldn't possibly let you go on your own, Beth, that would be very irresponsible.'

Beth was still chewing but you could tell she had her response ready.

'I mean, he might get angry,' added Marie before Beth could say anything. 'You never know, do you. He might get angry and then heaven knows what he might do. No, Beth, you really shouldn't go on your own, it could be dangerous.'

Beth was now wiping her lips with her napkin.

'You're not coming,' she said matter-of-factly. 'I'm going on my own.'

'But Beth,' said Sarah, putting her hand on her arm, 'that could be a bit reckless.'

Beth looked at them both and sighed. 'He won't get violent, he's a paramedic,' she said simply.

'But how do you know?' said Marie. 'Love does strange things to people. You don't know what he is capable of.'

'If the three of us turn up on his doorstep, it's going to totally freak him out. I'm going on my own and that's that. Cake, anyone?' she said, standing up and looking at them questioningly.

'No thank you,' they both said before Beth turned her back and went to peruse the laden glass shelves.

'She's probably right,' said Sarah, taking a sip from her peppermint tea.

Marie turned to her sharply. 'Well, I'm not happy about it,' she said. 'We must make sure she tells us when she is going and calls us as soon as she leaves, so we know she's okay. Just in case.'

'Just in case of what?' asked Sarah.

'Just in case something happens to her. We would never forgive ourselves, would we?'

JOURNALIST: So did your unexpected guest, Simon, ever invite you back? Should random guests always reciprocate, do you think?

BETH: Well, he did eventually, a while later, but that was the dinner party where it all went catastrophic, so he probably wishes he hadn't. Of course, I had soup with him before that. That was unplanned though. I spat it out. That was unplanned too.

Chapter Twenty-Five

Beth

'You're being ridiculous,' Beth said to herself as she looked in the mirror.

She'd put on her black trousers (slimming) and her folksy top from Monsoon. She couldn't decide if she looked feminine or frumpy. A few extra pounds could make that look go either way. She'd come home from work, jumped in the shower and then thought carefully about what to wear, whilst the butterflies had a jolly old dance in her stomach. She hadn't felt like this since she used to dash home from school at the age of fourteen ready to prepare for the monthly youth club disco.

What was she doing? She was a grown woman, married, with two sons and she was feeling giddy at the prospect of going round to a man's house and being alone with him. This was truly ridiculous. Totally stupid. She was going to deliver bad news, not to take part in a candlelit supper. What she wore was irrelevant. *She* was irrelevant. This wasn't about her, it was about Simon. Who knows, he might choose to shoot the messenger and then no feminine-looking top was going to preserve the kindling of a friendship they'd created.

She pulled off her blouse and put on a pale blue wool jumper that she'd worn pretty much all week and had a stain on the cuff. She looked at herself in the mirror. Much better. She looked much more like Beth, the bearer of bad tidings. Now she was ready.

She noticed that there was one car parked outside Simon's house. That was good. Hopefully that meant he was in and Candice was out. She fleetingly wondered what she would do if Candice happened to be in at 1 p.m. on a Monday afternoon. Ask them to dinner, she supposed. If they could bear another dinner party.

She stood for several minutes across the road staring at the house until an old man shuffled past and made a point of looking her up and down as though committing her to memory should he have to create a photofit of her later.

All she needed to do was cross the road, knock on the door, go inside and get it over with. Enough of this stupid butterflies and first date nerves sensation. It was ridiculous. That wasn't her. She needed to be Beth now. Good old reliable Beth, ready to solve a problem at the drop of a hat. That was who she was. That was her role in life. *Now cross the bloody road and get on with it.*

She shoved her hands deep in her pockets as she waited for him to answer the door. *Well-tended pot plants*, she thought. *Clearly him, not Candice.* Candice didn't strike her as the kind of woman to care about pot plants.

'Wow, hello,' said Simon, suddenly standing right in front of her. 'What a nice surprise. Come in, come in.'

He was wearing a tight T-shirt with a tea towel thrown casually over his shoulder.

Beth took a deep breath.

'Have you eaten?' he asked. 'I'm just having some soup. There's plenty.'

She stood there with her mouth open.

'Come on,' he said. 'I owe you a meal.'

Oh no, she thought. This wasn't supposed to happen. Her walking in and telling him his wife was preparing to cheat on him again was not supposed to include eating his lunch. What the hell was she supposed to do now?

She followed him in to the kitchen, trying to focus on the tea towel and not the tight T-shirt. Chris had said they had a kitchen to die for and he was right. It wasn't so much the decoration or the furniture but the dazzling light that poured in from the conservatory that the kitchen opened up onto. Walking in to the room, Beth suddenly felt her face bathed in sunlight.

'Take a seat,' he said. 'Take your coat off. I was literally just dishing up.'

'Please don't let me take your lunch,' she said, starting to feel anxious.

'No worries. My eyes are always bigger than my belly. And I have bread, fresh this morning. Look, a relative feast.'

He walked over with an unsliced loaf on a wooden chopping board and set it on the table, then walked back and dished up steaming hot soup in to two bowls. He set one down at the end of the rectangular table and one just round the corner. She sighed and sat down.

Moments later he was sitting next to her, energetically slicing up the crusty bread.

'Love fresh bread, don't you?' he asked.

She nodded.

'Candice is more of a processed sliced-white kind of girl,' he continued. 'I don't get it. But each to their own, eh.'

He dunked his bread in his soup before putting it in his mouth. Beth picked up her spoon and dipped it in to the hot liquid. She tasted it. It was of course delicious. She'd just put the spoon in to her mouth for the second time when he came out with the killer question.

'So, to what do I owe the pleasure then?' he asked innocently.

She spat her soup across the table. Yes, actually spat it across the table. She had just been thinking about whether she should come up with a lie as to why she was there. She couldn't see how she could inform this man of his wife's indiscretion over the most delicious vegetable soup she had ever eaten. Seemed rude somehow. And then he had asked her direct. Before she could come up with anything that would have led her to rock up unannounced and eat his soup.

'Are you all right?' she heard him ask, before leaping up to get her a piece of kitchen towel. 'Is the soup that bad?'

'No,' she said, shaking her head and trying to mop up her mouth. 'No, it's really good.'

'Here,' he said, handing her another piece of kitchen roll. She used it to gather up the soup that she had jet-propelled onto the table, leaving a sticky clump of paper sitting awkwardly between them as though she had just been sick.

'Well, my home-made soup has never got that reaction,' he said, sitting down again and picking up his spoon. 'In fact, quite the opposite. My mum's recipe, you see. A classic.'

'Home-made?' she asked.

He nodded.

'I just spat your home-made soup across the table?'

'Not your finest moment,' he said.

She laughed and they looked at each other. Despite her rocky start she was having such a lovely time. Why did she have to be having such a lovely time?

'So?' he asked, raising his eyebrows.

'So,' she said, nodding. The nice time was over. She swallowed. 'No easy way to say this, Simon, so I'll just spit it out. Not like the soup… Oh, you know what I mean.'

'Oh my God, something's happened to Chris, hasn't it? I thought he must be off. He quite often posts a little note through my door to see if I'm okay and he hasn't this week. Why didn't you say, Beth? Here's me force-feeding you soup you hate and something's happened to Chris.'

'No,' she said, shaking her head. 'Chris is fine. In fact, the last time I saw Chris he was trying to make a golf net out of an old curtain, so I may actually kill him when I get home, but for now he's fine.'

'Oh,' said Simon. 'So what is it then?'

She swallowed again and looked up at him.

He smiled at her.

She was tempted to get up and run.

She didn't.

'Candice gave Tony her number at Marie and Duncan's dinner party.' That sounded like an awful lot of names to take in, thought Beth instantly. What if he got them muddled up? Marie gave Tony her number at Candice and Duncan's dinner party. That wouldn't make any sense, would it? Could he take in all those names and understand what she was trying to tell him? She looked at him. He did look confused. 'Candice gave Tony her number at the dinner party you both attended,' she clarified. Yes, that sounded better. A bit formal but more understandable and by the look on Simon's face he was finding it a lot more understandable too.

'What do you mean, gave him her number?' he said slowly.

'She gave him her phone number.'

His face was even more screwed up now.

'Because… she thought we might need an extension designing?' he said.

Seriously? thought Beth. It was obvious Candice had no interest in his professional services whatsoever, other than possibly the salary she thought he must be earning given his lucrative occupation.

'Have you been talking about an extension?' she asked him. Perhaps she had better check. Just in case.

'No,' he replied.

'Do you think you might need an extension?' she asked.

'No,' he said. 'Not unless we got rid of the conservatory.'

She nodded. 'And it is a lovely conservatory,' she agreed.

'Exactly.'

She could see him searching her face for answers to the puzzle she had presented him with. He was squinting at her. Trying to decipher what she was trying to tell him.

She looked around in desperation and then screwed her eyes up before letting it out.

'She gave him her number because she wanted to have sex with him.'

He didn't move. He didn't flicker. She was aware she was holding her breath. The room seemed very still.

'How do you know she wanted to have sex with him?'

She raised her eyebrows. 'Why else do you think Candice would give him her number?'

He stared back at her. The colour drained from his face.

She mentally went through the recovery position in her head. Always the nurse.

He got up abruptly, his hands flying to his head. Beth thought she had never been in such a tense moment in her life. Such a life-changing moment. Even when she agreed to marry Chris, it hadn't felt life-changing. It had felt predictable. Saying no would actually have changed her life. Saying yes was just more of the same.

'It was definitely Candice who gave him her number, not the other way round?' she heard Simon ask.

She nodded.

'And you believe him,' he said. 'You trust him. I mean, he has form, doesn't he? He had an affair. He's done it before, chased another woman whilst he was married?'

She was shaking her head the whole time he was spitting out this urgent tirade.

'I know him, Simon. He's no serial adulterer. He's devoted to Sarah. They discovered each other too late to save him from his first marriage, that's all.'

Simon was nodding now.

'And Candice is not his type.' She regretted saying this the minute she opened her mouth.

'What do you mean?' flared Simon.

'I mean… I mean… I mean…' Why didn't she know what she meant? 'I mean, he only goes for brunettes,' she said. 'Always has. One of the few men I know who isn't turned by a pretty blonde.'

He was staring at her. Blinking at her. Speechless. Uncomprehending. In shock.

'Please sit down,' she said. 'There are too many sharp edges around here.'

He sat down on his chair with a bump.

'We thought you should know,' she added. She wanted to touch his arm but she was too aware that it was naked.

'We!' he exclaimed. 'What do you mean, we? Does Chris know too?'

The truth was that Chris was just about the only person who didn't know. Beth had thought about telling him, but she didn't know how he would react. Whether he would want to tell Simon or, probably more likely, Chris would advocate a bury-your-head-in-the-sand approach and decree that it was none of their business. So she had decided not to tell Chris until a later date when it was safe to do so, but this might seem an odd decision to Simon.

'Yes, Chris knows,' said Beth. 'Just me and Chris.'

'And Tony?'

'Of course. And Tony.'

'And he must have told Sarah?'

'Err, yes, I guess so. Yes, he probably has.' Wow, she was screwing this up really badly now.

Simon allowed his head to drop to his fist on the table. She stared at the top of his headful of tight bouncy curls. She swallowed.

'I'm so sorry,' she said. 'I didn't want to be the bearer of bad news but... but I thought you would want to know.'

His head reared up suddenly. 'You must think I am such an idiot!' he spat out, banging his fist on the table.

Uh-oh. Here comes the anger.

'No, of course not,' she said. 'You weren't to know. How could you have known?'

He looked at her.

'Probably when she slept with my best mate six months after we started dating,' he replied.

Beth tried not to let her jaw drop open.

'Wow.' It was no good. She couldn't stop herself. 'Seriously?'

He nodded. 'She's good at being sorry,' he said bitterly. 'Very good.'

Clearly, thought Beth. She tried not to think what their make-up sex must be like.

★

JOURNALIST: So, what did you make of Simon's culinary skills when you first went round? Were you thinking that he would be a good asset to the dinner party group? Was he up to standard?

BETH: Oh, the soup was delicious. And the bread was out of this world. I meant to ask him where he had bought it afterwards, but I was worried it would bring back painful memories.

Chapter Twenty-Six

Simon

The look on Beth's face said everything. He was an utter idiot. Of course he was. In fact, she looked confused more than anything. Which was totally understandable. After all, he'd married the woman who had slept with his best friend. He'd married the woman who had an affair with the chocolate vending machine salesman down the road. He'd married the woman who came on to a stranger at a dinner party within hours of meeting him, having only just got back together with her husband. Who could comprehend that? Simon wasn't even sure if he could comprehend that.

'How?' he moaned, staring at Beth.

'Tony said she just took his phone off him and put her number in.'

Simon stared at Beth.

'I meant how could I be so stupid?' he said.

'Oh,' she replied. 'Sorry. I thought you meant how did she give him her number.'

Simon shook his head. He really didn't know what to say, his head was a jumble of thoughts crowding his brain.

'She promised me,' he told Beth. 'She promised me that it would never happen again. She sat there, where you are sitting, and said she loved me. Said she was an idiot, that Ricky meant nothing to her.'

'Ricky?' asked Beth.

'The chocolate vending machine salesman,' said Simon.

'Of course.' Beth nodded.

He bit his lip.

'She said I was the only man she ever loved.' He could feel the tears springing to his eyes. He screwed them shut and shoved his fists in his sockets, hoping that would somehow quell the outburst. Next thing he knew he was heaving. His shoulders uncontrollably humping up and down.

He felt Beth's hand on his back. He felt a gentle squeeze. He felt her sympathy ebb in to his body and he was gone. The heaving exploded in to a full-on sob as he heard a chair scrape back and felt Beth's arms around his shoulders. He turned to bury his head in her jumper, his arms automatically reaching up for her. He grasped her like a life raft and she grasped him back.

Chapter Twenty-Seven

Beth

Beth felt her own tears flow as Simon held onto her, his desperate sadness somehow triggering her own. She felt something give. Like when the hosepipe flew off the end of the tap because the pressure had got too much for it and the water sprayed everywhere. Her cheeks were as sodden with tears as Simon's.

She didn't really know why she was crying. She suspected it was simply because she was sad. She thought perhaps she had been sad for a while. But she was tired of feeling sad. She didn't want to wake up in the morning and think, *oh shit, I've woken up again*. Woken up to something that feels like such hard work. Coping with the mundane. Coping with her everyday life. Coping with the same shit, different day. She was sick and tired of coping. Sick and tired of pretending she was coping. Her life felt grey, muted and woolly and she wanted it to be vivid and sharp and in full technicolour.

A bit like this. Holding Simon as emotion poured out of them. This felt vivid, this felt real. This was feeling something, unlike the state of numbness she was used to existing in. Simon was making her emotional. Something her husband hadn't managed to do for a long time.

Chapter Twenty-Eight

Chris

Chris whistled as he strode along the street. It was a good day. First day of the year in postman shorts. Always one of his favourite days. A true sign that spring was just around the corner, even though it was still early March. He'd opened the curtains that morning and he knew. He just knew that spring was in the air and he would put on his postie shorts and he would wear them, come what may, until October. His aim was always to be the last in the team in shorts. It gave him a feeling of accomplishment.

And he had a parcel for Candice. He grinned as he put it in the van. Great. It was a Monday, so Simon should be at home and he could call in and have a cup of tea. Break the round up a bit. He'd been dying to have an excuse to knock on the door to see how he was. See how him and Candice were getting on. He could totally understand why Simon had been so devastated now that he had met Candice. She certainly was a stunner and funny and lively. He was so glad it had worked out. He couldn't imagine what Simon had been through.

God, if anything like that ever happened to him and Beth. Well, his world would end, he knew that. He couldn't imagine his life without her. Chris and Beth, that's who they were and that's who they would always be. Solid till the end. Sometimes he even had daydreams about them ending up in some old folks' home together and the local paper would come along and take their photo on their diamond wedding anniversary and he would be able to say – 'I knew, I knew the day I clapped eyes on her in Mrs Heath's class on the first day of secondary school. I knew I was going to spend the rest of my life with her.'

He couldn't remember if he'd thought exactly that all those years ago, but he knew when she smiled at him it made him feel funny. No one else before or since had made him feel funny when they smiled at him. Just Beth.

Chris paced his round that day, so it was about two o'clock by the time he got to Simon's. He didn't want to interrupt his lunch. He turned in to the street and saw his car parked outside and smiled with relief. He was in. He was so looking forward to a chat. It was such a lonely job being a postman. Okay, so there was a bit of banter in the mornings when you collected the post, but you didn't really get that much time to bond or anything and then you spent the rest of the day on your own, catching snatches of the radio in the van or snatches of stilted conversation on doorsteps. Of course, some of them didn't want to talk to you at all. Looked affronted at you interrupting whatever daytime TV they were watching. But not Simon. No. He'd always gone out of his way to ask him how his day was and looked pleased to see him. He always enjoyed a day when he had to deliver a parcel to Simon.

He strode up to the door and rang the doorbell, reaching in to his bag for the floppy plastic bag addressed to Candice. Clothes, he thought. He shook his head. So much for the ban on online shopping to save money. Still, he hoped Candice would carry on sourcing her outfits online. He would miss seeing Simon if she stopped.

He was taking a while. Normally Simon was quite quick. It was rare he had to ring twice. But he might have to now. He would give it a few more seconds, then try again.

He rang again and stepped back from the doorstep, peering in to the front window. It looked empty, but then he presumed they spent most of their time in that fabulous conservatory at the back.

He saw a shadow flicker behind the glass in the door and put a smile on his face as the door opened.

'She's at it again.' He grinned, holding up the parcel. 'Or perhaps she's buying for you… Are you all right, mate?'

Simon looked off. Drained, pale. Certainly not his normal self.

'Erm, yeah, just woke up actually, that's all,' Simon said, pulling his hand through his hair.

'Oh, I'm so sorry,' exclaimed Chris. 'So sorry, mate. You on a late then last night?'

'Err yeah,' said Simon, looking dazed and confused.

'I had no idea or else I would have just put a note through the door. I'm so sorry.'

'No, no, it's all right,' said Simon, shaking his head. 'You weren't to know.'

'I'll leave you to it,' said Chris, backing off. 'Let you get back to bed. Here,' he said, remembering he still had the parcel in his hand. 'Sorry, but I do need a signature.' He handed the electronic device to Simon, who took it, still in a daze.

They stood together in awkward silence as Simon signed for the package.

'Cheers,' said Chris, taking it back. 'Good to see you both at Marie's the other night. Hopefully we'll all get together again soon, eh,' he said, unwilling to end his one conversation of the day quite so soon.

'Yeah.' Simon nodded. 'Course. Look, if you don't mind I really…'

'No worries, mate,' said Chris. 'Sorry to have disturbed you. Really. I'll see you another time. Okay?'

'Great,' said Simon, raising a limp hand and shutting the door.

Chapter Twenty-Nine

Beth

'Was that who I think it was?' asked Beth.

Simon nodded, sinking himself back in his chair at the head of the table.

'I'm sorry, I… I… I just couldn't face his relentless positivity,' said Simon, holding his hands up in submission. 'I panicked. I didn't know what to do. If I told him you were here then he would have of course wanted to come in. Does he know you were coming by the way?'

Beth shook her head.

'I thought you said he knew about Candice and… and the phone thing.'

Shit, thought Beth. *Rumbled.*

'I lied,' she blurted.

'Oh,' said Simon.

'I didn't want him rushing round here and telling you and doling out his relentless positivity, as you call it. Can you imagine? He would have come in here and said, "Simon, your wife gave her number to another man, but I'm sure it's nothing to worry about." That would probably have been how he would have handled it, as though you shouldn't give it a second thought.'

She knew she was babbling and Simon was looking at her as though she were babbling. *Make sense*, she told herself. *For goodness' sake, just try and make some sense.*

'Chris always, always looks on the bright side,' Beth explained. 'You could be telling him that you have just found out you have cancer and you have three months to live and he probably would respond by telling you to be positive, you've seen Leicester City win the league so you can die happy now.'

Simon nodded. 'Must be nice to be like that,' he said.

'I guess,' replied Beth. 'Can make him impossible to talk to though. Like playing tennis against a wall. He just keeps returning the ball, when you just want to get it past him. See how he deals with that. Make him see how it feels to watch the ball go past you every single day.'

Simon had a faraway look in his eyes, like he wasn't really there. He wasn't thinking about Chris now, Beth could tell. He was probably recalling some happy memory with Candice. Recalling a time when his life was on track rather than totally derailed. Funny how it's easier to remember the good stuff when the bad stuff is happening. What's the saying? You don't know what you got till it's gone. Beth suspected Simon never really had Candice, however. His memories were glimmers of happiness achieved with someone who would never be happy with the everyday joy of contentment and security. Candice would always strive for the drama and the heady rush of risk. She'd clearly thought she had wanted to settle down at some point, but temptation of new pastures was probably something she would never learn to decline.

But, unfortunately, Simon was the collateral damage of her wish to try such a lifestyle. He had entered in to the marriage in good faith, thinking they were headed on the same track, but she couldn't stick with him.

Was Beth the same? Was she the collateral damage of Chris's ever-optimistic view on life, where problems were never addressed, issues never faced, because in Chris's eyes there were no problems? She could just imagine his face if she ever told him she felt sad. She felt unhappy.

'Have the Co-op run out of dips?' she could imagine him asking.

How could she explain to a man so deeply entrenched in his own contentment that she wasn't content even if he was as happy as a pig in taramasalata? That something was missing. Worse still, she couldn't even tell him what was missing because she didn't really know. It wasn't so much of the grass being greener on the other side, it was the fact that she had never even visited the other side, never even had a day trip. And it gnawed away at her, the older she got. Increasingly, she felt the need to see the other side before it was too late.

What had she missed marrying Chris so young? Marrying her first proper boyfriend. She didn't know, but she felt like she should find out. And it wasn't that there was anything particularly wrong with their relationship. Sure, Chris took her a bit for granted, but they got on okay really.

But she just didn't feel anything. She wanted to feel something, anything, and she couldn't see that coming from Chris. She felt like she was in a trench that she had no way of knowing how to get out of and she suspected the last person who could throw her a rope was Chris. The very person who unintentionally had dug that rut for her.

This image was suddenly so vivid in her head, she wanted to shout and scream. She was in a ditch. A deep dark ditch, and she could see Chris standing at the top of it totally oblivious. Looking up rather than down. Oblivious to where she was in their marriage. Did he have a rope to throw her? She couldn't see. Did anyone have a rope?

She shook her head, trying to rid herself of the image. Today wasn't about her. She'd come here to try and help Simon. She wanted to help him and all she was doing was sitting here raking up irrelevant thoughts. She looked up. He looked like his thoughts were a million miles away. Should she leave him there or should she try and bring him back to reality?

'What am I going to do?' he said to her suddenly. 'I don't know what to do. What would you do?'

'I'm not you,' she replied. 'I can't tell you what to do.'

'But… but you're smart, sensible…'

Beth felt her heart sink to her shoes. He'd say cuddly any minute, she was sure.

'You're wise,' he continued.

Better, she thought. Though it made her sound like Yoda or Gandalf or some other wizened old man, so still not really flattering.

'You're practical.'

Fuck off, she wanted to say to him. Practical! Like a pair of wellies. Like having a foldable umbrella in her bag at all times in case it rained. Like never being without a packet of wet wipes. She so didn't want to be that woman. She hated wet wipes. The smell made her heave and yet… and yet she kept them in her bag at all times.

An image of Simon helping Chris dig the trench even deeper flashed through her mind.

'Fuck you,' she said, getting up suddenly.

'What!' he exclaimed. He was staring at her now. He wasn't thinking about Candice any more.

'Fuck you, I said. I didn't come here to be told I'm boring. I came here to do the right thing. I don't want to be fucking practical or sensible or wise. I don't, I really don't.'

'Okay, okay,' said Simon, getting up, a terrified look in his eyes. 'I didn't mean to hurt your feelings, honestly I didn't, and I can't tell you how glad I am that it's you here telling me this. I wouldn't want it to be anyone else really, I don't know why, but it's true. It's just… it's just… I don't know what to do, Beth. I really don't know what to do.'

Beth's heart was pounding. She hadn't spoken like that in years. Sure, she'd said things in jest. Her sarcasm was legendary, of course, but there was nothing sarcastic about what she had just said. It was the truth. And it felt so good to be saying exactly what she was feeling for a change.

'What should I do, Beth?' Simon asked her again.

She looked at him. He clearly expected her to have all the answers. She thought about what she wanted to do at this precise moment.

'Get your coat,' she instructed.

Chapter Thirty

Beth

'I've walked past this place so many times and I always wonder who is leading a life that allows them to go to the pub in the middle of a Monday afternoon?' Beth said to Simon as they walked down the high street. 'Of course, there will be the odd alcoholic in there, won't there, but when I've I peered through the windows they don't look like alcoholics. They look like normal people. Normal people who go to the pub on a Monday afternoon? I just don't get it. I don't know who they are, but, *I* want to be them,' she told him. 'If you asked me to make a wish, I'd say please let me be the type of person who can go to the pub on a Monday afternoon. And not be sensible or wise or practical, because that type of person goes to the pub once in a blue moon and has a spritzer. I want to go on a Monday afternoon and drink... What should we drink?' she asked, turning to him.

'Whatever you want,' said Simon. 'Look, I'm so sorry about the sensible comment. I really, really didn't mean to upset you. I thought I was paying you a compliment.'

'Does it sound like a compliment? Sensible Beth. Do you see my features lighting up at that?' she demanded.

'No,' he admitted.

'Correct. So let's be unsensible and order a bottle of wine and then we will think of an unsensible answer as to what you are going to do about Candice.'

'Okay,' said Simon, looking a little bewildered. He had his hands sunk deep in his pockets as he glanced around nervously entering the pub.

It was quiet and calm in there. The stresses and the strains of the day had clearly been left on the street. A middle-aged couple were eating in silence. An older man sat reading a paper with a pint. Three men in suits were talking earnestly. It felt good. Not like when you walk in to a pub on a Friday night. Then the air is electric with anticipation and everyone is on hyper speed as the release from work for the weekend accelerates them through alcohol and food. No, this was slower. This was where you could take your time and enjoy the novelty of being in a pub, on a *Monday* afternoon.

Beth walked to the bar, where two twenty-somethings were flirting with each other.

'Wine list?' she asked. She could hear Simon shuffling behind her.

The girl handed one over without a word whilst the boy drifted off to pretend to be doing something. She leant on a beer pump whilst she waited for Beth to choose. Beth could sense Simon was in no fit state to make an alcoholic beverage decision, so she dived in.

'The rosé Prosecco please?' she said.

'I'm sorry, we don't do that by the glass,' replied the girl.

'Oh no, we'll have a bottle,' stated Beth.

She wasn't sure when she had ever been so pleased with a phrase, especially as she watched the girl raise her eyebrows a fraction. She wondered what she was thinking. Was she thinking, *who is this sensible cuddly-looking woman coming in to a bar on a Monday afternoon with a buff younger man and ordering rosé Prosecco?* Beth smiled to herself again. She didn't know who she was either but she liked her.

'Can you bring it to that table over there with two glasses?' she asked. 'Shall I leave my card behind the bar?'

'Oh no,' she heard Simon protest. 'Let me pay. Please.'

'No,' Beth said firmly. 'You gave me lunch. This is my treat.'

She handed her credit card to the girl behind the bar and then went to sit at the table by the open fire. She could barely believe it. This was like a dream come true. A Monday afternoon in a bar by a fire with Prosecco? The top of the ditch suddenly seemed just a little bit closer.

She took her coat off, then grabbed a chair at the table. Simon was already sitting down, staring in to the fire. She left him to his thoughts as the girl approached with the Prosecco in a bucket of ice and two glasses.

Beth grasped the bottle and poured the ice-cold liquid in to the glasses.

'To Monday afternoons,' she said, raising her drink to him.

He sighed. 'Not sure I'll forget this one in a hurry,' he replied. 'Not what I was anticipating.'

'What would you normally be doing?'

'Probably be down the gym by now. It's a good time to go.'

'Oh yeah, me too,' she replied. 'Oh no, actually I would be doing battle in Tesco, thinking for the five hundredth time, what the *hell* shall we have for dinner.'

'What will you have for dinner?' asked Simon.

Beth sighed and leaned back in her chair.

'Prosecco,' she announced.

Chapter Thirty-One

Simon

'Why did you marry Candice?' he eventually heard Beth ask.

They'd not spoken in a while. Both lost in their own thoughts and in the Prosecco and in the dancing of the flames in the hearth in front of them. It hadn't felt awkward. In fact the opposite. It felt like exactly where he was supposed to be. Today. On this day when he had discovered he had been let down by his wife yet again. He felt cocooned from the outside world. Suspended from real life for a brief time so that he could contemplate how he was going to live the rest of it.

He looked over at Beth. Her question wasn't a challenge. It was a genuine question, like she was honestly interested, like it was an important question for him to be asking himself today.

He gave it genuine thought, something he may never have done before. Not even when he had asked Candice to marry him.

'She bowled me over,' he said eventually. 'She was like a force of nature. I had never met anyone like her. She walked over to me that night in the bar and changed my life.'

Beth nodded.

He stared in to the fire.

'I'd not long finished a long-term relationship,' he continued. 'I'd been seeing her for over five years. Caroline, she was called. She was ideal in every way. Everyone said we were perfect together. Everyone told us we were going to get married.'

'Why didn't you?'

'When I thought about marrying Caroline all I could see was this long uneventful life ahead. Comfortable but uneventful. I felt like I was going to live my parents' life. Never move from the town I was born in, stay in a dead-end job, the highlight of the week being fish and chips on a Thursday.'

'We have fish and chips on a Thursday,' muttered Beth.

'Sorry,' said Simon.

'It's not your fault,' replied Beth.

He took another sip of Prosecco.

'I just couldn't bear it. I didn't want to settle for that. I wanted more.'

Beth nodded. 'I can understand that.'

'So I finished with Caroline, much to my mother's shock. She told me I would never find another girl as nice as Caroline. I told her I didn't want nice. Nice wasn't enough.'

'Right.' Beth nodded.

'And then Candice came along. Maybe not so nice, but, man, she was exciting. She made me feel exciting. She made me feel alive.'

'Right,' said Beth again.

'Then she kind of asked me, really, to get married. One of her mates had just got engaged and she said she really wanted to get married, so I said marry me then and she said yes. I couldn't believe my luck, to be honest. This crazy gorgeous girl wanted to hook up with me for the rest of my life. I never thought I'd bag someone like that. Thought I was too sensible for her. As I say, I couldn't believe my luck. I didn't ever think beyond that. In my eyes she was amazing and if she wanted to marry me then no one was going to stop me.'

'Did anyone try and stop you?' asked Beth.

'My mum and dad did their best. Told me that she wasn't the marrying kind. Told me it would end in tears. But I wasn't going to listen, was I? They had wanted me to marry Caroline. They loved Caroline.'

'So do you think you did the right thing?' asked Beth.

He looked up sharply. She was looking at him intensely. Her cheeks were flushed. A combination of the open fire and the Prosecco no doubt. He could see his reflection in her glasses. He thought he looked old.

'The right thing marrying Candice?' he asked.

'Yes.'

He looked deep in his glass and cast his mind over their three short years of marriage. Eventually he looked back at Beth.

'Yes,' he said. 'As broken as I am now, overall she made me feel better than she made me feel worse. She made me live. *We* lived. I just wish I had been enough for her.' He bit his lip. He could feel the tears springing back up.

'So it's over then?' asked Beth gently.

He realised for the first time that he had been talking about his marriage in the past tense. That, somehow, from his bewilderment at home to the calm of now, he had realised exactly what to do. He had to end his marriage.

'Yes it is,' he replied.

Beth nodded and pulled the bottle out of its ice bucket and passed it to him, dripping cold water all over his leg. His topped his own glass up before reaching over to top up Beth's.

She raised her glass to him as he placed the bottle back in the bucket.

'To love and to cherish till she wants to sleep with other men do us part,' she said.

They clinked glasses.

'Thanks for that,' he said.

'You're welcome.' She smiled.

'Here's to you getting to the till death do us part bit,' he said, offering his glass to her again. He noticed her face change. A flicker of confusion.

'Sure,' she said, hurriedly clinking his glass and looking away. She seemed troubled.

'He is all right isn't he, Chris?' Simon asked.

'Yes, why do you ask?'

'You just looked worried.'

She stared back at him.

'Ask me,' she said forcefully.

'Ask you what?'

'Ask me why I married Chris.'

'Okay,' he said slowly. 'Why did you marry Chris?'

He watched as she took a large swig of her drink.

'Because I didn't think I could do any better. Because he was nice and he liked me. Because I thought he was my limit. Because I thought all I was going to get in life was the highlight of my week being fish and chips on a Thursday. I didn't marry a Candice, Simon, I married a Caroline.'

Chapter Thirty-Two

Beth

He clearly didn't know what to say to that. He stared at Beth open-mouthed. Gobsmacked. Poor lad. As if he didn't have enough to cope with. The demise of his own marriage and the awful fact that he had just shone an unflattering light on Beth and Chris's.

'I figure there must be loads of us,' said Beth, settling back in her chair. 'I can't be the only one who married a Caroline, can I? It can't be just me whose first and lasting response to a marriage proposal is one of utter relief. Just simple happiness that it's over, being single. That I proved to the world that someone loves me irrespective of my true feelings for them. That I was just grateful that a nice person was willing to take me on. I can't be the only one, can I?'

Simon was looking carefully at Beth, clearly still unsure of the right words for this situation.

'I think it's pretty common to marry a Caroline,' he finally said. 'I mean, I almost did. And, actually, in some cases, I'm sure a Caroline is the right answer. I mean, you and Chris seem so happy together. You might think he is a Caroline, but maybe you need a Caroline?'

Beth wasn't sure what depressed her more. The fact she'd married a Caroline or the fact that Simon thought she should be with a Caroline.

She shrugged and dug her chin deep in her neck.

'I mean, I'm not saying you're not worthy of a Candice, but imagine having to deal with a male Candice. Think how miserable that would make you. There's no way you would be happy with a Candice. No way.'

He had a point of course. Her insecurities could never cope with a Candice. A Candice would have destroyed her, whereas a Caroline had slowly but surely worn her down in to feeling nothing.

I would have liked a Simon, she thought to herself but she didn't say. A man who could capture her heart and keep it safe… to love and to cherish, till death do us part.

Chapter Thirty-Three

Duncan

Duncan and Issy were just going over the following week's schedule whilst sharing a bag of wine gums that Issy said she'd picked up in Aldi at lunchtime for just 49p. Duncan felt a sense of peace. He felt in control. He felt very happy to taste sugar during what was now known as no-sugar March. Little did he know that the calm was about to be shattered.

'What the fuck are your stuck-up mates doing messing with my marriage?' announced Candice, barging in unannounced, causing Duncan to guiltily grab the packet of wine gums and shove it in a drawer.

'Candice, what on earth are you doing bursting in like this?' he said, standing up.

'You heard,' she demanded, her mouth twisted in a way he had never seen before. She looked evil. 'I've just spoken to Simon and he's told me to go home and pack my bags.'

'Why? Is he taking you away somewhere nice?' asked Duncan, feeling confused as to why this would make her so angry. He noticed that Issy stifled a giggle.

'No!' exclaimed Candice. 'He wants me to move out and he says it's because someone told him I gave your poncy mate Tony my number.'

Duncan's mouth dropped open. His immediate thought was what a smooth bastard Tony was.

'Did you tell him?' she demanded.

'No!' replied Duncan. 'Of course not. I had no idea. Did you give him your number?'

'Yes, but it's a free country. I thought he was a very interesting man. Thought we could have a coffee or something at some point and talk again. No harm in that, is there?'

'You just said he was poncey,' said Issy still sitting steadfast in her chair.

'Well, he was, but that doesn't mean he's not interesting, does it? He builds stuff.'

'He's an architect,' Duncan told Issy.

'Oh,' she said. 'Loaded then?'

Duncan daren't nod.

'Whatever, it's none of anyone's business who I give my number to and now your bloody mates have interfered, saying there was more to it, and Simon wants me out. Like I would ever do that to him.'

'What about the chocolate vending machine salesman?' asked Duncan before he could stop himself.

'That was before. I told Simon I would never do anything like that again and I meant it.'

'Until you gave a bloke your number,' said Issy.

'For coffee!' exclaimed Candice. 'Not that it's anything to do with you. Just because you are mooning after the boss doesn't mean you can judge my life. You're no better than me!'

The room went quiet.

'Don't think we don't know what's going on in here,' said Candice, waving her hand around disparagingly. 'What with your cakes and your sweets and your answering to his every whim. It's as clear as day what you are after, Issy Barker, and don't you try and tell me otherwise.'

Duncan gaped, not knowing who to stare at, Candice or Issy. He couldn't understand what Candice was saying. She couldn't be implying that Issy had a… thing for him, could she? That was ridiculous. There was no way that someone like her could…

He looked over to Issy, who had gone bright red, her mouth opening and closing as she looked up to Duncan.

'I… I…' she started to say. 'I should go.' She got up and pushed past Candice, slamming the door behind her. 'Fuck off, Candice,' he heard her say under her breath.

'You… you shouldn't go saying those sorts of things, Candice,' he said.

'Oh really,' replied Candice. 'Just like your friends shouldn't go spouting off that I gave my number to your mate and so obviously I want to have sex with him.'

Duncan gasped yet again. What should he do? This had not been a scenario when they role-played sexual discrimination in the workplace. There had been no acting out of what to do if one of your employees accuses your friends of spreading gossip about them or indeed if one of your employees accuses your personal assistant of wanting to sleep with you. No, none of that. All he remembered was, no touching, no using of demeaning sexist names that didn't sound demeaning to him at all and look in to the eyes, always look in to the eyes.

'Look,' he said, trying to compose himself. 'Why don't you take a seat and tell me exactly what has happened and we can see if we can draw up a solution plan together.'

'Oh fuck off, Duncan. This is nothing to do with work. This is my fucking marriage that you have fucked up.'

Jesus, this was getting worse, he thought. But she was right, this was nothing to do with work. He really didn't need to be having this conversation here, with his entire team looking through the glass partition and Issy crying on Abigail's shoulder. Oh shit! Issy was crying on Abigail's shoulder.

He needed to get out. He needed to get Candice out. Off work premises. Then they could talk properly. This was a personal matter that needed to be dealt with away from public eyes.

'Go and get your coat and your bag,' he said to her as calmly as he could. 'We can't do this here. I'll meet you in the car park in five minutes.'

She pouted before she turned on her heel and left the office.

Duncan was just in the process of picking up the phone to tell Issy he was popping out when he remembered that Issy was part of the problem. He looked up to see that she had disappeared along with Abigail. He reached for a Post-it and scribbled that he was going out and stuck it to her phone before he walked out of the office, his entire staff of fifty-three sales executives watching him.

'Let's just get out of here, shall we?' he said to Candice when he found her waiting in reception.

'Where are we going?'

'I don't know, somewhere. I think we both need some air.'

He made sure she had buckled herself in before he started the engine. He was certain there would be a rule somewhere about a senior manager being responsible for a junior member of staff's safety at all times. Whether that extended to outside of the workplace he wasn't sure, but it was a company car so he wasn't going to risk it.

'So do you want to tell me exactly what happened?' he asked her as they drove out of the entrance.

'I rang Simon to tell him I would be home late because I was going out with Jill and he said I should go home and pack my bags because he knew everything. Just like that. He sounded a bit pissed actually. I reckon he was in the pub. On a Monday afternoon!'

'So what did you say?'

'I asked him what he was talking about and he said that he knew I had given Tony my number. Apparently that's all it takes to split a marriage up these days.'

'When exactly did you give him your number?'

'Err, when you went through to sing karaoke. Then Beth came in to shout us through.' Candice paused for a moment. 'Of course it was that bitch Beth who told him. She gave me a proper funny look when she came in.'

'Beth is not a bitch,' said Duncan.

'She's trying to break my marriage up. And she fancies Simon.'

'No she doesn't. You just can't say things like that, Candice. Not everyone is hunting around like a dog on heat, you know.'

'She so does. I saw her looking at him. As if he'd look at a frump like that twice!'

'Candice! These are my friends. If you want my help, you cannot be mean about my friends.'

Candice said nothing.

'Shall I take you home?' asked Duncan.

'Suppose so,' said Candice.

'Sounds like you need a proper chat with Simon. Give him your side of the story.'

'Suppose,' she said, shrugging again. 'Wouldn't have to, would I, if we hadn't come to your stupid dinner party. My God, that dip! What the fuck was in that dip?'

'Tahini,' said Duncan.

'What's that, then?'

'No idea.'

'What's the point in eating something that you don't know what it is? Your wife never heard of salsa?'

'She likes trying new things,' replied Duncan

'Must be thrilling,' replied Candice sarcastically, putting her arm on the sill and staring out of the window.

'So tell me where you live and I'll drop you home,' said Duncan

'Just head towards Checkley,' she said despondently.

'Oh, and whatever happens between you and Simon you need to apologise to Issy tomorrow. You were totally out of order saying what you did.'

'If you say so,' murmured Candice. 'She so does fancy you though. That much is true.'

They drove in silence for the rest of the way, only punctuated by Candice giving him begrudging directions.

'Oh shit, it looks like he's in,' she said as they pulled in to her road. 'That's his car. He said he was going to be out for the rest of the day.'

'Perhaps he's walked somewhere,' said Duncan, pulling on the handbrake and switching off the engine.

'Where?'

'I don't know. Perhaps he wanted to clear his head?'

'Will you come in with me?'

'What? No! I don't want to come in with you.'

'But what if he's there.'

'Don't you want him to be in so you can talk to him?'

'But what if he's angry. What if… if… he gets violent?'

'What, Simon! No way. He wouldn't, would he, I mean has he ever before?'

'No, no, but he's never told me to come home and pack my bags before.'

'Well, you are going to have to face him at some point.'

'Please,' she said, turning to him. 'Please come in with me. You might be able to talk some sense in to him.'

'I do not want to talk to Simon. Well, I do, of course I do, I mean he seems like a nice guy, but I do not want to talk to him about your marriage. That has nothing to do with me.' He mentally cast his mind back to the sexual discrimination manual. He was pretty sure there was no mention of assisting in marital woes.

'Just come in with me. That's all. Just to check he's mentally stable. Just so I know he's not going to do anything stupid. Please!'

Duncan looked at Candice. How had he got himself in to this situation? He should be at work now in a budget meeting. Christ, he hoped that Issy had cancelled the meeting. Explained what had happened. Perhaps he should just call her to make sure. But what would he say? How would he get past the awkwardness of Candice's theory to ask her politely to ring the finance team to tell them the monthly budget meeting was postponed until further notice?

He unbuckled his seatbelt. 'I'll see you to the door, say hello, then that's it,' he said. 'I'll leave you to it.'

'Oh thanks, Dunc,' said Candice, leaning forward and putting her arms around him suddenly. 'Thank you,' she breathed in his ear.

Duncan watched an elderly man walk past and peer in the window.

'Come on, let's get on with it,' said Duncan, untangling himself and reaching for the door handle.

At the front door, waiting whilst Candice rummaged in her bag for her keys, Duncan could feel his heart beating faster for no apparent reason other than wondering what you say to a man who has just told his wife to pack her bags and leave.

Candice turned the key in the lock and pushed the door open.

All was quiet.

'Hello,' shouted Candice.

No response.

'You don't think he's done anything stupid do you?' she asked just as Duncan's mind was thinking the worst.

'Where's the bathroom?' he gasped, pushing past her.

'Just there,' she said, pointing at a door right next to him.

'No! The main bathroom upstairs?' he said, starting to feel frantic.

'Door opposite the top of the stairs,' she replied, looking puzzled.

Duncan turned and dived up the stairs two at a time, his heart threatening to leap out of his chest. He crashed through the bathroom door to find it empty, a faint smell of lime shower gel lingering in the air. There was no Simon collapsed on the floor beside a bottle of empty pills. No Simon immersed mummy-like in an overflowing bath.

He clutched his chest, trying to get his breath back. Maybe he should check the bedroom. But which one? He felt like an intruder now, not a potential lifesaver.

'Come and look at this,' he heard Candice shout from the bottom of the stairs.

Shit, she's found him, he thought.

He raced back down the stairs and ran down the hall towards the back of the house, where he presumed Candice had shouted from.

She was standing at the table, staring down at it. Her hand rested on the back of a chair.

'What!' he exclaimed. 'Is he here?'

'No,' she said, shaking her head, 'but what do you make of this?'

He looked at the table. There were some bowls, some glasses, a chopping board with some delicious-looking bread half cut (his stomach spontaneously rumbled) and what looked like a tub of butter that had been left out. So Simon hadn't cleared away after his lunch. Hardly a crime relative to her misdemeanours of late.

'Looks like nice bread,' he said, shrugging his shoulders.

'No, look!' she said, pointing agitatedly.

It still looked like really nice bread and it had been a long time since he'd had a wine gum.

'What?' he asked.

'Two bowls?' she said, folding her arms and nodding her head. 'Two bowls. Two glasses and, if I'm not mistaken,' she said, picking up one of the glasses and holding it close to her face, 'that'll be lipstick. Now, unless Simon has taken to a spot of cross-dressing whilst I'm out, I'd say he had a woman here, wouldn't you?'

Of all the things he'd expected today, he hadn't expected to be playing Watson to Candice's Sherlock Holmes.

'I don't think you can assume that,' said Duncan. 'There is probably a very simple explanation. Perhaps his mum popped round.'

'She works in a charity shop three days a week and she wouldn't wear pink lipstick. In fact, I don't think I've ever seen her wear lipstick at all.'

'Oh,' said Duncan. He didn't know what to say.

'He had a woman here, Dunc. Can you believe it? As he's on the phone telling me to pack my bags because I'd given my number to a man, he had a woman hear right under my nose. It's just an excuse to get rid of me. That's what it is. An excuse. He's got someone on the side and wants to replace me, that's what is happening here. Go upstairs and check the bed,' she said.

'What, me?'

'Yes! See if they've been shagging in it. Under my own roof, I can't believe it.'

'W-what do I look for?'

'Signs of shagging!' she said. 'Just go and look, will you.'

Duncan blew his cheeks out and turned to head out of the kitchen door and walked wearily up the stairs. He didn't want to be here. He had to get out. He'd check for shagging, then he'd tell Candice she was on her own.

He pushed open one door and found the usual household rejects in the spare room. Stuff on its way to the garage then on its way out. He pushed open another door and found himself in what must be the master bedroom. He was praying he wouldn't find anything. Evidence of shagging was not high on his list of treasure-hunt challenges.

He peered in. The bed was unmade. But that could mean anything. A house with poor tidiness routines in the morning? Simon had been on nights and had only got up at lunchtime, intending to go back for a couple of hours? Confirmation of illicit sex would need further investigation.

He stepped gingerly in to the room and pulled at the corner of the duvet. *What am I doing?* he thought.

He turned and walked out, slamming the door behind him and running downstairs for the second time.

'I'm not going in there!' he exclaimed as he reached the kitchen.

'Why not?'

'This is nothing to do with me, Candice. I really don't want to be involved. You need to do whatever you need to do and I need to go. I'll see you tomorrow, okay?'

'Oh, I doubt I'll be in tomorrow,' she said over her shoulder, still staring down at the table.

'Why not?' he asked.

'I've just found out my husband is having an affair?' she said. 'Do you expect me to be able to come to work with that hanging over me?'

Duncan didn't know what he expected any more. This had all certainly been unexpected. 'Well, just see how you feel in the morning, okay? Now, I really have to go.' He took one last longing look at the half-loaf of bread, then turned and left, leaving Candice still trying to work out the significance of two empty soup bowls.

JOURNALIST: Hang on a minute. Are you telling me that one of your dinner parties caused a marriage break-up? Can we put that in the article?

DUNCAN: Well, actually more than one... eventually. In one way or another.

Chapter Thirty-Four

Beth

'I can't believe you just did that,' said a giggling Beth.

'Did what?' asked Simon, tucking his phone back in his pocket.

'Told her to pack her bags.'

'I don't think she did either.'

Beth raised her glass to him.

'A brave move,' she said. 'Very brave.'

'Doesn't feel very brave,' he said with a sigh, clinking her glass. 'Just feels shit.'

'Funny that, isn't it. How can doing the right thing make you feel so rubbish. I don't really get that.'

Simon stared in to the fire. 'Because even though it's the right thing it's still not what you want.'

'Mmmm,' she said, thinking. Thinking that she hadn't felt this relaxed in a long time. Sitting here in front of a fire with Prosecco in her belly whilst Simon split up with his wife. She decided to share that with him. 'Do you know,' she said, pulling herself up in her chair slightly, 'I haven't felt this relaxed in a long time.'

'Should I split up with my wife more often?'

'Yes,' she said. 'Quite frankly you should. Around about one o'clock on a Monday afternoon every week would do nicely,' she replied.

'I'll see what I can do.'

She smiled at him and reached over and squeezed his arm. To show companionship, she told herself. To show she knew how hard this was for him, but, boy, she was having a nice time.

'I have to say it's a very pleasant way to end a marriage,' said Simon, peering in to his empty glass. 'As break-ups go, I've had much worse. I think I could recommend it. You know, if you have to do it, this is a good way of doing it.'

'Maybe it's a business opportunity for me,' said Beth. 'I could be the divorce whisperer. This could be my office. I could just sit here all day and people could come to me with their relationship issues and drink rosé Prosecco and then sit in that chair and make the call.'

'Well, you are very easy to talk to,' stated Simon.

'Thank you,' said Beth. 'I try and listen. Not many people do. Most people these days just want to be heard.'

A heavy silence fell between them.

'Did you say something?' Simon eventually said.

'No.'

'I was listening,' he said. 'Did you see that?'

'Idiot.' Beth grinned. 'Someone does have to be saying something for you to be able to listen.'

'Ohhhhh,' replied Simon with a grin. 'I get it. Now, I've got something very important that you need to listen to.'

'Oh yeah?' said Beth, leaning forward.

He leaned forward too. She could see the pores on his nose. She could smell him. He leaned closer still.

'Shall we get another bottle?' he asked.

'I thought you'd never ask,' she replied.

★

Another glass had been poured and she had just leaned back in her chair allowing the indulgence of it all to sink in when she heard the dulcet tones of her mobile starting to ring. She thought about ignoring it. This was a bubble she didn't want to burst. But it could be work. It could be the kids. She put her glass on the table, praying it was a PPI company for the first time ever in her life.

But it wasn't a PPI company, it was Marie. She sighed. Everything told her not to pick up and everything told her she should. Just in case. Of what, she had no idea.

'Hi, Marie,' she said when she had tapped the call accept button. 'What can I do for you?'

'Well, Duncan has just called me…'

'Don't tell me, he's eaten a sandwich in Greggs and you need to know where to get his stomach pumped.' She watched as Simon satisfyingly snorted with laughter. 'They don't do carbohydrate overdose on the NHS any more,' she continued.

'Oh, very droll,' said Marie. 'I was just ringing to let you know that Duncan has just called to say that he's just had to drive Candice home because Simon has thrown her out.'

'I know,' replied Beth, taking a sip from her Prosecco.

'How can you know? Duncan has only just got back to the office.'

'I didn't know about Duncan, but I knew about Simon and Candice.'

'How come you know? Simon told her to pack her bags like an hour ago. Did Simon tell Chris?'

'No,' said Beth.

'So who told you? Has Duncan called you? Did he call you before me?'

'No.'

A moment's silence.

'Did Candice call you? Did she give you her number as well as Tony?'

'No.'

'So then how?'

Beth took a lingering look at Simon. He was deep in thought. Clearly churning the day's events as he sipped on his drink. Sure, he seemed very calm now, but she knew that it might not last. That come tonight, when he walked in to an empty home stacked full of memories, that he may not be feeling like this. That the enormity of what had happened would come crashing down on him. That this was the calm before the storm.

'Are you still there?' she heard Marie ask.

'Yes,' said Beth.

'So?' asked Marie. 'How did you know about Simon and Candice?'

Beth sighed heavily and mouthed a silent sorry to Simon.

'Because I'm with Simon now,' she said.

'What!' exclaimed Marie.

'I'm with him now. I went to tell him that Candice gave Tony her number.'

'You said you were going to tell us when you were going.'

'I know I did. But I just decided to go and, well, we had lunch and…'

'You had lunch!' gasped Marie.

'Yes.'

'Where?'

'At his house.'

'You went to his house?'

'Yes.'

'For lunch?'

'No. I went to his house to tell him about Candice and then he offered me lunch.'

She could here Marie breathing heavily.

'We had bread,' Beth decided to tell her. 'A lot of really nice bread.'

There was silence at the end of the phone.

'You should have told me you were going. I would have come with you,' said Marie.

'What for?' asked Beth.

'For moral support.'

Beth thought for a moment.

'I thought you were still on your no-carbs diet,' said Beth.

'We've cut out sugar this month,' replied Marie. 'So I'm back on bread. *Small* amounts of bread.'

'Oh,' said Beth.

'So how is Simon?' asked Marie.

'He's okay.'

'Where are you now?' asked Marie.

Beth blew her cheeks out. She could lie, but she knew it would somehow catch up with her.

'We're in the White Swan,' said Beth.

Simon looked over at her, raising his eyebrows.

Beth braced herself. There was a moment's silence.

'I'll come down,' said Marie in a manner that asked no permission. 'See you in twenty minutes.' The line went dead.

Simon still had his eyebrows raised.

'Sorry,' Beth said to Simon. 'Marie's coming.'

He shrugged.

Chapter Thirty-Five

Marie

'There you are,' exclaimed Marie. *What on earth are they both doing sitting in the bar area when the lounge is so much nicer?* she thought.

'Hi, Marie,' said Beth. 'Oh, and Sarah! Didn't realise you'd planned a girls' trip out and not invited me.'

'Marie texted me so I could let Tony know,' said Sarah. 'He's pretty cut up about it all. He's on his way.'

'Why?' asked Beth.

'To come and make sure Simon is okay,' said Sarah. 'He didn't do anything, Simon. Honestly. Nothing. He's really worried that you think he's to blame. He's really quite stressed out about it,' she continued, looking concerned.

'Of course he's not to blame,' said Marie before Simon could open his mouth. 'It's not his fault, is it, it's Candice's. So, are we going to go and sit in the lounge?' she asked. 'There's loads of space, rather than being cramped in this corner, especially if Tony and Duncan are joining us.'

'Duncan's coming too!' exclaimed Beth.

'Yes, he's traumatised. Says he's had a nightmare with Candice. He had to drive her home, you know,' she said to Simon.

'That's very good of him,' said Simon. 'I really didn't mean to get him involved in this.'

'Yes, well that's Duncan, isn't it? Always happy to help. Look, let's go and grab a table next door and you can tell us all about it.'

Marie turned her back on Simon and headed through the door in to the lounge, where she spotted a low table with a couple of comfy sofas clustered around it. She sank down gratefully in to one, happy to take the weight off her feet, which were crammed in to high silver stilettos. It was the first pair of shoes she could grab. It was only then that she realised that Beth and Simon hadn't followed her yet. Where were they?

'He looks terrible,' said Sarah, placing her Prada bag on the table. 'Broken.'

'I know,' hissed Marie. 'But you would be, wouldn't you? Candice has humiliated him. What with the chocolate vending machine sales-man and now Tony… Honestly, what was she thinking?' She broke off as the door to the lounge swung open and Simon and Beth struggled through with their glasses, coats and an ice bucket.

Marie leapt out of her seat and grabbed Simon's glass and the bucket from him.

'Come and sit here,' she said, putting his glass down next to her. 'What are you drinking?'

'Prosecco,' said Simon, falling onto the sofa.

'What a marvellous idea,' said Marie. 'Do you want to get another bottle, Sarah?'

'Oh yeah, great,' said Sarah, grabbing her bag and heading towards the bar. 'I'll get this one.'

'So,' said Marie, sitting down and putting her hand on Simon's knee. 'Why don't you tell us exactly what happened.'

'For goodness' sake, Marie,' said Beth.

'What?' she asked.

'He doesn't need to go over it again.'

Poor Simon, thought Marie. He'd been subjected to Beth's bluntness and sarcasm over this whole drama. He clearly needed some TLC.

'He might want to talk it through with a sympathetic ear?' she said, turning to Simon.

'Not really,' he said, shaking his head. 'I think I've talked enough.'

'Oh,' replied Marie.

Simon silently took a sip of drink, glancing between Marie and Beth.

'So how do you feel then?' asked Marie. 'Pretty shit, I imagine.'

'Marie!' exclaimed Beth. 'You heard him, he doesn't want to talk about it.'

Marie glared at Beth. Nobody spoke.

Sarah arrived back with two more glasses and another ice bucket with chilled Prosecco poking out from it.

'So how are you feeling?' Sarah asked Simon as she began to pour.

'For fuck's sake,' Beth muttered under her breath.

'Oh, here you are,' gasped Duncan, suddenly appearing at the door. 'I assumed you would be in the bar by the fire at this time of day,' he said, putting his bag down and starting to take off his coat. 'I'm so sorry about all this, Simon,' he continued. 'Gutted for you. I don't know the ins and outs. None of my business. *So* none of my business. And what Candice made me do, well, I'm so sorry. She asked and I couldn't say no and now I feel terrible, absolutely terrible. But, anyway, enough about me. How are *you* feeling?'

Chapter Thirty-Six

Beth

'How's Candice?' asked Simon, ignoring Duncan's well-meaning question.

'Well...' said Duncan. 'Look, do you mind if I get a pint and then I'll fill you in.'

'A pint!' exclaimed Marie. 'Have you any idea how much sugar is in a pint of beer?'

Duncan looked at her. 'I need a pint,' he said steadily and walked off.

'I'm trying to get his weight under control, I really am,' she said, reaching forward and taking a big gulp of her Prosecco. 'But what do I do when he insists on drinking beer. And what he consumes when he goes to work, I dread to think. I've told his PA, Issy her name is, to keep an eye on him, but I'm not sure she took me seriously. She's not married so has no idea what it's like to have to manage your husband's health.'

Duncan arrived back with his pint and sat down before taking a long gulp and downing nearly half of it.

'That's better,' he said, leaning back in his chair. 'This is nice, eh,' he said, looking round. 'In the pub on a Monday afternoon. We should do this more often.'

'So how is Candice?' asked Simon again.

Beth wanted to reach out for his arm. She could hear the pain in his voice. But she was miles away from him now, on the opposite side of the table in an uncomfortable chair, whilst Marie sat next to him on the comfortable sofa. She was like a magician sometimes. She could magic herself in to the right spot at the drop of a hat.

'Oh, sorry, mate,' said Duncan, wiping his lips. 'Well, let's put it like this... How should I say this... Well... she thinks you are having an affair.'

'What!' said Simon.

'What!' chorused Beth, Marie and Sarah.

'How... Why... I don't understand,' said Simon. Again, Beth felt the pain in his voice.

'Well, she burst in to my office, making all sorts of accusations,' Duncan continued. 'All sorts, she did, so I thought I'd better get her home so she could sort herself out. Anyway, she insisted I see her in. She said she was worried that you might be angry, violent even. As if! And then she found the table set for two and jumped to all sorts of conclusions, which basically led to her demanding that I go upstairs to see if the bed had been slept in. And I mean *slept* in.' He raised his eyebrows dramatically and took another swig of beer. 'What was I supposed to do? I was totally mortified. I didn't know what to do with myself. I'm so sorry, mate, but she was getting in a right state.'

'So had it?' asked Sarah, clearly forgetting for a moment that the suspect was in the room.

'No!' exclaimed Simon. 'Of course it hadn't. I mean...' Simon suddenly looked at a loss for words. 'I mean, I'd slept in it the night before with Candice, but I hadn't slept *with* someone in it since then.'

'It was only Beth,' said Marie calmly. 'You went round, didn't you, Beth, to tell Simon? And ended up having lunch. Nothing to worry about. It was only Beth.'

It was only Beth. Suddenly she could picture the flipchart paper again and someone had written ONLY BETH in red next to the word CUDDLY in green.

'Oh,' said Duncan. 'All right then.'

There were no further questions. Duncan was completely and utterly satisfied that there were no potential shenanigans taking place as it was 'only Beth'.

'How did you leave her?' she heard Simon ask Duncan.

'Pretty angry with the world, I should say,' Duncan replied. 'I left her staring at a glass with lipstick on.'

'Lipstick?' said Marie instantly. 'Beth doesn't wear lipstick. Especially not during the day.'

Beth bit her lip. She felt tears spring to her eyes, but she fought them back.

'Tinted lip salve,' she said quickly. 'I was wearing tinted lip salve.' She felt ashamed. She was as bad as Marie. She'd gone to another woman's husband's house wearing lipstick. What was she thinking?

'Oh.' Marie nodded, looking vaguely satisfied.

'Well, all I can say,' said Sarah, 'is she's got some cheek really, hasn't she? Accusing you of an affair when she's given her number to my husband.'

'I'm so sorry, Sarah,' said Simon immediately. 'I… I… mean, I don't know what to say. I can't believe she did that.'

'It's not your fault,' said Sarah. 'You shouldn't feel bad. Tony is mortified, honestly. He wants you to know that he did absolutely nothing to encourage her. You know that, don't you?'

'Of course,' said Simon, picking his drink up. He looked away.

Beth knew that he wasn't convinced. She knew exactly what he was thinking. *Tony and Sarah got together whilst Tony was married. He's an adulterer.* Maybe he was wondering if being an adulterer was like being an alcoholic. That is what you always are. You can't get away from it. In fact some men start out like that from day one.

'Do you remember that night we had in London when we went down to see Sarah at uni?' said Beth a memory from their past suddenly flooding back to her. 'That guy kept sending cocktails over to our table.'

'I remember,' said Marie. 'It was fun… for a while.'

'Worst night of my life,' muttered Beth, shaking her head. 'I'd never had a pina colada before and I drank six in an hour. I was soooo sick.'

'But it *was* the most appropriate throwing up incident of all time,' added Sarah.

'I agree that my timing *was* impeccable' said Beth.

'You should have seen this guy,' Marie said to Simon. 'He sauntered across to our table and was all over Sarah. He was being such a letch. We knew we needed to leave and get out of his way but he suggested we move on to a club together, at which point Beth rears her head up and throws up all over him. And guess what he says?'

'No idea,' said Simon.

'Bloody hell, I'm getting married in this suit tomorrow!'

Chapter Thirty-Seven

Tony

Tony sighed heavily as he drove along the high street. He wished he was going to a difficult client meeting. He wished he was in London pitching for business. He wished he was skiing. He wished he was absolutely anywhere but here, in his car, driving to the White Swan to cross-examine every inch of the breakdown of bloody Simon's marriage. What he was particularly dreading was that he knew he would come under much scrutiny regarding his own part in it. He knew in particular that Marie would be forensic in her interrogation. She was nosy. She'd want to know the ins and outs and really there were no ins and outs. Candice gave Tony her number, end of. Unsolicited. Nothing more to it. Move on. But he somehow suspected that moving on was going to take some time.

He needed a shield, a frontman. Someone to go in ahead and deflect the questions. A stooge, a distraction. Someone so clueless that they would have the unique ability to ignore what was going on around them, not tune in to the significance of the gathering, and it treat just as a casual incident.

He called Chris.

'Hi, mate,' said Chris after a couple of rings. 'Everything all right?'

'Yeah, sure,' replied Tony. 'Just wondered if you want me to pick you up? I'm on my way to the White Swan.'

There was a brief silence at the other end of the phone.

'Bit early for that, mate, but why not, I guess. Cheeky pint on a Monday afternoon sounds mighty attractive. Is Duncan coming?'

'He's already there, I think.'

'Right. Well, Beth isn't here, no idea where she is, so I don't know what we are having for tea, but I'll just leave her a note shall I? Say I'll be back in an hour or two.'

'Beth is at the White Swan.'

'Is she?'

'Yes.'

'Had we arranged to meet then? Have I forgotten something?'

Tony sighed. He should have known better than to call Chris.

'No. Has she not spoken to you? Simon has kicked Candice out. She, well… I'll tell you later. Anyway, they are all down the pub cheering him up.'

'Who, Simon?'

'Yes.'

'My mate Simon?'

'Yes.'

'But I only saw him a bit ago and he never said anything.'

'Well, it all must have happened since then.'

'And who's there?'

'Everyone. Everyone except me and you.'

Another silence down the end of the phone.

'Oh,' Chris said eventually.

'I'm on my way to your house now,' said Tony. 'I'll be there in about five minutes.'

'Right,' said Chris, still sounding confused.

'You all right?' asked Tony.

'Yeah,' said Chris. Another pause. 'Do you think we'll be having tea at the White Swan?' he asked eventually. 'I really like their fish and chips and they do proper mushy peas, you know, old-style. A bit pasty-looking, not like that bright green stuff you get these days. They're really good. You should try some, honestly. We should just stay for tea, shouldn't we? I'll suggest it when we get there. I mean, that's what us lot do when we meet. We eat!'

Chapter Thirty-Eight

Beth

Beth watched mesmerised as Marie talked… and talked.

'So why don't you come to my Pilates class with me on Wednesday? There are a few men there, but it's such a great class for stress. I tell you, when I'm lying there with my legs in the air, pulling on my core strength, I totally forget about the pain-in-the-arse customer who comes in every Saturday and spends two hundred quid on clothes and then returns them all on Monday.'

Simon was nodding at her, but Beth could tell he wasn't really listening. And if he was, she wasn't sure he'd appreciate his marriage break-up being compared to an overly fussy compulsive shopper.

'Well, isn't this great?' she heard over her shoulder, instantly knowing that Chris had just arrived. Only her husband could miss the fact that the reason behind why they were all gathered was far from great. 'What a bonus. Monday afternoon in the pub! We are having tea here, aren't we?' he said, looking at Beth. 'You know how I feel about their mushy peas. Honestly, if you haven't had them you are missing out.'

Beth was long past the point when anything Chris said could cause her mouth to drop open in horror, but at that moment she felt dismayed that his response to their gathering was so predictable that all she was capable of was of a very long deep sigh.

'People have children to get home for,' Beth pointed out.

'Actually, Annabelle is at dance, then she's going back to her friend's,' said Marie.

'Chloe is on a play date,' said Sarah, without thinking. 'So we are okay for another couple of hours.'

Tony glared at her from behind Chris's shoulder.

'I'll text the boys then,' said Chris. 'They can fend for themselves. Now, what's everyone drinking?'

'We're drinking Prosecco,' Beth told him.

'Why?' Chris asked, looking confused.

'Because it's nice.'

'If you say so.'

'You could get another bottle in. Simon's drinking it too. Because he really needs a drink because HE JUST SPLIT UP WITH HIS WIFE!'

'Oh, God, shit, yes, I forgot all about that for a minute. Sorry, mate, what was I thinking?' Chris sat down heavily next to Simon and threw an arm around him. 'How are you? So tell me what has happened.'

'Oh, for goodness' sake,' said Beth, exasperated. 'He doesn't want to go through it all again. Marie's already given him the third degree.'

'No I did not!' she exclaimed. 'You wouldn't let me!'

'So asking him when he and Candice last had sex is not giving him the third degree?' Beth had been shocked by Marie's bluntness but secretly would have been very interested in the answer.

'It can be an indicator of gaps in a relationship, Beth. We all know that. And an indicator of whether your spouse is straying.'

'Candice had only just finished shagging the vending machine salesman. It's hardly a sensitive question to be asking, is it?'

'Whether or not they have had sex post the affair is an important question,' said Marie. 'To me it would signify the depth of Candice's commitment to going back to Simon.'

Beth glanced over to Simon, who was blinking rapidly as though trying to block out the conversation. She must move things forward.

'So, Chris,' she said to her husband slowly. 'Just to bring you up to speed – you remember that Simon and Candice got back together, right?'

'Yes – you were so happy!' exclaimed Chris, looking bewildered. 'And you changed your shifts for her. You were pulling out all the stops, mate.'

'Anyway,' continued Beth, knowing that Chris's observations weren't really helping. 'When Candice and Simon came round to dinner at Marie and Duncan's, do you remember that she got on really well with everyone?'

'God yeah. I was so pleased. We had a blast. And Candice does a brilliant Britney Spears,' he told Simon seriously.

'Well, that night Candice gave her number to Tony.'

Chris screwed his face up.

'Are you building a house?' he asked Simon.

Simon shook his head.

'She wanted sex,' said Marie.

Chris gasped. 'What!'

'You can't be sure that is what she wanted,' interjected Tony. 'She *only* gave me her number.'

'Why else would she give you her number?' asked Marie. 'I'm telling you, she wanted sex. She's clearly that type of girl.'

Simon looked up at her sharply.

'I'm sorry, Simon, but I think you need to face facts here.'

Beth watched Simon go pale. She wished she was sitting beside him. She wanted to put her hand on his arm again. She wanted to be back by the fire alone with him.

'But why would she want sex with Tony?' asked Chris.

No one said anything. Tony looked awkward.

'Well, he is a catch,' muttered Duncan, nodding at Tony. Clearly feeling the need to fill the silence.

'Anyway,' said Beth to Chris. 'I heard about what Candice had done and I thought that Simon should know so he could decide what to do about it. So I went round to tell him at lunchtime.'

'Lunchtime?'

Beth nodded.

'I delivered a parcel at lunchtime.'

Beth glanced at Simon. *Shit. What now?*

'You just missed her,' said Simon. 'She arrived just after I saw you.'

'What a shame,' said Chris. 'We could have told him together. If you'd let me know. '

Everyone stared at Chris.

He gazed back at them.

'So, who's up for fish and chip tea, then, with mushy peas?' he asked.

JOURNALIST: So do you ever go *out* to eat as a group?

CHRIS: We did once, by accident. We all ended up in the pub at the same time and decided to stay and eat. I can't even remember why. It was a brilliant night though.

Chapter Thirty-Nine

Sarah

She could see Tony eyeing the large menu suspiciously. He was shaking his head gently. Almost imperceptibly. She wasn't sure if he was shaking it at the fact that he appeared to be somehow involved in sparking the end of Simon's marriage through no fault of his own or that he was about to order food in a pub where Chris regarded the mushy peas as the height of their culinary expertise.

They had now moved to the dining room, which was really an over-grand name for a room off the lounge that had proper tables and chairs in. There had been an embarrassing scrum over seats as Marie had virtually pushed Beth out of the way in order to sit next to Simon, to which Beth had rather tipsily responded by commenting, 'For goodness' sake, Marie, Simon could see your tits from Mars today, you don't have to sit on top of him!'

Marie had gasped and Duncan had tried to distract everyone by describing in minute detail the last time he had had a meal in the White Swan. He'd had steak with a pepper sauce, apparently. And peas. Oh, and broccoli, although the broccoli was a tad overcooked and he'd asked for fries but got chips. Today he would be making sure that if he had steak he would be very clear that he wanted fries and not chips.

He liked fries. Marie said nothing about his over-eagerness to get the carbohydrate portion of his meal exactly to his liking. She just glared at Beth as Simon pulled out her chair for her.

'So are we having starters?' asked Chris, looking around hopefully.

'Not for me,' said Marie.

'Nor me,' added Sarah.

'Beth loves the deep-fried Brie, don't you, Beth?' said Chris. 'Are you going to have some deep-fried Brie?'

Sarah looked up. Beth took another swig of her Prosecco before replying.

'Not today,' she said.

'Oh,' said Chris, clearly disappointed that his chances of being able to partake of a starter were diminishing fast. 'Simon, you'll have a starter, won't you, mate? You need to eat. You know, if you are sad. You need to eat.'

Everyone raised their eyes and looked at Chris before looking back down at their menus.

'I'm not hungry,' said Simon. 'Honestly.'

'Nachos?' said Chris, now getting desperate. 'How about we share some nachos?'

'All right then,' agreed Duncan before glancing furtively at Marie.

'Brilliant!' said Chris, looking mightily relieved. 'We'll have loaded, shall we? Beef or chicken? Or shall we just have one of each and then everyone can have a dip in. Because you know you all want to. I know what's going to happen,' he said, looking around and waving his finger at everyone. 'Me and Dunc will order nachos and then one of you will ask to try some, then I'll say, "Go ahead", and then I'll have to say "Does anyone else want to try?" and then you'll all have some nachos and there will be none left for me and Duncan. So let's just be upfront, shall we. Order two bowls of loaded nachos, one with beef and one with chicken and no one goes without. Agreed?'

Everyone silently nodded.

'But is it all right if we put an extra portion of chillis on one because I like my nachos hot, really hot?' added Chris.

Still no one spoke.

'I don't mind which one, beef or chicken. Doesn't matter to me in the slightest. You tell me which one you would prefer to not have the extra chillis on?'

Still silence.

'Tony?' asked Chris. 'Any preference?'

Sarah watched Tony look at Chris like he was an alien. He shook his head ever so slightly again.

'Chicken,' he said finally and looked back down at his menu, dismissing Chris.

'Chicken,' repeated Chris, nodding. 'So do you want the extra chillis on the chicken or not on the chicken?'

Tony very slowly raised his eyes from the menu again.

Sarah held her breath. She wasn't sure how he would respond to this deep and meaningful question.

'Put-the-extra-chillis-on-the-chicken-nachos,' Tony said deliberately and menacingly. He was losing patience with Chris, she could tell. He didn't want to be here. He had the look of someone who was stuck in the lift and resigned to the fact that a rescue was not coming soon. In fact, he had that brooding atmosphere hanging over him that last time had led to him punching a French waiter and Tony spending the night in hospital. Chris needed to shut up about the nachos soon.

Sarah glanced round the rest of the table. Tony wasn't the only one who looked out of his comfort zone. Duncan was openly staring at

Marie as she did her damnedest to insert herself in to the conversation between Simon and Beth. Mostly with her chest. But Beth was doing a great job of putting her shoulder between herself and Marie, making it difficult for Marie to feel included. Consequently, Marie looked a little confused and bewildered. She wasn't used to standing behind Beth in the queue for anything, least of all a man.

Sarah glanced back to Tony. He was staring at her. 'Can we leave?' he mouthed.

'Soon,' she mouthed back. They'd have to wait until after they had eaten, but then it would probably be wise to flee as she couldn't see how this evening was going to turn out to be anything other than a disaster.

She looked at her menu again to try and see if she'd missed something that had the potential to have been cooked fresh and not jammed in a microwave. There was a salad, but she highly suspected that this was a token item. No one expected it to be ordered. It was there to make the lard eaters feel like they could have salad but they had made a conscious decision to treat themselves to lard. Token salad it was. She suspected that when she ordered it they would see the chef dash out to the Co-op next door to find some green stuff.

She looked up at Tony again. They really could do without all this nonsense. She could tell it was winding him up and she needed him in a good mood. She needed him to be calm when she dropped her bombshell.

He was now telling the waitress who had come to take his order exactly how he expected his steak to be cooked. He told her to write his exact words down. 'A warm red centre,' he said slowly, observing her as she wrote. 'That is how medium rare *should* be cooked.'

The waitress nodded.

'Mushy peas with that?' she asked.

Chapter Forty

Beth

They were all standing in the car park attempting to go home. It was only 7.30 p.m. on a Monday, but they were all a bit drunk.

Beth thought it was probably one of the best days of her life.

Simon had just taken her to one side and hugged her.

'Thank you,' he said.

'I didn't do anything,' she replied.

'You did. You had the guts to come and tell me what had happened and then you had the guts to stay and listen whilst I worked it out. I won't forget that.'

'Rosé Prosecco,' she said. 'Works every time.'

He smiled. She thought she could see a tear in his eye.

'You'll be fine,' she said, reaching out and rubbing his arm.

'I know I will,' he replied. 'Just not yet.'

'These things take time.'

'I don't know what I would have done without you today.'

She shrugged. 'I just happened to be there. Anyone would have done the same.'

'No,' he said. 'They wouldn't have done it like you.'

'You ready to stagger home, love?' said Chris, wandering over. 'Do you want us to walk you back?' he asked Simon.

'I think I can find my way,' he replied.

'I was just saying we should do this more often,' Chris said in Beth's face.

'What?' she asked. 'Eat nachos?' She nearly keeled over as she smelt the chillis on his breath.

'Well, I'm always up for that, but I meant we should go out more often, as a crowd, you know. It's been fun. Don't know why we haven't done it before.'

'We've not had a divorce to celebrate before, I guess,' said Beth.

'Shit,' said Chris, his hand flying to his face. 'I forgot about that. Sorry, mate.' Chris flung his arms around Simon, leaning on him for drunken support, causing them both to topple over onto the gravel. 'Bloody hell,' said Chris, scrabbling around. 'What happened there?'

'What are you doing on the floor?' said Duncan, dashing over.

'He was getting too friendly with my wife so I knocked him out,' laughed Chris, giving Simon a friendly punch as he hauled himself up. 'We're going to have to watch him now he's single, lads,' he announced.

Beth felt herself go bright red.

'Not sure I'm quite ready for that,' replied Simon, dusting himself down.

'Oh, mate, we'll soon get you back in the saddle, won't we lads? Boys' night out, eh? What do you reckon, Duncan, Tony?'

'Defo,' replied Duncan.

'I've got a lot of work coming up,' said Tony.

'Right,' said Chris. 'Right. We'll get something sorted. But for now we shall wish you adios,' he said, flourishing his arm. 'See you anon. At Sarah and Tony's, isn't it?'

'I believe it is,' replied Beth. 'Next week in fact.' She had been thinking of asking Tony to do a soufflé to get her own back following the fondue debacle but a better idea had just come to her.

'Brilliant,' said Chris. 'Looking forward to your fine hospitality as always.'

'And you'll come, won't you?' Beth said to Simon. 'It's all right if Simon comes, isn't it, Tony?' she said, turning to him. She so enjoyed the look on his face. A faint cloak of politeness over utter horror.

'Of course,' said Tony curtly. 'Unless he has any better offers of course.'

'Please come,' said Beth. 'You're part of the gang now. You have to come.'

Beth could still see Tony just in her eyeline. He was shaking his head ever so slightly.

'Well, if you're sure?' Simon asked Tony.

'Very sure,' replied Tony. 'Looking forward to it.'

JOURNALIST: So your random guests ended their marriage as a result of one of your dinner parties? Did you keep in touch after that?

SARAH: We did with Simon. Someone invited him to the next dinner party that we hosted. Tony wasn't happy about it though. He'd done with him. And then me disappearing upstairs with him for over half an hour didn't help either.

Chapter Forty-One

March – Dinner at Tony and Sarah's

Tony

'Did you get the sticky rice?' asked Tony, dashing in at six-thirty.

'Yes,' said Sarah, hastily putting her iPad down. She smiled at Tony brightly.

'Good day?' he asked.

She nodded, still smiling brightly.

'What did you get up to?'

'Oh, this and that,' said Sarah. 'Nothing interesting. Tidied up ready for tonight mostly.'

'What, all day?'

'Pretty much.'

She was lying. He knew she was lying. He'd popped home at lunchtime to check on his marinade and she wasn't there. No big deal. He hadn't told her was popping in. He wasn't expecting a hero's welcome or anything, but still, she normally mentioned it if she was going out. Then he'd rung home later and she didn't answer. He wanted her to check the white tablecloth was clean. He'd tried her mobile and still she didn't answer, which was unusual. Very unusual.

'Sorry I missed your call,' she said. 'The battery died on my phone at some point. It's just charging now.'

She was lying. If the battery dies you don't get an engaged tone – it just goes straight to voicemail.

She'd been acting strange ever since the night at the White Swan. He'd had a good moan about the fact they'd had a disrupted evening just because of Simon's marriage breakdown… again. He'd expected her to react. Defend someone, anyone, but she hadn't. In fact, she hadn't reacted at all. Instead she'd asked him to repeat what he had said because she wasn't listening. She never did that.

She wasn't here. For the last week she'd been somewhere he couldn't reach. Sure, she was there physically. But mentally, no. Whenever he looked over to her, she had a thousand-mile stare on her face. She was thinking about somewhere else, or possibly someone else.

The trouble with having had an affair is that you can identify all the signs very quickly in others. Tony could spot it a mile off. The faraway look. The rapid processing of information whilst the rest of the world goes on around you. Sarah was processing something inside but he couldn't see what and she clearly didn't want to tell him. A bad combination. Because that meant whatever she was processing he wasn't going to like.

'Can I help with anything?' he heard Sarah ask as he lifted his marinating chicken out of the fridge.

'Smell this,' he said, offering it up to her, hoping she'd spot that he must have been home whilst she was out. That chicken was not marinating in the fridge when he left that morning.

'Wow – smells great, what are we having?' she asked, completely oblivious.

'I'm doing Thai,' replied Tony. 'Fishcakes with chilli jam and then a red curry.'

'Perfect,' she said.

'You could make the chilli jam if you like?' he asked.

'You're making it?'

'Yes.'

'Don't we normally buy it from the shop?'

'Yes. But I thought home-made would be good.'

Sarah shrugged. 'If you can be bothered,' she said.

'Well, clearly you can't,' he replied petulantly. He waited for a response. It didn't come.

He turned round. She was looking at her phone.

'Do you want to make this jam or shall I?' he asked.

'Why don't you make it,' she said. 'I'll lay the table.' She got up and floated out of the room to heaven knows where.

He was secretly pleased she didn't want to make the jam. Sarah was an all right cook but not brilliant. She just wasn't interested really. And he wanted to show Marie, if he was perfectly honest, that he could make just as good a dip as her.

He went to pick the iPad up that Sarah had left on the kitchen table to search for the recipe. He clicked onto the web browser and was shocked to find it open on a page for high-end women's lingerie. Now normally he would have enjoyed looking at the attractive women in lace and silk and pretty bows, but why on earth would Sarah be searching the web for expensive underwear? Sure, she was the type of woman who wore matching pants and bra (unlike Beth, he suspected), and sure, a lot of this stuff would look very good on his wife, but somehow it wasn't her usual style. This was man-bait underwear. This was new-relationship underwear. This was secret-affair underwear.

★

JOURNALIST: So, tell me, who does the majority of the cooking when it's dinner at your place?

SARAH: Tony. He likes to be in control. Likes everything to go according to plan. He isn't good with deviation. Gives him high blood pressure. I told him so many times he needs to learn to take things more in his stride but he wouldn't listen.

Chapter Forty-Two

Duncan

Duncan stood in the supermarket feeling out of his depth, as he always did when he was trying to decide what wine to take to Tony's house. He was no wine connoisseur. He'd rather have a beer, to be honest, but taking beer to a dinner party seemed to have gone out of fashion and he certainly couldn't imagine taking beer to a dinner party at Tony and Sarah's – certainly not. He suspected there were no beer glasses in their extensive glass collection. There would be glasses for every other type of drink, he imagined: cocktails, gins, even sherry probably, but not beer. A pint pot was about as likely in Tony's house as a pot to piss in.

He walked up and down the aisle again. He needed a recommendation really – perhaps Richard and Judy should do a wine club. How good would that be? You walk in to the supermarket and buy a wine endorsed by some well-known celebrity. These supermarkets were missing a trick there.

He picked up the premium supermarket brand of Chardonnay, but he didn't really trust the supermarket to recommend wine. More than likely they'd got a job lot at a bargain price and needed to get rid of it so they'd added some premium branding to make it look fancy – to make people think it was posh – and sat back and watched it fly off the shelves despite the fact it tasted like every other wine but cost you a fiver more. No, he wasn't falling for that trick.

He put it back. He watched a very smart, slim man in an expensive suit pull a bottle off the top shelf and put it in to his basket, along with a ready meal for one. Duncan followed his lead and grasped the same wine. It was a sad sight to see a man in an expensive suit clearly buying supplies for a Friday night alone. But the man looked like he knew more about wine than Duncan did, so a recommendation from a sad man spending the night alone would have to do.

Duncan strode towards the checkout, past the flower racks. It crossed his mind that he could buy a bunch for Marie. Flowers might actually jolt her in to acknowledging his existence.

Again, he considered the vast choice that the supermarket had to offer and thought about his recipient. Just as Tony would be judgemental about Duncan's wine selection, so would Marie be about his flower selection. Why did supermarkets make life so complicated? Please would someone invent a supermarket with less choice? Or perhaps Richard and Judy could do a flower club?

A pre-made bouquet with a variety of blooms or a bunch of the same variety? Below five pounds or above? This shopping trip was proving to be a nightmare.

No, he wouldn't buy her any flowers. The possible consequences were not worth it. He could buy her the wrong flowers and therefore disappoint her and, to be perfectly honest, he didn't really feel like she deserved them anyway. There had been a change since the group had last met on masse. Since he'd got food poisoning from the dodgy fish, chips and mushy peas he had at the White Swan.

Marie was barely talking to him. She was spending all her spare time at the gym. She said it was because she wanted to be fit for their skiing holiday, but this was borderline obsessive.

And Beth's comment had really stuck in his brain. What had she said? 'For goodness' sake, Marie, Simon could see your tits from Mars today – you don't need to sit on top of him.'

He was used to Beth's sarcasm, but this had hit a nerve. Marie was generally flirtatious. Always had been. She liked to be admired by men. He knew that. And, to be honest, he was secretly proud of how men did admire his wife. Of course he was. Secretly proud that most men found Marie attractive. But she'd chosen him and that made him feel good. Then he'd watched Marie for the rest of the night. He saw her quizzically study Beth and Simon engrossed in conversation. She'd tried to insert herself, but to no avail. Simon didn't appear to be reacting in the way she expected and it bothered her.

Duncan had tried showering her with compliments, but they had all fallen on deaf ears. She clearly didn't need compliments from her husband. She needed them from elsewhere. What does a husband do about that?

He walked away from the flowers. Then he stopped. He saw a daisy plant sitting alone at the end of the display.

Issy had worn a black shirt decorated with white daisies that day. It suited her. It was pretty. He'd wanted to tell her that, but they were barely speaking these days either and surely such a comment would now be misconstrued in their post-#MeToo environment and particularly in their post-Candice's revelation environment.

Candice had phoned in sick the day after the drama. Duncan had finally got in to work at lunchtime, having thrown up several times due to his belly's reaction to the much-lauded fish and chips at the White

Swan. First, he'd looked to Candice's chair – he'd been very happy to find it empty. Then he'd looked to Issy's chair and felt an anxious jump in his heart as he saw her sat there. He'd called her that morning. She'd been polite and professional. He should have read the warning signals then. She was never professional to him on the phone.

'Hi, Issy,' he'd said as he approached her desk.

She looked up. 'Hiya,' she'd said with a forced smile, then looked down again. No chat. No gossip. No swearing. No sarcasm about his late arrival. All was not well.

Ever since Candice's outburst all representations of their special relationship had been withdrawn. There were no guiltily shared sweets and no free cakes delivered to his door when there was a birthday in the office. She no longer ripped to shreds his healthy lunch, offering to bring him back a quarter pounder from McDonald's. She didn't even wink at him when she went to collect the new recruits from reception whilst he masqueraded as one of them. Nothing. They had a normal healthy relationship between boss and PA and he hated it.

What's more, he had no idea as to whether her change of attitude had been sparked by the outing of her secret desire for him or by the desire to deny any such hideous rumour.

He thought of going to HR to ask their advice. But what would he say? 'My PA no longer swears at me or takes the piss out of me and I don't know what to do about it'?

He could just imagine the response.

'Excellent management skills, Duncan. Keep it up.'

Duncan picked up the daisy plant. Issy would love it. And two weeks ago he could have bought it for her and made her day. She probably would have jumped in the air and thrown her arms around him and no one would have thought anything of it. It would have been a good moment. Not now though. It wouldn't just be a daisy plant. It would be a peace offering. But for what, he wasn't really sure.

The thought that perhaps he should buy it for Marie crossed his mind. He shook his head and put it back down.

She'd hate it.

Marie wasn't a daisy person. Issy was a daisy person.

'Hello,' he heard to his left as he was still gazing at the daisy pot.

He looked up and there he was. In all his glory. Simon.

'You doing the same job as me?' asked Simon jovially. 'Wine for tonight?' He nodded down at the bottle clutched in Duncan's hand.

'Oh yeah,' said Duncan, struggling to wake up from his distracted thoughts.

'What have you got?' asked Simon. 'I went with what was on offer.' He held his bottle up to show Duncan.

'Oh, that's a good one that,' Duncan found himself saying. 'You've done well there.'

'Really?' said Simon, studying the bottle. 'Haven't got a clue, to be honest. But I get the impression Tony has, so it's a bit daunting, isn't it?'

'Not really,' replied Duncan. 'Tony won't mind what you bring.' He knew this was a lie. Once, Beth and Chris had taken a bottle of Lambrini and Tony had been unable to hide his disdain. It was immediately opened, unchilled, and force-fed to Beth and Chris until it was gone. Everyone else seemed to have preferred red that night.

'So I thought I'd take some flowers for Beth, what do you think?' asked Simon. 'She has been so good to me, I can't tell you. Do you think she'd like flowers?'

'Err, yeah. Most women like flowers, don't they?'

'I guess so. What about this daisy plant?' he said, picking up the pot that Duncan had already pictured on Issy's desk. 'It's nice. Happy.

I think that would suit her, don't you? Maybe better than flowers? Something a bit different. Roses don't feel right somehow.'

Duncan stared at the plant in Simon's hand.

'I think she would love it,' he told him.

'Good. Right. I'll see you later then. Thanks for the help, mate.'

Simon strode off to the self-checkout, leaving Duncan standing next to the empty daisy plant stand.

JOURNALIST: How important do you think atmosphere is at a dinner party? Do you do anything special to try and create the right atmosphere?

TONY: I generally find that one's wife disappearing with one of the male guests for forty-five minutes creates the wrong atmosphere. I would advise your readers against it.

Chapter Forty-Three

Beth

'Simon just texted me to ask what type of wine he should take to Tony and Sarah's,' Beth told Chris as she came out of the bathroom. 'I told him the expensive kind. He sent me a smiley face back.' She chuckled to herself.

'You tell me off for taking my phone in to the loo,' Chris said to Beth.

Beth stopped and looked at him.

'I forgot it was in my pocket when I went in,' she replied. 'Then it buzzed and I thought I'd better check in case it was work. But it was only Simon.'

'Right,' said Chris, opening his wardrobe door. 'Blue checked shirt, do you reckon tonight?' he asked.

'Would that be your small checked blue shirt or the medium or the large?' she asked.

'They're all the same size, aren't they?' asked Chris. 'All large?'

'I meant the size of the check, idiot,' she said, looking over his shoulder. 'You have every variety of blue checked shirt known to man.'

'I like blue checked shirts, nothing wrong with that. And it's not like I have twenty or anything. Only one, two, three, four, five… six!' he said as he counted them out.

'You should have seen the clothes we cleared out for Candice,' Beth told Chris. 'I have never seen anything like it. She must have been a shopaholic, seriously. I bet I found at least thirty dresses still with labels. Not even worn. It was unbelievable.'

'What's he doing with them all?' asked Chris, shrugging a medium checked blue shirt on and starting to button it up.

'His mum works in a charity shop, so he's giving them to her. Apparently Candice packed her stuff, forgot all about the piles of clothes in the spare room and then he watched her walk out the door and straight in to the house of the chocolate vending machine salesman.'

'You are kidding me.'

'I'm not.'

'So she's gone straight back to him.'

'Apparently so.'

'He's going to a conference in Las Vegas next month,' said Chris. 'He told me the other day when he signed for a registered delivery. He said they were his plane tickets. First time he's ever spoken to me. Showy bastard.'

'Las Vegas? Candice will be with him at least until then, then,' said Beth.

'Poor Simon,' sighed Chris. 'Look, I've been meaning to say this for a while, but thanks by the way. For helping him. It's good of you. I'm sure he really appreciates it. I know he's my friend really, so it really is above and beyond for you to go out of your way for him.'

Beth shrugged. 'Well, I consider him to be my friend now,' she said. And she really did.

They talked most days. She'd check in to see how he was and he'd call to update her on the latest development with Candice. Whether it be knocking on his door at midnight drunk and in hysterics or having to watch her arrive back from work and walk calmly in to the house of the vending machine salesman.

They even shared a WhatsApp group. It was called Beth & Simon. She doubted if anything could have made her happier.

Apart from when he laughed at her jokes, her sarcasm, her bluntness. When he did that, the sun came out.

And, curiously, that was enough. To have a man want to be her friend. To want to spend time with her. It felt good. She felt good. Just by wanting to spend time with her, he made her feel attractive despite the fact he wasn't attracted to her. And that was enough. For now.

Chapter Forty-Four

Sarah

Sarah was sitting on the bed gazing at her phone. There it was in black and white. A life. Sarah reincarnated.

She thought it had gone well. To be honest, she'd been a bit distracted. Worried that Tony was going to pop out of the woodwork at any minute and track her down, or that she wasn't going to get back in time for school pick-up. How would she explain that? But then they started asking her about her previous buying experience and suddenly she was in her element. Telling them how she increased sales by over thirteen per cent in the three years she was womenswear buyer and then by a further twenty-two per cent when she took over as overall buying manager. She told them that she had followed what was happening in the market ever since she had stopped work to have Chloe and then proceeded to tell them exactly what she would do with the lingerie section of their brand. What categories she thought they might consider withdrawing from in order to reduce stockholding and increase their open-to-buy. Why she thought that attractive control underwear could be a big new opportunity for them and how she'd seen that there were factories opening up in China now specialising in control fabrics but who had the skill to embellish. That would set their product apart from everyone else's. She talked about her contacts that she had kept in close touch with all this time. Suppliers, factory owners, retailers, you name it, her contact book was as up to date as it had been the day she left work.

She faltered slightly when they asked her why she was applying for a more junior position than the one she'd left. She could have told them the truth. That despite the fact that they were living in the twenty-first century, she didn't think her husband could cope with his wife in a senior role. That he would feel like he was losing part of her to someone else and he couldn't handle that. He pretty much needed her full attention, even though the majority of his attention was lavished on his work.

She didn't say that.

Instead she said that she was looking for a good work–life balance. That she wanted to add value to a company whilst still having time for her family. She pointed out to them that she was well aware they might think she was overqualified, but she didn't see it that way. She knew that her experience would mean that she could get the job done more efficiently and effectively than someone younger. Thus she expected to be able to achieve amazing results on a four-day-week basis with two days a week working from home. She told them this was a win-win situation. They were getting a lot more experience for their money and she was getting the work– life balance she needed.

The head of buying, who looked about twenty-five, had nodded thoughtfully, as had the head of HR. She didn't think she quite had them yet, so she went with her killer line.

'In my eight years as a buyer I never once missed my target. My team and I always got our bonus. Always. If you give me this job, I will not be tarnishing that record. I will hit my target and we will get our bonuses.'

The two ladies had nodded harder then. She might have just nailed it.

And she had. Less than twenty-four hours later she got the call from the headhunter to say they had made an offer and he would be forwarding it to her. And there it was. Four days a week. Two days in London and two days working from home. It was a dream come true. All she had to do now was convince Tony.

She got up and walked in to her closet and for the first time in a very long while she headed towards the dressier end of the rail. She suddenly had the urge to dress like a buyer again. Something stylish but a bit edgy – fashion-forward, you might say. She sifted rapidly through the rack until she came upon an exquisitely cut slate-grey sheath dress with a puff sleeve and asymmetric hemline. She loved it, but she knew it was slightly off the wall. It was the type of dress that someone without insight would say looked like a sack of potatoes. She slipped it over her head and selected a pair of red patent platform shoes that contrasted beautifully with the grey.

She walked to the mirror and looked at herself.

I'm back, she thought.

'You've not worn that in a while,' said Tony when she arrived in the kitchen having applied minimal make-up but a bright red lipstick.

'Fancied a change,' she said.

'Trying to impress someone?'

Sarah looked quizzically at Tony.

'No,' she said. 'Who on earth would I be trying to impress around here?'

He shrugged.

Perhaps she should talk to him about the job offer now. Get it over with. No. Not before the dinner party. It was likely to put him in a bad mood and Tony in a bad mood could kill a good dinner party. She might tell him later. After everyone had gone. When they'd both had a bit to drink. That sounded like a better idea.

'Can I get you a drink?' she asked him.

'I'm doing a hot champagne cocktail to start,' he said. 'Shall we try it?'

'Hot champagne?' said Sarah. 'I think we better had.'

Chapter Forty-Five

Tony

'That is amazing,' said Sarah, taking a sip. 'What's in it?'

Tony looked at her. For the first time in days she looked him straight in the eye. For the first time in days she looked truly engaged. In fact she positively glowed. Was it the hot champagne cocktail or something else that was setting her off like that?

'So it's a syrup made from honey and hot water, then some fresh lemon, cognac and fresh ginger. Then you add the champagne, of course.'

'This is excellent,' said Sarah, taking another sip. 'Cheers to you.' She held her glass up towards him.

'To us,' replied Tony, holding up his own glass. He had a slight lump in his throat. He noticed that Sarah looked at him intently but said nothing as she clinked her glass against his.

The doorbell rang.

'I'll get it,' she said, scampering off without a backwards glance.

He'd prepped two more hot champagne cocktails by the time Sarah came back in to the room with the first arrivals. He'd put them on a silver tray, carefully making sure they were symmetrically placed. Then he turned, ready to greet his guests with a plastered-on smile.

'Ooh, Tony,' said Beth, walking in. 'You are spoiling us.' She bent forward and sniffed the glasses. 'Honey? Lemon? Beechams Powders, is it? Do you have the flu, dear?'

'Actually it's a hot champagne cocktail,' announced Tony, gritting his teeth. 'Would you like to know what's in it?'

'Hot champagne?' enquired Beth.

'No. It's hot water and honey and lemon juice…'

'Aaah, Beechams Powders, you see,' said Beth.

Tony looked down at his carefully crafted and selected cocktail for the evening. He'd thought it would be ideal for a cold night. He'd thought it was a real crowd-pleaser. He should have known it would be wasted in this lot.

'What else is in it then?' asked Beth.

'Cognac and fresh ginger,' he replied. 'As well as champagne of course.'

'Did you say ginger?' asked Chris, peeping his head over Beth's shoulder.

'Yes. Fresh ginger.'

Chris bent down and sniffed suspiciously.

'You got any lager, mate?' he asked, looking back up at Tony.

Tony wondered why he bothered.

The doorbell rang again.

'Sorry we're late,' said Marie, bustling in in a cloud of perfume and chiffon. Yes, chiffon.

Tony looked her up and down. She'd really outdone herself this time. Marie looked like… well, what did she look like? Possibly an older version of Candice! Her skirt was up her backside and her top was so deeply cut you could park a lorry in it, never mind a bike. Her only nod to modesty was a pale pink translucent chiffon shawl cast over her shoulders.

'Eden recruiting again are they?' asked Beth, raising her eyebrows at her friend.

'Eden?' replied Marie. 'What's Eden?'

'Ask Tony,' replied Beth with a mischievous grin, glancing towards him.

He sighed. Beth never forgot anything. She was like an elephant, in many ways.

'It was seven years ago!' he exclaimed.

Beth merely raised her eyebrows further.

'It's the lap dancing bar on Sadler Gate,' said Sarah. 'Don't you remember that Tony's brother insisted they all go there on his stag do?'

'It was a good night.' Chris nodded, tucking in to a bottle of craft ale that Tony had managed to find him. He looked round when no one agreed. 'It was! Best Greek I've ever tasted.'

'I hope you mean Greek food?' enquired Sarah.

'Of course I do. What else would I mean?' he asked, oblivious.

'We were just talking about you lot being taken to the lap dancing club,' said Beth.

Chris shrugged. 'It was all right, I suppose. If you like that sort of thing. But the tzatziki – now, I would never forget that tzatziki.'

'You look amazing,' Tony told Marie. Anything to get Chris off the subject of food.

'Well, thank you, Tony,' said Marie, doing a small curtsey. 'I'm starting to put things to one side for skiing now, so I'm having to wear things I know I won't be taking. Hardly think this is appropriate for the slopes, do you?' She laughed.

'Hardly appropriate full stop,' Tony heard Beth mutter behind him.

'So, has Simon not arrived yet?' asked Marie.

Tony glanced over to Duncan and saw him grimace. He'd not said a word yet. Not like Duncan at all. He was annoyingly cheerful most of the time, the type that Tony actually found quite irritating. But this quiet version of Duncan? Well, he could actually get to like him.

'I saw him in passing at the gym this morning,' Marie continued. 'But he had to dash off so I didn't really get the chance to talk to him.'

'He'll be here in a minute,' said Beth. 'He was stopping off at Sainsbury's to get some wine before going home to change. He's not had a great day. Did you know that Candice has moved in with the chocolate vending machine salesman? He keeps bumping in to them together in the Co-op. It's killing him. That's why he went to Sainsbury's.'

'Oh, I bumped in to him at Sainsbury's,' said Duncan. 'I forgot to mention it.'

'Did you?' exclaimed Marie.

'Yes. He was buying flowers for Beth.'

'For Beth!' exclaimed Marie.

'For me!' exclaimed Beth simultaneously.

'Yes,' replied Duncan. 'Sorry. Perhaps he meant for it to be a surprise, sorry, Beth.'

'No, it's fine,' said Beth, a slight blush rising to her cheeks. 'No idea why he would be buying flowers for me though.'

'You have been helping him with a lot of the donkey work this week, love,' said Chris. 'She was there all day the other day sorting out Candice's old clothes with him. She really has been a trouper.' He walked over and put his arm around her. 'I'm not surprised he's bought you flowers,' he said.

Chapter Forty-Six

Beth

She couldn't wipe the grin off her face.

Simon was on the way with flowers... for her.

She looked up and Marie was staring at her. She knew exactly what she was thinking. Why was an attractive man like Simon buying flowers for someone who arrived at a dinner party wearing last year's faded black linen trousers and cardigan, when she had arrived with all her assets on show? Tits, bum and legs. The three things Beth was at constant pains to cover up. In fact, if she could cover everything up she would. There was nothing about her body that she wished to display for the world's perusal. Nothing. And yet she was the one being bought flowers. This was just brilliant. Just superbly brilliant. She didn't think she had ever felt like this in her whole life.

The doorbell rang and she felt her heart leap in to her mouth.

He was here. Simon was here.

She pushed her hair over her ear. She had okay ears.

'Sorry I'm late,' he said, coming through the door. 'No excuse, I'm afraid. Just late.' He lunged forward and kissed Sarah on one cheek, then shook Duncan's hand before he turned to Marie and kissed her without even looking down at her spectacular outfit. He hurried through his arrival until he reached Beth, then he finally paused.

'Hey, you,' he said, giving her a hug. 'I hope you don't mind, but I bought you a little something. A thank you for the other day. I don't know what I would have done without you.' He pulled a daisy plant out from behind his back and thrust it at her. A sheepish grin on his face.

'Oh, it's gorgeous,' said Beth, gazing down at the plant in his hand. 'You really shouldn't have.'

'I hope you like it,' he said. 'I had to get you something, but I didn't know what and, well, I thought this looked about right.'

'I love it,' she gushed. 'I'm going to put it on the windowsill in the kitchen and every time I see it I'll think of the look on Candice's face when she realises all of her dresses have been sent to the charity shop.'

Simon laughed.

'Isn't it lovely?' said Beth, holding the plant up for everyone to admire.

'Very cute,' said Sarah.

'Beautiful,' added Marie.

'Putting me to shame, mate,' said Chris. 'She'll be expecting flowers off me next.'

'Sorry,' said Simon. 'I didn't mean to…'

'I'm only joking,' said Chris, slapping Simon's back. 'I buy her a takeaway once a month, that normally suffices.'

Ignore that, thought Beth. *Just ignore it. Do not let the bubble burst. Stay in the bubble.*

'Shall we go and sit down?' said Tony.

'Yes!' declared Chris. 'I am starving!'

'I meant the lounge,' said Tony.

'Oh,' said Chris. 'Dips first, is it?'

'Chris!' said Beth, thumping him. Honestly.

Stay in the bubble, she said to herself again.

As they walked through the door in to the beautiful vaulted-ceilinged lounge, she could hear Marie whisper slightly too loudly behind her to Duncan.

'A daisy plant!' she hissed. 'At least he could have bought her roses!'

Chapter Forty-Seven

Sarah

Sarah watched as Simon entered the room. He did as everyone did. He looked up in awe and then around in astonishment. The high vaulted ceiling and enormous fireplace came as a complete surprise in contrast to the Georgian formality of the farmhouse. It had been Tony's vision when he'd first bought the run-down wreck. He knew he wanted to add the surprise element and he did. A large barn was attached to the house and he'd knocked through and turned this in to the imposing lounge. It was his pride and joy and he loved the reaction of anyone who first saw it.

'Wow,' said Simon. 'This is stunning. I was not expecting this.'

'It was pretty dilapidated when we first saw it,' said Tony. 'But I saw the potential straight away.'

'I feel like I've walked onto a set of *Grand Designs*,' remarked Simon.

'Oh, Tony thinks he is Kevin McCloud,' said Beth. 'Watch out. Any minute he will describe the majestic beauty of the humble barn reappropriated to fittingly comfort and nurture the humble family.'

'I would not say that!' exclaimed Tony.

'You did,' added Sarah. 'In *Architects' Weekly*.'

Tony looked crestfallen.

Not a good move, thought Sarah belatedly.

'Well, it's amazing,' said Simon. 'I hardly dare sit down.'

'Tony puts extra-care spray on the upholstery when we come round,' said Beth.

'No I don't.'

'You only let Chris sit in the black chair.'

'He spilt hummus on the white Chesterfield,' replied Tony.

'If you'd have provided nachos for scooping, it wouldn't have happened. Carrots do not hold dip well,' butted in Chris.

'We are not allowed to eat food in this room any more,' Beth told Simon. 'Banned since hummus-gate.'

Sarah could see Tony looking really uncomfortable. There needed to be a distraction.

'Would you like the tour?' she said to Simon.

'Oh yes!' said Simon. 'If you don't mind. To be honest, I LOVE *Grand Designs*, so please, please let me look round.'

'Come this way,' she said, grabbing his hand. 'We'll start from the top, shall we? I can give you the interior spin. Where I sourced wallpaper from and light fittings, that kind of thing.'

'I think I may have died and gone to heaven,' was the last thing they all heard Simon say as Sarah dragged him up the sweeping staircase that led to a minstrels' gallery-type landing. Sarah breathed a sigh of relief. Hopefully she had averted the potential for Tony to be put in a bad mood. She really needed to put him in the right frame of mind for her news.

'And this is our bedroom. Solid oak floors, wardrobe sourced via a vintage shop on Portobello Road. Light fitting from an old school on the Dordogne.'

'Wow,' said Simon for the hundredth time. 'Did it come with wine?'

'Actually yes. We drove there to collect it over a weekend. We hired a van and, well, we had room for a lot of wine as well. So, rude not to really. It was really good wine.'

'How… how did you find the time to source all of this stuff?' he asked in wonder.

'I had nothing else to do,' she replied simply. 'Come and look at this,' she said, grabbing his arm, keen to get off the subject of what she did or didn't do with her time. 'This is definitely the best room in the house.'

She flung open the heavy oak double doors leading to her closet. Rails lined the room, hanging the collection of clothing accumulated during her career. When she was really, really bored, she would come up here and reorganise it. Sometimes by colour palette, sometimes by year purchased or her most recent theme had been by trend. She'd enjoyed that. Thinking about what each design had been inspired by. In fact, it had filled up a whole two days whilst she scrutinised each and every item, placing it carefully in its new home.

'Wow,' said Simon again as he followed her in. 'All yours?' he asked.

'Yep.' She nodded. 'Quite a collection, hey?'

'You're telling me. You make Candice look like a reluctant shopper!'

Sarah laughed. 'Well,' she said. 'It was what I did for a living.'

'What? You bought clothes?'

'Yes. I was buying director for a women's chain in London.'

'You never said,' he replied. 'That sounds really important.'

She shrugged. 'Well, it's hardly life and death, is it? Not like what you and Beth do.'

'You got to buy clothes for a living,' he said, looking round in wonder. 'It's a good job actually that Candice didn't know that. It would blow her mind. Can you imagine?'

She could actually. Candice would have peppered her with questions and then told her she must have been the luckiest woman alive. To do that for a living. Not clever, not smart, not brave, no, just lucky. When you do a job like that, no one seems to think that you had to work your arse off to get there. Oh no. It was obviously luck.

'How you coping without her?' asked Sarah.

'Okay, actually,' he replied. 'I'm all right.'

She nodded. She doubted it. He'd mentioned her too often already. She was clearly at the forefront of his mind still.

'So when do you get to wear all this stuff?' asked Simon.

'I don't,' she replied.

'Oh,' he said.

There was silence as he looked around.

'So it's like a shrine,' he added, 'to a previous life?'

'I guess,' she admitted.

'Beth said I had to get rid of all Candice's stuff or else I would always be living in the past. It was harsh but fair, I think.'

'Well, that's Beth for you,' replied Sarah. 'Beth's actually never been in here. I bet she would tell me to sell it all. It's probably worth quite a bit and, after all, I hardly wear any of it.'

'Why don't you then?'

Sarah looked at him.

'Actually I've just been offered another buying job,' she found herself blurting out. She was so desperate to tell *someone*.

'Wow. Congratulations.'

'Thank you.'

'When do you start?'

She hesitated. Now what?

'Not sure. I've not told Tony yet.'

'Oh,' said Simon, staring at her. 'Why not?'

She looked at the floor.

'Because it would mean me being in London two days a week. We'd have to get a nanny. There's a lot to think about. I don't know how he's going to react.'

'Right,' said Simon.

She looked back up.

'He'll be supportive though, won't he?' he asked. 'He seems so... you seem so... so together, you know, like a team.'

Sarah looked at him. Were they really? Is that how they appeared? They probably did seem like that as long as they were doing what Tony wanted. Was that a good team?

Simon was waiting for her response. Did she tell him what he thought he should hear or did she tell him the truth?

'I suspect he'll say no,' she answered.

Simon's eyes flared in surprise.

'Oh,' he replied eventually. 'And what if he does?'

She didn't know. That was the big question. What would she do? She'd thought about that moment a lot. She'd gone over and over in her head how to tell him about the job in order to secure a positive response, because the alternative was impossible. She thought about her future carrying on as it was. No change, just emptiness, and it didn't bear thinking about. She couldn't do it. She couldn't carry on like this. So if he said no, she really didn't know what would come next.

'I don't know,' she admitted.

'Right,' he replied.

He looked away. She'd put him on the spot now. Not where he'd expected to be. He'd wanted a gawp round her beautiful home, not deliver a counselling session. He was the one who had just split up with his wife after all. This conversation had gone topsy-turvy.

'Have you talked it through with Beth?' he asked eventually.

'No,' she replied, shaking her head. 'No, I couldn't talk to Beth about it.'

'Why not?' said Simon in surprise. 'She was brilliant with me over Candice. Not that I'm suggesting… not that I'm suggesting that this is anything like… you know…'

'I… I…' faltered Sarah. 'Me and Beth don't talk about stuff like this.'

'But why? You're such good mates, aren't you?'

'Yes… but… how can I say to Beth that I'm anything but delighted with my life, anything but completely satisfied. I mean, she goes out to work and is up to her armpits in bodily fluids all day, every day, and then she comes home and does everything for that family, and I mean everything. And look at me. I've always had it so much easier than her – well, in her eyes anyway. I shopped for a living and then I married a millionaire. I can't go running to Beth saying I'm not happy with that. I can't talk to Beth about the fact that if I don't take this job I am literally going to die of boredom. She won't understand that. Boredom to Beth is an aspiration. But it's killing me. Literally killing me.'

'Really?' said Simon, his eyes wide now.

'Yes,' Sarah replied. 'I know I should feel so, so lucky. I don't have to work, I don't have to earn a living, I can live a stress-free life away from the workplace, but I have never ever felt so stressed out in my life.'

Sarah suddenly felt on the edge of tears. The release of saying it out loud overwhelming her. Her guilty secret. She hated her oh-so-perfect life. And she felt ashamed of herself for having to confess that. Something she hadn't even been able to confess to her closest friends, never mind her husband. Her husband who thought that he had given her everything.

A tear rolled down her cheek and Simon stepped forward. He put his arms around her shoulders and she sank in to him, sobs suddenly wracking through her body.

They said nothing for a few minutes. She could feel him start to rhythmically rub her back and it felt good. Soothing.

Eventually, she felt him pull away as her sobs subsided. He reached in to his pocket and offered her his handkerchief.

'You might need this,' he said, holding it up.

'Do I look like a panda?' she asked.

'A bit,' he agreed.

'Oh no. I've got mascara all over your shirt!' she cried, looking at his shoulder.

He looked down and shrugged. 'Not to worry.'

'We'll have to get it off. You can't go downstairs like that,' said Sarah. 'They'll all want to know what we've been up to. Take it off and I'll get it under the tap.'

'Okay,' he said and began unbuttoning his shirt.

She stood patiently waiting for him, but as the well developed pecs were revealed, she had to look away. She pretended to study her shoes.

'There you go,' he said.

She looked up to take it from him, catching sight of his hairy chest. She looked away again, before glancing back to take another peek. He was in good shape. Really good shape. She remembered that he was down the gym all the time, according to Marie.

'Wait there,' she said, grabbing it off him, needing to put some distance between them. 'I won't be a minute.'

'I think you're wrong about Beth, you know,' said Simon just as she turned to leave the room. 'I think she'd understand more than you think. You should talk to her.'

'Maybe.' She shrugged and went to go and scrub her mascara off his shirt and pull herself together.

JOURNALIST: So I'm wondering if you have any rules you would like to share with our readers regarding dinner party etiquette, seeing as you managed to keep yours going so long.

BETH: Not saying what you really think is probably key to harmony at a dinner party. When the truth comes out is when it all goes pear-shaped.

Chapter Forty-Eight

Duncan

Duncan watched Tony closely as Simon and Sarah finally descended the stairs forty minutes later.

'She been to show you the holiday home in Norfolk as well?' asked Beth.

Sarah blushed.

'No, I just was giving Simon a demo of the walk-in shower that converts in to a steam room. You think you might get one, don't you, Simon?'

'Oh yeah,' said Simon, nodding vigorously. 'I've never seen one of those before. Just amazing.'

'Where would you put one?' asked Beth. 'Your bathroom is tiny.'

Duncan swivelled to look at Beth, and then back to Tony.

'Well, err, I was thinking that maybe I could convert the spare room. Not going to have much use for it now, am I.'

'Not a good idea to lose a bedroom,' said Tony gravely. 'If you are thinking of doing home improvements you can lose a lot of value if you get rid of a bedroom. You very rarely add value if you do that. It's a common mistake a lot of people make.'

'What, even if you converted it in to a steam room?' asked Marie.

'Yes,' replied Tony without looking at Marie. He never took his eyes off Simon, Duncan noticed.

'Right.' Simon nodded, not quite meeting Tony's gaze. 'Perhaps I won't then. Perhaps I'll stick to a really good shower.'

'You can't go wrong with a decent shower,' added Chris. 'Every home needs a decent shower. We spent more than we could afford on ours, to be honest, but that was nearly ten years ago and we've never regretted it, have we, love,' Chris said to Beth.

Beth wasn't looking at Chris. She was looking at Simon.

'So what did you think of the view?' she asked.

'What view?' said Simon, looking startled.

Beth paused and narrowed her eyes before she spoke.

'The view in the bedroom, what did you think of it?'

'Oh,' said Simon. 'Just amazing. Stunning. What a great spot this is.'

'Isn't it?' said Beth. 'Even in the dark.'

Simon didn't reply.

'I love being able to see the lights of Grangewood in the distance,' announced Sarah. 'It's amazing that we can see that far. Now, is everyone all right for a drink. Who wants a top-up?'

'We've already had a top-up,' said Tony frostily. 'We've finished the hot champagne, Chris has had two bottles of lager left over from last Christmas and is very hungry. We were waiting for you.'

'God, I'm sorry,' said Simon. 'I got carried away. I'm so in awe, Tony, of your property. It's just… it's just amazing. I just couldn't stop looking at it.'

Duncan shifted awkwardly in his chair. Tony pulled himself up out of his.

'I'm a very lucky man,' he said slowly, directly to Simon. 'But I worked very hard to secure it and turn it in to what you see now. These things take time, but I always knew I was in it for the long haul. That there was destiny at play. That we were meant to be together and stay together. And that is how it will be. Now, shall we go through to the dining room and eat?'

.

'Duncan… Duncan… are you there?'

Duncan shook his head. He'd drifted off somewhere else. Marie was digging her nails in to his wrist and grinning at him. He'd not really paid attention since they'd sat down. He and Tony had exchanged a glance as they'd walked in to the dining room with its twelve-seater distressed oak table laid out exquisitely with white china and sterling-silver cutlery. Their eyes had met in a knowing fashion. A troubled fashion. But Duncan was wary of trying to read anything in to Tony any more. Not since the phone call when he'd totally misjudged him.

But then their eyes had met again. When Marie insisted on sitting next to Simon and had immediately launched in to the absolute need to discuss the relative merits of the new Pilates instructor at the gym. She declared that she would be fascinated to hear Simon's views on Shakira and whether he thought that she would be better suited to a yoga class instead as she hadn't taken to Shakira at all. She had this entire conversation with him with her back facing Duncan and boobs thrust forward. Duncan watched as Tony markedly looked down at her cleavage, which was difficult to avoid, and then back up to Duncan as if to say 'I wouldn't let my wife thrust her tits at Simon like that.' Duncan was tempted to point out that at least his wife hadn't spent forty minutes upstairs with Simon only to arrive back downstairs looking flustered.

'Duncan,' Marie said again as he tried to focus. 'Did you hear that? Simon's going to train me to do a half-marathon!'

'What?' said Duncan.

'A half-marathon,' repeated Marie. 'He reckons it'll be a lot better for me, fitness-wise, than all these classes I've been doing.'

'Right,' said Duncan. He glanced over to Tony. They shared a look again.

'So how long do you think it will take?' asked Marie.

'Well, we'd have to see really, but given you're pretty fit anyway then maybe three to four months.'

Tony and Duncan exchanged yet another look.

'So is there a half-marathon locally around that time that I could aim at?'

'You could always do the Night Lights Run. That's a great one.'

'Wow, I've always wanted to do that but never thought I could. Do you really think I'm capable?'

'I would have thought so, if you commit to a training plan.'

'Oh, I am willing to commit. Really I am. When I say I am going to do something I do it, don't I, Duncan?'

'Yes,' replied Duncan, refusing to look at Tony.

'Why don't you join us?' asked Simon.

'Who?' said Duncan. 'Me?'

'Yes,' replied Simon.

Marie laughed. Duncan didn't.

'Duncan couldn't run thirteen miles,' she said, still cackling. 'I've been telling him to do some exercises, so he's ready for skiing, but he's not even done any of those. No, no way he could do that.'

'I bet he could,' said Tony. 'If he felt like he wanted to.'

Duncan had to look at him now. Was this a vote of confidence from Tony or was he trying to tell him something else?

'I can't run,' piped up Chris. 'Just not built for it.'

'I don't need to do one,' said Tony.

'It's not for me,' said Sarah, shaking her head.

'I wouldn't mind a go,' added Beth.

The table went quiet.

'Maybe you should do something a little less challenging first,' said Marie. 'I'm not sure you'd be able to keep up with me and Simon.'

'You do get puffed out just going up the stairs, love,' offered Chris.

Beth slowly turned to Chris but said nothing.

'She could do it,' said Simon. 'If she put her mind to it, of course she could do it.'

'Thanks, Simon,' she said, without averting her gaze from Chris.

Chris shrugged. 'You go for it, love. If that's what you want to do. I'm just saying, you might need to take it steady. It's a while since you did any exercise.'

'On her feet all day, marching up and down wards,' said Simon. 'That is pretty energetic, if you ask me.'

'Thanks, Simon,' Beth said again.

'Maybe you should take up one of those couch to 5K courses first,' added Marie. 'I've heard lots of people have done really well on those.'

'When did you last run five kilometres?' Beth asked Marie.

'Well, err, not a straight 5K in a while, but I have been going to the gym four times a week and I actually think I'm in the best shape I've ever been. My spinning instructor said I looked like I was still in my thirties.'

'Was he referring to the fake tan or the Botox?' asked Beth.

'Botox!' exclaimed Sarah and Chris.

'Isn't that for, like, movie stars?' added Chris. 'I thought you could only get that type of thing in Hollywood.'

'Botox? Since when?' said Duncan. 'Why?'

Marie glared at Beth, clearly unhappy that she had let the cat out of the bag.

'It's for my migraines,' Marie told Duncan. 'It's good for migraines, that's all. The doctor suggested it.'

'But you don't get migraines,' stated Duncan.

'Exactly!' said Marie.

Duncan stared at Marie. 'Why didn't you say?' he asked.

'Because I knew you would kick up a big fuss about it and tell me we couldn't afford it,' bit back Marie.

'I meant why didn't you tell me you were getting migraines?' he said.

'Oh,' said Marie. 'Because I didn't want to bother you.' She laughed a nervous laugh. 'You're so busy with work, you didn't need that on your mind. So I bothered the doctor instead and the first thing he recommended was Botox. Can you believe it? Who would have thought it was such a miracle worker?'

Duncan knew she was lying. Marie had a very low pain threshold and if she hurt herself or was ill then the whole household had to live through it with her. Every single step. Marie normally couldn't take a single dose of paracetamol or ibuprofen or any other remedy without it being witnessed by at least one member of the family, who would be required to issue soothing comments as she took her medicine. There was no way Marie could hide an onslaught of migraines. Marie with a migraine would require complete attention, closed curtains, quiet rooms and bed rest, all normal services cancelled until she recovered.

'So they put the Botox in to your forehead, do they, even though it's for migraines?' asked Beth.

'Oh yes,' replied Marie. 'Well, they can put it where you like, I just thought I might as well get some added benefit. I mean, why not?'

Why not indeed, thought Duncan. *Because it's probably bloody expensive and unnecessary and... and... who are you trying to kid, Marie.*

'So what does your forehead feel like?' asked Beth.

'It feels fantastic,' replied Marie defiantly.

'So, let me get this straight,' said Chris. 'You had plastic surgery to get rid of your migraines?'

'No!' said Marie. 'It's not surgery, it's just an injection that so happens also to be used to reduce the signs of ageing. But that is not why I had it, I had it to get rid of the terrible migraines I'd been having.'

'Migraines can be very debilitating,' said Simon.

'Oh they are,' agreed Marie. 'Just awful. You can't do anything.'

'You must have been difficult to live with if you were in so much pain,' said Tony. He looked at Duncan and nodded.

Duncan nodded back.

JOURNALIST: So do you get together on any other occasions outside of the dinner parties or are they your main point of contact?

DUNCAN: Not really. I guess the girls occasionally meet up for coffee, but it's rare for the men to. Of course, Marie started training for the half-marathon with Simon so they began meeting up regularly. But the less said about that the better.

Chapter Forty-Nine

Tony

'Will you come and help me plate up the starter?' Tony asked Sarah once they had got everyone settled at the dining table.

'Of course,' she replied.

He walked in to the kitchen and started laying out plain white plates on the kitchen island, then went to the fridge to take out his garnish of rocket, cherry tomatoes and cucumber.

He checked his watch. He'd taken the Thai crab cakes out of the oven half an hour ago when they were ready, but then Sarah and Simon had failed to appear. He'd put them in the warming oven, hoping that it wouldn't dry them out. He couldn't cope with false admiring noises from his guests, not tonight.

'What do you want me to do?' asked Sarah.

'The chilli jam is in a bowl on the side. Can you divide it between the six ramekins?'

'I still can't believe you made chilli jam.'

'It's not rocket science. Just peppers, chilli, a bit of fresh ginger, garlic, cherry tomatoes, sugar and vinegar.'

'Don't tell Chris,' replied Sarah.

'What about?'

'The ginger. Remember, he said he didn't like ginger.'

'But he loves dips. I don't think he'll notice somehow.'

'You're right. It tastes delicious by the way.'

Tony didn't reply. He was concentrating. He'd not practised his plating. He normally did. He liked it to look good on the plate. He liked to show care and attention where the others didn't.

Sarah started bringing the ramekins over just as Tony headed towards the oven to check on the crab cakes. He eased them out and brought them back to the island, then laid the tray on a chopping board. He took a sharp knife and carefully inserted it in to the fishcake before withdrawing it and touching the blade with his finger. Good, they were still warmed through and they didn't look too shrivelled. They might have got away with it. No thanks to Simon.

'You were a very long time up there,' he said, looking up. He lifted the knife as he did so, pointing it at his wife.

She looked startled. He watched as she swallowed. The colour drained from her face before she looked away.

'He, err, wanted to talk,' she said.

'What about?'

'Well, Candice mostly,' she replied. 'He's clearly struggling to process what has happened.'

'So, did he want advice from you?' he asked. He kept the knife raised. She glanced at its point, then looked away again. 'Because you know about affairs? Did he think you'd be best placed?'

'No!' said Sarah, shaking her head. 'No, nothing like that. I think he just wanted to talk and I guess I was there.'

'You were just there?'

'Yes.'

'Right.'

Tony looked down and decided to slice the crab cakes in two and then place them on the plate, end down, so that they looked like two bread-crumbed humps. He liked it. A bit unusual. He carefully dissected the next one, then he looked up, the knife again poised in the direction of Sarah.

'I don't like him,' he said. 'I don't trust him. He's turning us all in to liars. All of us.'

Sarah stared back at him. She went to say something but he silenced her. Raising the knife by just an inch.

'I don't want to talk about it any more,' he said. 'I'm done.'

Chapter Fifty

Chris

'Fucking hell, Tony, you have surpassed yourself here, mate. What is in that dippy thing?' Chris asked.

'Nothing special,' replied Tony. 'Peppers, chilli, garlic, you know, stuff like that.'

'Restaurant quality, mate, that starter. Restaurant quality, I reckon. Don't you, Beth?'

'Better than the White Swan,' agreed Beth.

'Oh my God, yes. It just needed their mushy peas on the side and that would have been a dish made in heaven. Actually, that would go, wouldn't it? Crab cakes and mushy peas. That's just posh fish and chips really, isn't it? I reckon that could be a winner. I might suggest it next time I'm down there. You got a recipe for these fishcakes, Tony?'

'I have,' replied Tony. 'And if you think the White Swan would serve up Thai crab cakes as good as these, with or without the mushy peas, well, I might even be tempted to go there again myself.'

'I tell you what, that was a good night, wasn't it?' said Chris, leaning back in his chair.

'Well, it was an afternoon really,' pointed out Beth.

'Always the best,' said Chris. 'A spontaneous Monday afternoon in the pub. Can't beat it. When we doing it again? Do you know what, we should do it every week. I mean, if you lot can get babysitters. We can leave our pair to it as long as they don't start scrapping. We should be down the pub every Monday now, what do you say? Have some food. Simon? You'd be up for that wouldn't you?'

'I usually go down the gym on a Monday afternoon,' admitted Simon.

'Well, how about we do it once a month?' said Chris. 'That wouldn't hurt, would it? We could do it in between our regular dinner party night. How about that? Give you ladies a night off from the cooking.'

'I cooked tonight actually,' said Tony.

'Oh, yeah right, of course you did. Well, you know what I mean. Give everyone a night off from cooking.'

'Except you,' said Beth. 'You never cook. So how can you have a night off?'

'Aww, come on, love. You know I can't cook. Never have been able to. You are so much better at it than me.'

'You could cook if you put your mind to it,' said Simon.

'Bloody hell!' Tony suddenly exclaimed. 'Who are you, some self-help guru? Beth doing a marathon? Chris cooking? Are you serious?'

No one moved.

'I am serious,' said Simon steadily. 'I think that sometimes people put up their own barriers. They think they can't do something, but actually the only people stopping them are themselves. You have to ignore the voice in your head and then just get out there. Get on with it.'

'So do you apply that to relationships as well?' asked Tony.

'What do you mean?'

'Perhaps you think that you can have anyone you want. That no one can stop you but yourself.'

'No, I don't think that,' said Simon, holding Tony's gaze. 'Of course I don't.'

'More chilli jam, anyone?' asked Sarah, getting up quickly.

'Hell yes,' said Chris. 'You mean there's more? Any more of that fishcake too?'

'The crab cakes have all gone,' said Sarah.

'Not to worry,' replied Chris. 'You got any crackers or maybe even some crisps? I bet crisps dipped in to that chilli dip would taste amazing, don't you? In fact, I bet anything dipped in that chilli dip would be delicious. I have to say, I don't usually like home-made dips. I don't think you can actually beat a classic sour cheese and chive but I think I might be willing to make an exception for your chilli dip.'

'It's a jam, not a dip,' said Tony.

'A jam?' questioned Chris. 'But it's not sweet. You wouldn't put it on a scone, would you.'

'It's got sugar in it,' replied Tony.

'Are you serious?' said Chris. 'A dip with sugar in it. No wonder I liked it.' He laughed heartily as he banged Tony on the back with his fist.

Chapter Fifty-One

Beth

'And there goes the cuckoo clock,' said Beth. She looked over at Tony, who was sitting stony-faced. Normally it made her smile when she heard the novelty clock in Tony's house. But not tonight.

'Look at the skier,' said Chris, urgently pointing to the clock on the wall. 'Look at the skier coming out of the clock, Simon. Quick, quick before it stops chiming.'

Everyone turned to look at the old man on skis pop out of the cuckoo clock, raising his poles as he did so. They'd all seen it a hundred times but tonight they were grateful for its intrusion.

'Wow,' said Simon. 'I've never seen a cuckoo clock like that before.'

'Isn't it the coolest thing you have ever seen?' chuckled Chris. 'We bought it for Sarah and Tony for their wedding. Can you imagine a better present for these pair who love Switzerland and love skiing?'

Beth glanced over to Tony. He still looked stony-faced. She knew he hated it. She knew it looked totally out of place in this house of oh-so-carefully selected furniture and household accessories. Everything else screamed money and authenticity and style. The skiing man cuckoo clock screamed cheap tat. That was why she'd agreed to let Chris buy it for them. She thought this house was desperately in need of some light relief.

She'd been amazed that they had even had put it up, to be honest. She suspected that it had been Sarah who'd insisted. Sarah who would appreciate the message from Beth. *You may have a fancy house and husband but that doesn't mean you can't have a piece of trash hanging up in your dining room.*

'So we all know what time it is *now*,' announced a delighted Chris. Beth groaned.

'Well, it's nine o'clock, isn't it?' said Simon.

'Well, yes, but we have a tradition, you see. I started it,' said Chris. 'When we come here for dinner and the cuckoo clock goes, then we all have to tell a joke.'

'Do we have to?' asked Beth, shaking her head.

'No... no... no one has to, but I'm going to,' said Chris with a big grin.

'Do *you* have to?' said Beth with a sigh.

'Yes. I've been saving one up for weeks for this very moment. It's a good one, I can assure you.'

'Okay, well put us out of our misery then,' muttered Beth.

'Well,' said Chris. 'What is brown and sticky?'

'A stick,' replied Beth.

'What! You knew it. Did you hear it before or have you just guessed?'

'I've heard it like a thousand times before.'

'Really! Well, you could have kept quiet.'

'How many people round this table have heard that joke before?' asked Beth.

Everyone raised their hands.

'Sorry, mate,' said Duncan.

'Ah well,' said Chris. 'Hopefully we will still be sat here at ten o'clock and I can share the other joke I had as back-up. I don't think it's as good, personally, but if it's one you haven't heard before then you might like it.'

'I can't wait,' muttered Tony. 'Sarah, would you clear the starter away while I plate up the main course?'

Plate up? thought Beth. Who did Tony think he was, Gordon bloody Ramsey? She could pretty much bear Tony when he came to dinner at their house, but when he hosted, he got right up her nose. Every time, it was as though he was trying to display how a dinner party should be done. It was as though he took pains to point out every failing of your own offering. Like your husband turning up with a four-pack of dips and Pringles and serving them on a bar stool. That would never happen under Tony's roof. Oh no, it was all pretty food on matching crockery with everything made from scratch.

A movement suddenly caught Beth's eye. *Oh! What just happened there?* she thought, as she looked around to see if anyone else had noticed it.

Tony wouldn't have seen it as he had already left the room. Duncan had excused himself to go to the bathroom and Chris was talking to Marie. But Marie had spotted it too. Beth could see her staring at Simon. Simon didn't look up after he had reached behind him and squeezed Sarah's arm as she left the room. He just leaned forward and took a large slug of wine. But Beth had spotted it.

He'd touched her. So something *had* happened upstairs. That was a touch of someone who had shared something. Something they didn't want anyone else to know about, except now both Beth and Marie did.

Beth had noticed the undone button on Simon's shirt after he arrived back from the so-called 'tour' of the house. And, of course, she couldn't fail to notice Sarah's flushed face and glistening eyes.

She felt sick to the stomach.

Had they?

No way, they couldn't have. Could they?

But that touch. That intimate touch. What had happened up there?

Beth actually thought she was going to be sick. This was so unfair. Simon was hers. He was her special friend. Not Sarah's. She couldn't have him. She had everything, absolutely everything. Couldn't she just leave Simon for her?

He'd even bought her a plant, for goodness' sake.

She didn't realise she was staring at Simon until he looked up and caught her.

He winked.

What the hell was that?

Of course, it was what it always was.

Every guy that had ever crossed her path had looked past her to her glamorous friends. *Every* guy. Sure, they'd given her the time of day. Chatted to her, laughed at her jokes. She was the funny one after all, the one with the 'personality'. The label given to the girl without the looks as some kind of compensation prize. Then Sarah would arrive and they would get that faraway look in their eyes. Personality never seemed to be adequate competition for a size eight figure. Never.

Why would it be any different now?

But as far as Beth was aware, they had barely spoken to each other. She'd not spotted any real connection between the two of them around the dinner table. Perhaps that didn't matter. When two good-looking people met, the banter was irrelevant, the connection was irrelevant, they were like magnets, destined to bond, ignoring all outside factors.

She bit her lip. She couldn't lose what she had with Simon now. He made her feel worthwhile. She felt tears hover uncomfortably at the corners of her eyes. The last few weeks had had a remarkable transformation on her attitude to life. She didn't want to go back to where she had been. No way. It was a bleak place. A humdrum place. Simon had somehow brought life in to her life.

The thought of losing what they had, whatever it was, well, she couldn't bear it. She would somehow have to fight for his attention. She needed some, just a bit, just to keep her going.

But she knew in her heart of hearts that *if* Simon and Sarah had crossed a line, then it would be all-consuming. Affairs were. And Sarah should know. She had watched Sarah lose interest in her beloved career, for goodness' sake. Given it up even, for an affair. Affairs seemed to be like that. They were not confined. They damaged everything.

She scrutinised Sarah as she re-entered the room. She looked a little tearful. She didn't meet anyone's eyes, especially not Simon's.

Perhaps Tony had noticed something. Beth did well to stop herself gasping. What if Tony had noticed something? She dreaded to think how he would deal with that. She often joked about him being the Godfather and hiding bodies under the patio, but she was only half joking. There was a dark side to him. She could feel it. You wouldn't want to cross him. You wouldn't want to have an affair with his wife. Beth looked across at Simon. She dreaded to think what he might do to Simon if he suspected some misdoing.

Tony entered the room looking grim. There was definitely trouble in paradise. He laid bowls of steaming food in front of them all without a word.

'Chopsticks,' he barked at Sarah.

Bloody hell, thought Beth. Chopsticks were all she needed. Tony knew that she and Chris had never mastered chopsticks and yet he served Asian food every single time they came over for dinner, forcing them to embarrass themselves by asking for a knife and fork.

'What's brown and sticky?' asked Chris, gleefully holding his chopsticks up.

No one answered.

'I'll have a knife and fork, Tony, if you don't mind,' Chris said. 'You as well, Beth?' he asked across the table.

She nodded silently.

JOURNALIST: So it was always Thai food at your dinner parties then?

SARAH: Yes, well Tony's first wife was Thai, you see. He got a contract to design a hotel over there and came back with a wife. He gave her a lot of money in the divorce. The only thing she gave him were her recipes. So I guess he thinks he needs to make the most of them. They really cost him.

Chapter Fifty-Two

Early April

Duncan

It had been a pretty normal day until now. Well, a normal day in the current scheme of things. A normal day at the moment consisted of Marie rising at the crack of dawn to go and meet Simon for a run before she went to work. They were building up to the ten-mile mark apparently. Not that he particularly listened when she started talking about it. He found that he didn't really care for his wife banging on about this fabulous goal she was working towards, with another man.

Normally work was his therapy. Work took him out of himself. He loved his job, or he used to. Now he dreaded walking through the doors. Dreaded going up the stairs to his first-floor office only to be greeted by a sullen Issy, who was even more sullen now that Candice had returned. They circled each other like wary animals. He half expected there to be a massive catfight at any point. A scrap, to be honest, might clear the air. Anything had to be better than the thick, choking atmosphere that seemed to have settled over the three of them.

He didn't know how to break the stalemate. The air of professionalism was killing him. What he really needed was a frank conversation with both of them. Some bluntness wouldn't go amiss, but neither of them seemed to be in the frame of mind to make that acceptable. He feared mutiny if he dared tread anywhere close to it.

And so he was living through another day of torture, but then his phone rang and he was astonished to see that it was Tony calling.

Tony never called.

'Hello, mate,' he said, picking up the phone.

'Hello, Duncan,' said Tony, sounding formal. He was clearly in work mode.

'Fabulous curry the other night by the way. Been meaning to text you.'

'Thank you. Because of the delays to our evening the rice wasn't how I would have liked, but there you go.'

'There you go indeed.' Duncan wondered if he should acknowledge the cause of the evening's delays, i.e. Sarah and Simon disappearing for ages, but decided against it. Tony may be calling for the first time ever in their relationship but his reaching out probably didn't extend to a frank discussion about his wife's behavior.

'So, I was wondering if you would come and have a drink with me tonight. There's something I wish to discuss.'

Duncan was speechless. An invite for a drink and a chat. This was new. How to respond? He'd said he'd cook dinner, but he was sure Marie wouldn't mind if he texted to say he was meeting Tony for a drink first.

'Of course, mate,' he replied. 'I said I'd cook dinner but…'

'Marie can cook her own dinner can't she?' interrupted Tony somewhat sharply.

'Of course,' replied Duncan. 'I'm sure she won't mind.'

'Good. Shall we say Squires & Angels at 6 p.m.?'

'Err yeah,' said Duncan. 'Err…'

'Good. Bye then.' The phone went dead.

He looked at it. He had no idea what or where Squires & Angels was. He was just about to shout through to ask Issy, when he remembered their stand-off. He'd have to Google it.

He was busy looking at the overly designed interior of Squires & Angels online when an envelope dropped on his computer keyboard.

'What's this?' he asked, looking up. Issy was standing in front of him.

'Read it,' she said, nodding at it.

All that was on the front was his name. He picked it up and opened it, folding out the single sheet of A4.

'Dear Mr Mottershall,' he read aloud, 'I hereby give notice of my employment. Miss Pertry in HR tells me I am on a month's contract, but I have been offered another job and would appreciate it if you would let me leave within the next two weeks. I really appreciate the opportunity you gave me and I will never forget you. Yours sincerely, Isobel Barker.'

Duncan looked up, a lump in his throat.

'No,' he said, shaking his head.

'What do you mean, no?'

'I can't let you leave.'

'Why not?'

'Because… because…' The lump was getting bigger.

'You can make me work the month if you want. Helen Pertry said you can. I just thought that the sooner the better really.'

'But… but why?'

Issy said nothing just stared at him.

'Time I moved on,' she eventually said.

'But you love this job. You said at your last appraisal that you never wanted to leave and that I could pay you in jelly babies if I wanted to.'

'I say a lot of things I don't mean,' she muttered, looking away.

Duncan didn't know what to say. Didn't know what to think. The enormous elephant in the room looming larger than ever. Bloody Candice. Bloody, bloody Candice, what had she done?

'Have you really got another job to go to?' he asked.

'No,' she replied. 'But the agency said I should be okay. Be lucky to get another PA job due to lack of qualifications and the factory work has dried up post-Christmas for a bit, but I'll get something. I know I will.'

'But what about Kady and Callum and your mum?'

'We'll be okay. We always have been. I'll look after them. I'll find a way.'

'Why don't you stay until you find another job? You can do that, can't you?'

Issy was shaking her head before anything even came out of her mouth. 'No. No, I have to go.' She looked down at her hands, then started chewing her nails. 'Please will you let me go,' she said, looking at him. 'Actually I really would like to go now.'

He stared back at her. There was only one thing he could say.

'If that is what you want.'

She nodded. Their eyes met, lingered, then she looked away.

'I think it is for the best.' She turned round and left the room.

It didn't feel like the best. It felt dreadful. Truly dreadful. He felt like letting his head fall on the desk in front of his entire call centre team and banging his fists on the desk.

He looked over towards where Candice was sitting. She was in the middle of a call, twirling her hair idly, without a care in the world. What had she done?

He could see Issy collecting her things. Quickly stashing a picture of her nieces and nephews in to her bag and then the Smurf that had presided at the top of her computer for the last year or so.

She glanced behind her to find Duncan staring. She looked down at the Smurf, then strode back in to the office and put it on the desk in front of him.

'A memento,' she said, then left.

She walked out with her head held high. One by one the banks of desks turned to stare until eventually she went past Candice's area.

Issy paused and blew her a kiss in full view of everyone, then sighed heavily and pushed her way through the heavy double doors at the other side of the office.

Candice turned sharply round to seek out Duncan, a confused look on her face. He glanced back at her before getting up and shutting the door to his office. He walked back behind his desk and laid his forehead on the table and banged his fist.

Why hadn't he bought the daisy plant? he thought. He should have bought the bloody daisy plant.

JOURNALIST: So, I have to ask. What happened to Candice?

DUNCAN: I used to see her at work but then I fired her. Eventually.

Chapter Fifty-Three

Tony

Tony arrived at Squires & Angels at 5.45 p.m. He wanted to be settled in a leather Chesterfield with a paper and a whisky in the window before anyone arrived. Then he would feel in control of the situation. He'd told Duncan to arrive for 6 p.m. and Chris to arrive at 6.15 p.m. Given that Chris was bound to be late that would give him and Duncan plenty of time to discuss the matter at hand and come to an agreement on a plan. Not that Tony envisaged there would be much discussion. It was very clear to him what needed to be done and he was certain Duncan would agree. They just needed to convince Chris, that was all. And Tony thought that Duncan was actually more on Chris's level and would be better at putting it in to words that he would understand.

After everyone had left the dinner party, Sarah had announced a headache and retired to bed, apologising profusely that she wasn't up to helping clear up. He'd said it was fine, though it wasn't. Sarah was normally very resilient and certainly not work-shy. She wasn't one to let a headache get in the way of clearing away a few dinner pots. He suspected that actually she was avoiding him. As he stewed over the evening, he distracted himself by stacking the dishwasher as it reminded him of an architectural challenge. It was all about optimising space and it fascinated him how the various shapes represented by kitchen utensils could slot together. He never admitted it, but sometimes he got inspiration from the dishwasher. Seeing the grater sit alongside a lemon squeezer had inspired an innovative hallway design for a library in Edinburgh. Of course, he'd probably said his inspiration came from the juxtaposition of industrial forms and nature in early twentieth-century architecture rather than kitchen equipment. You could charge more for that kind of inspiration. A lot more.

When he'd finished he'd sat with a whisky on his white sofa in the dark for a while, playing over the dinner party, then gone upstairs where he found Sarah fast asleep. Or was she? Certainly, there was no invitation for communication or desire to discuss the evening's events. That would have to wait until another time.

But another time had not presented itself so far. Or rather, Sarah hadn't seemed to want to present herself. He'd barely seen her in days. That was why he'd decided it was time to take action.

'Hello, mate,' said Duncan, approaching him. 'Is this a new place then?' he asked. 'Not been here before.'

'Must have been open a couple of years,' replied Tony. 'We did a bit of consulting on the project. One of the trainees got involved. We get a discount.' He dug his wallet out of his pocket and handed Duncan a card.

'Wow – cool,' said Duncan, studying the card. 'Can I get you anything?'

'I'm good thanks,' replied Tony, nodding at his whisky.

Duncan ambled off and Tony watched as he fumbled in front of the uber-stylish young barmaid. He clearly didn't know what to drink in this achingly fashionable joint. He came back a few minutes later clutching a large bulbous glass with herbs and slices of grapefruit floating in it.

'I asked for a gin and tonic and ended up with this,' he said, looking dismayed. 'I didn't realise I was having dessert as well.'

'They do like their craft gins here,' replied Tony.

'I'm sure she said something about rhubarb.'

'Rhubarb gin maybe, or even rhubarb tonic?'

'Really? Is that what young people drink these days? What am I supposed to do with this?' he asked, pulling a large sprig of rosemary out of the glass.

'Leave it in. It flavours the drink.'

'Really,' replied Duncan suspiciously before raising it to his lips and getting rosemary up his nose. 'So, good day?' he asked after he'd poked the rosemary to the bottom of the glass.

'Acceptable,' muttered Tony. 'You?'

Duncan took another slug of his drink.

'Not great,' he admitted. 'My PA's leaving.'

'Oh dear. That is very inconvenient.'

'You're telling me.'

'Pregnant?'

'What? Oh no. No, nothing like that. Just wanted to move on, I think. Try something new. Not sure how I'm going to replace her, to be honest.'

Tony was done with the small talk. He really didn't need to know about Duncan's work issues. He couldn't imagine that it would be difficult to replace a PA at a call centre. No big deal, surely. Except Duncan was looking like it was the end of the world. Best snap him out of it and get onto more pressing issues.

'I actually wanted to talk to you about our little problem,' said Tony, leaning forward.

Duncan blinked back at him.

'What little problem?' he asked.

'You know, the one you called me about a few weeks ago?' *Bloody hell, Duncan, come on. That problem that was so pressing that you called me at work about it. I'm ready to talk about it now.*

'I'm not with you,' said Duncan.

Tony sighed. Perhaps this was going to be harder than he thought.

'I'm talking about Simon,' said Tony.

'Simon,' repeated Duncan.

'Yes, Simon,' said Tony. 'I think it's time we took action, don't you?'

Duncan looked at him over the top of his glass and then put it down. He rubbed his hands over his face and sighed.

'So has something happened?' he asked. 'I thought you were relaxed about him.'

It was Tony's turn to take a swig of his drink.

'No, nothing's happened,' he said firmly. 'I just think that enough is enough. He must be back on his feet now. He doesn't need us any more. And I don't think we need him, do you?'

Their eyes met. Did he really have to spell it out? After all, it was Duncan who'd picked the phone up first, suggesting that having Simon around wasn't going to end well. Why was he being so thick today? He'd been expecting Duncan to jump at the opportunity to join forces to oust the infiltrator, but he was acting all reluctant.

Duncan sighed.

'Him and Marie are training for this half-marathon nearly every other day,' he said.

Finally, thought Tony. *Progress.*

'Right,' said Tony. 'Sounds a bit over the top, don't you think? Spending that much time together?'

'I guess.' Duncan shrugged as though he didn't really care.

'Does it not bother you?' asked Tony.

'I guess.' Duncan shrugged again.

'Well, it would bother me.'

'Like it did when he disappeared with Sarah the other night for three quarters of an hour.'

Wow, thought Tony. *He's sussed it now.*

'I trust my wife,' said Tony. 'I know she wouldn't have anything to do with that brainless gym bunny, but I'm getting a bit sick and tired of him hanging around. Fawning over Sarah and Marie. I'm done with him.'

Duncan blinked back at him. 'You think he's fawning over them? Not the other way round?'

'Well, there is some fawning back going on. Not Sarah though.'

They held each other's eyes again.

'Marie's always been a flirt,' said Duncan. 'I knew that when I married her.'

'But I bet you don't want to see it in your face over dinner, do you?'

Duncan swallowed. 'Not really.'

'And now Beth's joined the fan club,' added Tony. 'Even her eyes are misting over when he walks in. Oh, and that pathetic daisy plant. I mean. He really shouldn't be encouraging her.'

They both sat in silence, looking at their drinks

'So what are you suggesting?' asked Duncan eventually.

'That we get rid of him.'

'What do you mean?' spluttered Duncan, looking vaguely horrified.

'We tell Chris that we no longer wish for Simon to be included in the group.'

'Right.' Duncan nodded. 'What's Chris going to tell Simon?'

'That's his problem. He brought him along in the first place. He needs to extract him.'

'Extract him?'

'Yes, remove him, get rid of him,' explained Tony.

'He's not going to like that. You know what Chris is like. Wants to be friends with everyone. Not a mean bone in his body. I'm not sure how he's going to react to having to tell Simon that he's not welcome any more.'

'Like I said, that's his problem.'

Duncan took another sip of his drink. 'What do I do about the marathon training?' he asked.

'Now that is your problem,' replied Tony, draining his drink. 'Shall we have another? Chris will be here any minute.'

'What! What do you mean he will be here any minute?'

'I invited him for a drink too. Thought we would strike whilst the iron is hot. Talk to him tonight. It's their turn to host the next dinner party. We need to be absolutely clear that Simon must *not* be invited.'

Chapter Fifty-Four

Duncan

Duncan watched as Tony leaned effortlessly against the bar. He could feel his heart racing. Would today never end? He was stressed enough already without having to gang up on his mate and demand he fall out with another mate.

'Eh up, mate,' said Chris, coming through the door. 'Isn't this great. Tuesday night beers. We should make a thing of this.'

'Sure,' replied Duncan, forcing a grin.

'You need a top-up?' asked Chris, pointing at Duncan's glass. 'What the devil is that? You had some food or something? Do they do food here? I'm starving.'

'No, it's a gin and tonic,' said Duncan.

'But there's a twig in it.'

'Don't ask,' said Duncan. 'Tony is at the bar if you want to join in the round.'

'Brilliant,' said Chris, striding off and throwing a casual arm around Tony's narrow shoulders. They really looked an unlikely pair. Duncan watched as Chris laughed and joked and Tony smiled back. The barmaid approached and Tony passed on the drinks order, turning to ask Chris what he wanted. Then Duncan watched as Tony's face dropped. He suddenly looked dismayed. What on earth had Chris asked for? A stout or something. Or maybe a bowl of nachos. Something not cool. Tony turned reluctantly back to the barmaid and repeated whatever Chris had said. Chris turned back to glance at Duncan and stuck his thumbs up.

Moments later, they walked back to the table holding two drinks each.

Two drinks? Had Chris been rude enough to get Tony to buy him in two drinks?

'There we go,' said Chris, putting them down. 'Simon should be here any minute. I happened to see him at lunchtime and said he should come along. We can talk about how we are going to fix him up with a new woman, can't we, lads?' he chuckled whilst sipping on his pint. 'I think this could be the start of a few lads' nights out, don't you? We can be Simon's wingmen, right?' he said, winking at them both.

Duncan exchanged glances with Tony and saw that he was shaking his head, looking at Duncan in wonder. Duncan shrugged. He felt oddly detached. He'd switched off. All he could do was keep going over and over his conversation with Issy that afternoon. Did she really want to leave? Why was she leaving? Was it because she was mortified at what Candice had said? But that wasn't like Issy. Normally Issy would give as good as she got, not cower in the corner, as she seemed to be doing. Not running away. Why was she running away? He didn't want her to run away.

He logged back in to the conversation just as Chris was going in to a detailed explanation of the golf he'd been watching on the television the night before. Tony stared back at him hard-faced. Clearly not listening to a word he'd said either.

'Hello,' said a voice from behind them.

Duncan watched Tony's face fall even further.

'Hi, mate,' said Chris, standing up to shake Simon vigorously by the hand. 'Good to see ya.'

'You too,' replied Simon. 'Can I get anyone a drink?'

'No, no, Tony's got the round in. We got you a pint. Hope that's okay?'

'Awesome,' said Simon, settling himself on the sofa next to Chris and picking his glass up. 'Cheers,' he declared, raising it up to his mouth.

'Cheers,' said Chris, raising his glass back.

'Cheers,' muttered Duncan.

Tony said nothing.

'How's Sarah?' asked Simon.

Duncan barely contained his gasp.

'She's fine.' Tony nodded. 'Totally fine.'

Simon nodded back expectantly as though he was waiting for something more.

'I think you know better than me how my wife is?' said Duncan out of nowhere. He was rewarded by a smirk from Tony.

Simon laughed. 'Well, she's certainly keeping me on my toes. When she decides to do something she goes for it, doesn't she? I'll be struggling to keep up with her soon.'

Duncan nodded. 'She can get obsessed with things. Starts to take over her life.'

'She clearly intends to do well. Her determination is quite incredible.'

'Mmmm,' muttered Duncan.

There was an awkward pause in the conversation.

'Beth popped round this morning, didn't she?' asked Chris. 'Said she was helping you take some more boxes down to the charity shop.'

'That she did,' replied Simon. 'She's a saint, she really is. Sorry for taking up so much of her time, Chris, but I honestly don't know what I would have done without her.'

'Aww, don't worry about it. She's really enjoyed it, I can tell. She's nagging me less, so you carry on, mate.' Chris burst in to laughter. 'She can come round to yours whenever she likes, as far as I'm concerned.'

'Well, that's very good of you really,' said Simon, taking another sip of his beer.

'Yes it is,' added Tony whilst looking at Simon.

'You might not want her round so much if you find another woman though,' said Chris.

'What do you mean?' asked Simon.

'Well, she might not take too kindly to another woman hanging round, even if it is only Beth.'

'Well, we will cross that bridge when we come to it,' stated Simon.

'Speaking of which, we were just talking about the fact that we need a proper lads' night out to get you back on your feet. Get you out there.'

'Really?' replied Simon. 'Not sure I'm ready.'

'You're ready,' said Tony firmly. 'You shouldn't be hanging out with a load of happily married couples just now. That's the last thing you need. You need to be out there with people your own age. Single people. Not coming to dinner with us lot.'

'But we can have a lads' night out as well though, can't we?' pleaded Chris. 'I really fancy a night out with us lot. It would be a right laugh.'

'Simon's never going to pull with us hanging round him, is he, Duncan?' said Tony, turning to him. 'Don't you agree that we are holding him back? He needs a social life with a younger crowd, not us.'

'Yeah.' Duncan nodded. He was still struggling to concentrate on the matter in hand. Was any of this relevant?

'I just can't bear the thought of going back to that scene,' sighed Simon. 'I've grown out of it now. I'm not in to pub crawls and trying to chat women up any more. I'd much rather… well, come to dinner with you lot, to be quite honest.'

Tony laughed almost deliriously. He shook his head. 'Haven't you got *any* other friends? I don't understand what makes you want to spend time with us. Why, Simon?'

Simon blinked a little before he answered.

'I have got other friends but… most of them have young kids, so they don't really have time for me now. Other priorities. And if we do go out, they tend to go a bit crazy, like let-off-the-leash crazy, and I'm just not in to that. So I guess it's been nice to hang out with people who are past all that. Past baby obsession. Past Friday nights out on the lash. You're all such nice people. You made me feel so comfortable in my hour of need. My other mates, well, most of them said I told you so. I didn't get much sympathy. But you lot, well, you've got me through a very difficult period in my life, to be honest. I really do appreciate it.'

'Aww, isn't that nice?' said Chris. 'You are so welcome, mate.' He grinned, holding his beer up to Simon's so they could chink glasses. 'It's been a pleasure and you are very welcome to hang around with us bunch of losers for however long you like.'

Duncan watched Tony's face as Chris responded to Simon's loving tribute.

It was full of pure loathing.

Chapter Fifty-Five

Beth

Sarah looked slimmer than ever.

How? thought Beth. How did she do that? How did anyone at their age get thinner? Beth read all the articles about weight being harder to lose the older you got and she felt a mixture of disappointment and relaxation. Disappointment that despite her best efforts she was probably never going to be thin. After all, time was against her now. But maybe that meant she could relax as she could just settle in to middle-aged spread and leave it at that. Time to hang up her dieting boots and blame it on how old she was rather than the packet of Oreos she seemed to have consumed since she got home.

But Sarah – now she seemed to defy the laws of genetics. The older she got, unbelievably, the more attractive she got. *And* the older she got, the more loaded her husband seemed to get, thus allowing her the luxury of an extremely laid-back life. The exact opposite to Beth.

She wondered what Sarah had summoned them for. Perhaps she'd won the lottery? Perhaps the bank manager had written and told her that they had run out of zeros to add onto their balance and she needed advice on what to do? Or maybe, of course, it was to tell them why she had disappeared with Simon for forty-five minutes the other night. Perhaps they were here for a confession. Beth felt her stomach churn. Whatever it was, she wasn't sure she was going to like it.

'I would have suggested Squires & Angels,' said Sarah as she sat down in the pub they had arranged to meet in. 'But Tony said he was going there. His practice consulted on the design. Have you been there yet?'

'Where?' asked Beth.

'Squires & Angels.'

'Is that some high-class strip joint or something?'

'No. It's a bar in town. Tony said it's really cool. Unlike anything else in Morbeck.'

'Right.' Beth nodded, relieved to hear that she hadn't been forced to enter a 'cool' establishment. 'Sore thumb' sprung to mind.

'What do you want to drink?' asked Sarah. 'I'll get them.'

'Erm, gin and tonic, I think. A normal one though. No plant life added, if you don't mind.'

'Sure,' said Sarah as she drifted away. Beth watched as two men leaning against the bar paused their conversation to watch her float by. The barman served her immediately despite the fact that two other women had been waiting longer. She didn't even notice them, just ordered her drinks oblivious to their vicious stares.

'Hiya,' said Marie, coming up behind Beth. 'You been waiting long?'

'No, just got here,' replied Beth.

'Hi, Marie. I got you a mineral water,' said Sarah, returning to the table with drinks. 'Are you still in full-on training mode?'

'Absolutely,' said Marie. 'I'm off alcohol until after the half-marathon. Totally not missing it, to be honest.'

Beth tried not to snort. Marie was always the one who would suggest the bus or a taxi to avoid driving at all costs. She'd been known to get her mum to pick her up at the end of the night rather than drive.

'Wow,' said Sarah. 'Well, you're looking good on it, I have to say.'

'Thanks,' said Marie, taking a sip of her drink. 'It's doing wonders for my calves. Finally they are getting in to shape.'

Beth started to mentally count down in her head.

'Simon says that I'm currently ahead of schedule. That actually I should think about doing a marathon next year.'

Just five seconds to mention Simon. Simon had told Beth that morning that he'd advised Marie she was overdoing it. That she was getting obsessed and she needed to be careful about burnout. Marie clearly had heard his words of advice in an entirely different way.

'I asked him if having bigger boobs would be a hindrance to my running,' continued Marie. 'He said that he can't imagine they are helpful, but I should see them as an asset rather than a drawback.' She laughed. 'Simon says…' began Marie again.

'Jesus Christ,' interrupted Beth. 'No wonder it's called Simon Says, if this is how much saying he does.' *My God*, thought Beth, *if it isn't Sarah fawning all over Simon, it's Marie.* She couldn't bear it.

Marie looked at her crossly for interrupting.

'Well, he is my trainer so I have to listen to what he says,' she added.

'Clearly,' sighed Beth. 'So what does he say this time?'

'He says that I have impressive stamina,' she continued. 'I think he's amazed that I can keep up with him.'

'Well, it is impressive, Marie,' said Sarah. 'We'll be there to cheer you on, won't we, Beth?'

'Of course,' agreed Beth. 'Wouldn't miss it. So,' she continued, turning to Sarah, 'to what do we owe this pleasure then?'

'Well, err, I, err…'

'Come on, spit it out,' said Beth. She needed to get this over with. She braced herself for painting a sympathetic smile over her crushed face.

Sarah took a deep breath. 'I've been offered a job,' she said.

Blank looks from Beth and Marie.

'Back in fashion,' she added.

'Thank Christ for that!' said Beth enthusiastically. Maybe this wasn't going to be so bad after all.

'How amazing,' said Marie, clapping her hands. 'I didn't know you wanted a job. You could have asked me. I bet there's something going at our place. I could have asked for you. I bet they have some shop floor work going.'

'It's a buying job,' explained Sarah.

'Oh,' said Marie.

'Lingerie actually,' she continued.

'Cool,' said Marie. 'You know where to send your samples,' she said, pointing at her boobs.

Beth didn't bother getting involved in that one. Lingerie wasn't something that suited her. Never had. Flimsy didn't wrap cellulite up well.

'Who for?' asked Marie.

'Ascots,' replied Sarah. 'It's actually a much more junior role than I had previously, but I figure that means I should be able to do it in my sleep so I can have a decent work–life balance, unlike before.'

'Sensible,' agreed Beth. 'Chloe still needs to see you around.'

'Exactly,' said Sarah.

'So when do you start?' asked Marie.

'Well, not sure. I've not actually accepted it yet.'

'Why not?' asked Marie.

'Well, it's just a bit tricky. Which is why I wanted to talk to you two. I've managed to negotiate it down to a four-day week, with two days working from home, but it will still mean I need to spend two days in London.'

'Two days in London?' said Beth. 'How are you going to manage that?'

'Well, I was thinking it will only mean being away one night a week and Chloe will be at school most of the time and Tony has said he wants to be more hands-on with Chloe. Well, he said it once, just after she was born. So I figured that Tony could do the pick-up and the drop-off the night I'm away. He can work from home if he needs to. It's a great opportunity for him to spend time with Chloe. I think it could work out really well for everyone.'

Beth looked at Sarah. She was all flushed with the effort of the explanation. She was searching their faces for approval of this plan. But Beth knew very well it wasn't their approval that she needed.

'So what does Tony think about this?' she asked.

'I've not discussed it with him yet.'

'What!' gasped Marie. 'Why not?'

Sarah looked away. 'Not been the right moment somehow,' she said.

'Well, you really need to talk to him,' urged Beth.

'I know, that's exactly what Simon says,' sighed Sarah.

'Oh, for Christ's sake, don't you start,' erupted Beth. She swallowed. The sick feeling was back.

'You spoke to Simon about it?' questioned Marie, looking slightly aghast.

Sarah blushed and looked uncomfortable. 'I know I should have spoken to you guys first,' she said, 'but he just happened to be there and I needed someone to talk to.'

Marie and Beth said nothing. The silence was long and awkward.

'What if Tony says no?' Sarah suddenly spluttered.

Beth knew that Tony wasn't going to be overly happy about this new direction in their lives and there was a high chance that he would say no. But not in so many words. In a subtle way. He wouldn't so much say no but convince Sarah that there was no way she could say yes. She suspected that Sarah knew this as well.

'He's going to say no, isn't he?' blurted Sarah when Beth and Marie continued to be silent. 'It's too much to ask for, isn't it? To be away two days a week. It's not fair on Chloe. But I... I don't know what I will do if he says no.' She paused, then looked directly at Beth. 'Because I'm so unbelievably bored, I feel like I am literally dying of boredom. I can't explain it, but it is literally killing me.'

'I wish,' muttered Beth.

Sarah looked back at Beth desperately. 'I take Chloe to school, then I get home and I want to cry, every single day, because I have nothing. And yet I have everything, so that makes it even worse. I have an amazing husband, a gorgeous house, a wonderful healthy daughter.'

And Simon – do you have him? Beth wanted to ask.

'I want for nothing,' continued Sarah, 'and yet I have nothing. I feel so guilty for feeling so unhappy. What do I do, Beth? What do I do if he says no?'

Beth took a long slow sip of her drink.

'He's not said it yet,' she replied. 'All you can do is lay it all out for him and trust he will understand.'

'But he wants a wife not a lingerie buyer, I know he does.'

'He married a career woman. He shouldn't be at all surprised that you want to go back to work,' Beth pointed out.

'I don't just want to, I have to,' said Sarah. 'That's the problem. I think I might go mad if I don't.'

'Duncan has always understood that I have to work,' said Marie. 'I want to work, it's non-negotiable. In fact, I don't think we have ever even discussed it.'

'Chris knows I have to work or else we can't pay the mortgage,' said Beth blankly. 'Zero discussion required.'

Sarah said nothing but she looked half-broken.

Did Beth feel sorry for her? Could she feel sorry for her? Of course she could. Beth knew as well as anyone that you could seemingly have everything. That on the surface you could look like life is a fucking beach but deep inside you know something is missing. There's a hole that is destroying the rest of your seemingly wonderful life and you can't do anything until you sort that hole out. Sarah's hole was a career or, more precisely, a purpose. Without purpose, life was tough however rich your husband was.

'Ironic really,' said Beth eventually. 'If Tony wasn't as minted, then we wouldn't be having this discussion, presumably. You'd be out there grafting like the rest of us.'

'I guess so,' sniffed Sarah.

'What about if we brought down Tony's business?' mused Beth. 'Made him bankrupt. That would make you happy, wouldn't it?' she said, trying to lighten the mood.

Sarah managed a small smile. 'Maybe,' she replied.

'So, we need something terrible to happen. Something that would stop Tony being so loaded. We need to find those bodies under one of his buildings so he has to go out of business.'

'That would also mean he would have to go to prison,' pointed out Sarah.

'Even better,' said Beth. 'You become a single parent so need a full-time job and move to London. Problem solved.'

'Discovering that Tony is a murderer is your answer?' asked Marie.

'Yes!' exclaimed Beth. 'It could be the only way that Sarah can persuade him to let her go back to work, if you ask me.'

JOURNALIST: So Beth has now told me what happened when you all went to Simon's for dinner. I can't tell you how sorry I am. I had no idea what painful memories this interview was going to drag up. Did you have any idea what was coming?

DUNCAN: Of course not. It didn't come out until afterwards that Tony punched a waiter in Switzerland because he gave Sarah too much attention. Maybe if I'd known that I would have been more understanding of Tony wanting to get rid of Simon.

Chapter Fifty-Six

Duncan

'So who is it then?' said Candice, barging in to Duncan's office. *She wouldn't have done that had Issy still been here*, he thought. No one interrupted his salad-eating when Issy was here.

He put his fork down and stood up.

'You really cannot do this, Candice,' he said. 'If you need to see me, book an appointment with… with…' He didn't even have anyone to book his appointments any more. He'd half-heartedly spoken to HR about replacing Issy and they'd sent him a candidate who'd started as a phone operator a couple of months ago and who'd said to him in reception when he did his customary sweep of the new intake that she was only here until her rich boyfriend asked her to marry him and then she didn't plan to work ever again. She was still on the phones as far as he knew.

'Who is it?' Candice demanded again.

'Who is what?' he asked, losing patience. Every time he saw Candice he fantasised about getting rid of her. Sadly, she was good at her job and so she needed a pretty heavy misdemeanour before he could justify giving her the heave-ho.

'Who's Simon messing around with?'

'What do you mean, messing round with?'

'Oh, don't give me that. I've seen 'em. Seen 'em all coming and going. It's got to be one of them.'

'One of who? You are not making any sense, Candice.'

She took a breath and sighed as though he were the one who was the poor communicator, not her.

'Which one of your wives is Simon messing around with?'

Duncan paused. Marie in her barely-there running gear immediately popped in to his mind. Who knew you could get hot pants that doubled as running shorts.

'What on earth makes you think that?' asked Duncan, trying to stay calm.

'Simon,' declared Candice with her hands on her hips. 'He told me he'd found someone. I think he was trying to get at me for moving in with Jack.'

'Is he the chocolate vending machine salesman?'

'How did you know that?'

'Lucky guess. So what exactly did he say?'

Candice shook her head in frustration. 'He said that he had found someone and I said, he'd kept that quiet, and he said he'd had to because she was married. Un-fucking-believable, right? And he chucked me out for giving your mate my number. Talk about double standards.'

'She's married? Are you sure?' said Duncan feeling his heart rate suddenly speed up.

'That's what he said. And I've seen all your lot round there, so I figure it's one of them, don't you?'

'What, all of them?'

'Oh yeah. In particular your wifey. She's in there most days, coming out with wet hair like she just got out the shower. She's my main suspect, if I'm honest. She looks the type.'

'I beg your pardon!' said Duncan.

'You, know, puts it all on show.'

Duncan tried hard not to look at Candice's skirt, barely skimming her thighs. 'That is my wife you're talking about,' he said.

'Yeah, I know. Poor you. And then there's the posh skinny one. Can't remember her name. She's been in and out this week. Often comes out in tears. It could be her, as she's more his type. More sophisticated. He likes that.'

Duncan was speechless.

'Oh, and the fat one's there all the time, of course, but I doubt it's her. She's just been binning all my dresses, the bitch. I bet if she were thinner she'd have bagged them all for herself, but there ain't no way that bitch is fitting in to my size eights.'

Duncan shook his head. If he regurgitated this tirade to HR, could he get rid of her? He considered having to explain that Candice had arrived in his office and accused his wife of having an affair with her soon-to-be ex-husband. He was sure a woman in a cardigan would politely clarify that Duncan, as a senior manager, should avoid being accused of a vendetta against a more junior employee just because she thought his wife was having an affair.

Duncan swallowed. He must brazen it out.

'I can assure you that none of your allegations are true, and even if they were, you and Simon are not together any more. You have no right to walk in to this office and make these claims. You *need* to leave.'

'We were all right, me and Simon, before you lot came along and interfered. We would still be together if it wasn't for you,' she said angrily.

Duncan tried to breath slowly and calm down, but he wasn't sure he was succeeding.

'I think sleeping with one of your neighbours had more to do with you and Simon splitting up than any of us.'

Candice shook her head in disbelief.

'You're all weird,' she started to shout. 'Wouldn't surprise me if you were all swingers. Keys in the middle of the table type of couples. That dinner party wasn't right. I knew there was something strange going on. No wonder Issy left. Did she find out? Did she find out you were all swingers? Put her off you, did it?'

'There was nothing weird going on,' said Duncan, slamming the table with his fist. 'You are deluded. You blame everyone except yourself. We are not perfect, but neither are you. Simon throwing you out was your own fault, no one else's. And you have no right coming in here making stupid accusations. No right, do you hear? Issy left because of what you said. You embarrassed her and that was unforgiveable.'

'You don't like me because I speak the truth. I can see that.'

'You can't see anything. Get out. Get out now! I never want to see your face again.'

Candice stared at him. 'What do you mean, out?'

'You're fired. I cannot bear to work with you any more. Get out.'

'You can't fire me.'

'I just did.'

'You can't. You are so going to regret this. I am going straight to HR to tell them that you fired me because I guessed you were part of a swingers' gang.'

'Fuck off, Candice.'

Chapter Fifty-Seven

Simon

He'd considered backing out. Making his excuses and saying he couldn't go for dinner, but something was stopping him. Every time he went to pick the phone up he couldn't do it. Because, actually, he really wanted to go for dinner. He wanted to see her despite the fact he knew he should walk away now. That he had to nip it in the bud before it went any further, before he found himself doing something that he shouldn't.

Perhaps it was the way she talked about her husband that made him hesitate. She was clearly dissatisfied with him, as well as life in general. If he thought she was happy, then maybe he could have left well alone. It broke his heart that she was unhappy, that's why he couldn't walk away. Couldn't bear to see her living this life. Maybe he should rescue her… But she was married. He believed in marriage… well, he used to. Until Candice blew his ideals apart. Maybe he shouldn't believe in marriage. What he should believe in was happiness. What was the point of marriage unless it drove happiness? Happiness was a higher order than marriage, surely?

In the end he decided to invite them all over to his house; it was technically his turn after all. He was also worrying that some members of the group thought he had outstayed his welcome. If he had them all over to his, then at least he wouldn't look like he'd been freeloading off them all. It was supposed to be at Beth and Chris's this time, so he'd done one full rota of dinner parties with the group, and so really it was his turn. It seemed like a lifetime ago since he'd shown up out of the blue on Chris's doorstep. A broken man. He was a different man now. They'd changed him.

Candice knew. She'd shouted at him that he was stuck-up now he had his poncey mates from the 'dinner club'.

He didn't know why he had told her. It just came out. She was taunting him with stories of going to Vegas with the chocolate vending machine salesman and so he'd said it to shut her up. To get rid of her. He told her that there was someone. He should have left it there, but he couldn't resist. It felt good to say it out loud. Show Candice that he had stuff going on in his life too. The minute he'd told her she was married, she demanded to know which one. She missed nothing, Candice. She demanded to know which of the stuck-up dinner party crowd he'd made a connection with. Of course he didn't tell her. That was his treasure. No one else's, until he worked out what on earth he was going to do with it.

Chapter Fifty-Eight

April – Dinner at Simon's

Duncan

What to do? His head was spinning with thoughts of daisy plants and accusations and threats and recriminations. What to do indeed.

There had been a last-minute change of venue for tonight's dinner party. Marie told him when he got home that Simon had offered to host and wasn't that good of him. He scrutinised her. She said it without any apparent hidden agenda. She said it freely and untroubled. He didn't know if this was a good thing.

'He knows exactly what to cook in line with my training,' said Marie. 'Unlike Beth, who sees it as her mission in life to force-feed us with whatever we are trying to cut down on.'

'Will there be carbs then?' asked Duncan hopefully.

'Oh yes. You need carbs to fuel your training. I imagine there will be some kind of rice or pasta dish. Not for you though, of course. Can you fit in that shirt yet? Honestly, Duncan, it'll be next Christmas by the time you have lost enough to wear it. It's such a waste of money if you are not prepared to lose the weight to get in to it.'

'Bitch' sprung to mind. But he didn't have the energy to put it in to words. He was starving without Issy's fillers during the day. Without the odd few sweets, half her sandwich that she didn't want, a couple of cakes off the obligatory birthday tray, quite frankly he felt like he was wasting away.

'Shall I ring Simon and tell him no carbs?' he asked wearily.

'I already told him this morning. And we are doing a 10K tomorrow, so he'll have some carbs lined up for me.'

Surely she wouldn't be this blasé if they were really having an affair, would she? He'd sense awkwardness whenever Simon's name was mentioned, surely. Her body language would give her away. And yet he detected nothing different. She was still ranting about his carb intake and Simon was still the best thing since sliced bread. Bread – Duncan laughed at the irony.

He'd toyed with calling Tony regarding Candice's outburst. Given the unproductive night out with the boys the other week, he knew that Tony would like to know. Would relish the confirmation that something was afoot. That things were going astray, just as he had predicted. But he feared that Tony's anger would put his feeling of slight indifference in to frightening relief. Tony would expect a plan, would expect camaraderie, would expect outrage and fighting talk.

Camaraderie? There was a time when that would have been music to Duncan's ears. Camaraderie with Tony. He'd never expected to achieve that. And now he had it handed to him on a plate. They could be a team. Team 'get rid of Simon', except he really wasn't bothered.

As he and Marie arrived at Simon's, Duncan shuddered as he remembered the last time he was there. Chasing Candice helplessly up the path, wondering what on earth he was doing.

What had happened to him since Simon had arrived in their lives? Somehow he'd turned Duncan's world upside down. Before Simon, or BS as he would now refer to it, he loved his job and now he hated it. He suspected there was a strong possibility he might get fired. Candice hadn't left the building when he'd told her to leave; she'd walked straight downstairs to HR and lodged a complaint. Of course she had! He had a meeting with the Head of HR and the MD on Monday morning, when he would be forced to explain Candice's allegations of unfair dismissal and her claim that Duncan was responsible for the demise of her marriage and that Issy only left because Duncan had led her on in some kind of twisted way that only Candice could dream up. He didn't know how it was going to go on Monday. He didn't know how to even begin to explain the sequence of events that had led to him firing Candice. He could barely explain it to himself. Perhaps it would have been better if Chris had never brought Simon along to that dinner party. Because then he wouldn't have brought Candice to the next one and then this whole can of worms would never have been opened.

'Hi, guys,' said Simon, flinging open the door. 'Come in.'

Duncan noticed he was wearing an apron and it suited it him. *Sums him up really*, he thought dejectedly.

'Wow, smells amazing!' exclaimed Marie, walking in and hanging her own coat up as if she had been there many times before. Oh, yes, of course, she had been there many times before as a result of their 'training'. He watched how they interacted. All seemed perfectly normal. All seemed natural. There was no awkwardness. Duncan was pretty convinced if Simon had fallen for someone it wasn't Marie and yet the funny thing was that he didn't know if he was relieved or disappointed.

'Go through to the kitchen,' Simon said to Duncan. 'It's through the door at the end of the hall. Downstairs toilet is just here, by the way,' he added, indicating a door to his left.

Duncan thought about pointing out that this wasn't the first time he'd been in the house but decided against it. Why drag that up now.

'Duncan has been here before, remember,' said Marie.

'Has he? When?'

Duncan sighed.

'I brought Candice home when you chucked her out,' he said. 'She forced me to check the bed for signs of you having had another woman here?'

He watched as Simon went slightly pink.

'Of course,' he said eventually. 'I'd forgotten all about that. Well, I'm glad to have you here under better circumstances. I can assure you I will not be asking you to check the beds at any time at all during the course of the evening.'

'Good to hear.' Duncan nodded grimly.

Five minutes later and Duncan was feeling better. He was sitting at the kitchen table, nursing a particularly nice glass of Sauvignon 'Bland' as Marie liked to call it and eating quite the tastiest dip he had ever experienced. Marie had given him the evils as he had taken up a nacho and delved in, ignoring the carrots and celery, but he didn't care. And then once he started, he couldn't stop. It was amazing. Warm and melt-in-the-mouth and it had green stuff in it so it had to be healthy, right? Marie couldn't complain about that, could she?

'This is just spectacular,' announced Duncan on his fifth dip. But, hey, who was counting. Marie was, he could tell.

'My auntie lives in America and can't believe she can't get spinach and artichoke dip here, so she makes it all the time when she visits.'

'What's in it?' asked Marie, looking at it suspiciously.

'Chopped spinach and artichokes and this recipe has mayonnaise, mozzarella, garlic and Parmesan in it. It's the baking that makes it though. There is something about a warm dip that is just amazing.'

'You're telling me,' said Duncan. 'And I know who is going to absolutely love this,' he continued.

'Chris,' they all said in unison.

'He'll be lucky if there is any left,' said Marie as Duncan took his sixth dip.

'Don't panic,' replied Simon. 'I made two. Thought it might be popular.'

'Thank goodness for that,' said Duncan as he took his seventh dip. Somehow the world seemed a better place just at that moment. It was amazing what carbs and a decent dip could do for your mental health.

Chapter Fifty-Nine

Tony

'What are we doing here?' said Tony, confused, as Sarah drew the car up in a road he didn't recognise. He'd been on the phone to a contractor the whole journey. A project in Watford was just about to go vastly over budget if the guy didn't stick to his original estimate. Tony hated nothing more than people not sticking to their promises.

'Oh sorry,' said Sarah, shaking her head. 'Did I not mention it? Simon offered to host tonight at the last minute. Beth's been run off her feet at work and Simon said it was his turn anyway, so we're eating here instead.'

'His turn?' said Tony.

'Yeah.' Sarah shrugged. 'I guess he's right. He's already been to Beth and Chris's. Remember, that was the first time we met him, so it must be his turn.'

Tony stared at her, horrified. How had this happened? How did Simon get a turn? Simon couldn't possibly have a turn. A turn implied he was a fixture. He was a permanent part of the rota. Who decided that? Surely everyone should have been consulted on such a decision. You can't just go inserting someone in to the dinner party rota without consultation.

Tony sat there for a moment contemplating not going in. Contemplating demanding to go home. Contemplating saying that he wanted no more to do with his man. But he wasn't sure how that would go down with Sarah. Relations between them were tense enough as it was. Ever since she had told him about this ridiculous job offer.

She needed to get over it now. Really she did. He had no idea why she ever thought it was a realistic option. Working in London two days a week? Employing a nanny? Asking him to make sure he wasn't ever away on a Tuesday night so he would be home with Chloe? What was she thinking?

Apparently she was bored, but he thought she seemed happy enough. She had everything after all. She never wanted for anything. Surely, she couldn't be unhappy about that?

And he'd even offered to set her up in business. Buy her a shop, design it for her. Give her cash to start up. A boutique could be perfect. She'd be brilliant at it. But when he had offered her that she'd looked at him with a face he had never seen before. He'd seen it displayed for the benefit of other people but never him. A look of confusion and bewilderment, like he was the stupidest man on earth.

'Do you understand,' he'd said slowly. 'I'll set you up in business, right here in Morbeck, if you are bored. Give you whatever you need.'

The look had only intensified. Then she had uttered one word before she left the room.

'No,' she'd said.

He wasn't used to people saying no. And if they did, he could always work out a way of turning it in to a yes.

Then he'd woken in the middle of the night with a realisation. He had no idea why it came to him then. But it did. He thought about waking Sarah up to ask her but thought better of it. He needed to see her reaction and so he saved it until the next morning.

'Is that why you were so long upstairs with Simon the other night?' he'd asked. 'Were you telling him about the job?'

She'd looked up, hesitated, then said, 'Yes.'

'You told him before you told me?'

'Yes.'

Tony didn't know if he trusted himself to speak. He was aware of his breath quickening. It hurt.

'Why?' he'd managed to say. He was struggling for breath.

'I didn't mean to, but I needed to talk to someone. He just happened to be there.'

Simon just happened to be there rather a lot, thought Tony.

'I needed to know if it was a stupid idea before I even talked to you,' Sarah had said.

Tony started shaking his head. This was not happening. 'And what did the mighty Simon have to say about it?' he'd asked.

Sarah had looked at him for a long time before she answered.

'He said I should talk to you. He said you would understand.'

She'd left the room on a conversation for the second time in twelve hours.

Fucking bastard Simon, thought Tony.

Shaking his mind of the memory, he looked up at Simon's house. It was a nice enough, he supposed. If you liked that sort of thing. A new build on a bog-standard estate. No personality, no style, no individuality. *I guess that sums Simon up, really*, Tony thought to himself grimly as they stood at the door waiting. The house didn't even have a name, just a number. He hadn't lived in a house with just a number for... well, never.

'Well hello,' said Simon, opening the door. 'Glad you could come.' He made a point of shaking his hand over-vigorously, thought Tony, before he grasped Sarah's shoulders and did the double kiss. 'I can't offer you the opulence of your place, but, well, you are very welcome. I will do my best to make up for it in the cooking.'

Unlikely, thought Tony to himself. His Thai fishcakes had been marvellous and it was hard to think how you could beat a genuinely good Thai curry.

'Man, you have to try this dip,' said Duncan as they walked in to the kitchen. 'Seriously, I think I might have died and gone to heaven. It's amazing. You'd better get stuck in before Chris gets here or else he is just going to inhale it in one fell swoop.'

Tony peered at the creamy mush flecked with green.

'What's in it?' he asked dubiously.

'It's spinach and artichoke,' said Simon. 'It's warm. Great for this time of year.'

'Oh my God,' said Duncan, seizing another nacho and delving it in to the mush. 'Was that the doorbell? Chris will be here any minute. Grab some whilst you can.'

Simon disappeared to let in the last arrivals, leaving Duncan shoving a bowl of nachos in Tony's face eagerly. Tonight was going to be a disaster. He could already tell.

Duncan grabbed his arm. 'I need to talk to you, mate,' he hissed.

'Okay,' said Tony, taking a nacho and dipping a tiny corner in to the dip. He tasted it. It was surprisingly good, which really irritated him! 'What do you want to talk about?' he asked Duncan.

'I can't say now, but maybe I could give you a ring tomorrow and we could have a chat.'

Tony looked up at Duncan and found himself trading quizzical looks. *What now?* he thought.

'We have to go here next,' said Chris, dashing in through the kitchen door and waving a flyer in Tony and Duncan's face. 'Oh hello, is that dip?'

'I'll put some more in the oven,' said Simon, coming in behind him followed by Beth. 'Let me get you both a drink.'

Chris didn't speak whilst he dug a nacho deep in the goo. He didn't then speak at all for a good few seconds whilst he concentrated on his appraisal of this new dip arrival.

'Oh my days!' he gasped eventually. 'Finally a home-made dip to topple the mighty classic of sour cream and chive. I never thought we would see this day. Have some, Beth. It's amazing.'

'I thought you said Tony's chilli jam was right up there last month,' said Beth, helping herself to a nacho.

'Well, I know but…' said Chris, looking sheepishly at Tony.

'Wow!' said Beth. 'That is delicious. I see what you mean.'

'Do you like it?' asked Simon.

'Like it?' she replied. 'More than fondue, I reckon.' She grinned.

Chris grabbed another nacho and pushed the flyer he still had clutched in his hand at Tony. 'Boys' night out,' he muttered, trying not to spit crumbs everywhere.

'Oompah Bar,' Tony read out slowly. 'What on earth is that?'

'It's a German-style bar with great beer and live bands and chicken wings, can't tell you how much I love chicken wings, and apparently everyone ends up dancing on the tables by the end of the night! It sounds like a perfect boys' night out and apparently it's full of women. We are bound to get Simon here fixed up. What do you say?'

Tony walked over to the counter, grabbed a glass and poured himself a drink. He wasn't sure if he could stand many more of these dinner parties.

★

JOURNALIST: So I understand you had a raclette at Simon's?

CHRIS: Yes. Don't think we will be having one again. Lethal, as it turned out.

Chapter Sixty

'A raclette?' asked Chris. 'What's a raclette?'

It had taken a while to get everyone seated after the excitement of the dip, but now they were all sitting around Simon's kitchen table looking at some strange cooking contraption he had placed in the middle.

Beth rolled her eyes. She wasn't really sure what a raclette was either but trust Chris not to be shy about coming forward with his ignorance.

'It's another Swiss way of cooking,' said Simon. 'I got the idea from the fondue that you did.'

'But what is it?' asked Chris, looking suspiciously at the large stone slab in front of him.

'Well, I've already plugged it in. Look, there's an element underneath the slab that heats it. It gets really hot, so be careful. I don't want to be treating anyone for burns tonight. And what you do is you put bits of steak and chicken and peppers and mushrooms on the slab and cook them yourself.'

Chris eyed warily the platters of raw meat and vegetables that Simon was placing on the table in front of them.

'You just put it on the top and let it cook for as long as you want,' explained Simon. 'And underneath the slab there are little pans like frying pans and you can lay the cheese in there and melt it. It tastes really good over the steak and chicken.'

Beth shook her head. The thought of Chris being trusted to cook raw meat was scary. She predicted food poisoning by the next morning.

'Of course this isn't a proper raclette,' said Tony. 'A raclette cheese is round and in Switzerland they suspend half a cheese over a flame that melts the surface, then you scrape it off.'

'I know that,' said Simon patiently. 'But this works just as well. You'll see. Now dig in, everybody,' he told them, sitting down. 'There's plenty of French bread and new potatoes as well to have with it. Don't be shy.'

'So we are due to run a 10K tomorrow, aren't we, Simon?' chipped in Marie. 'So it's all right to load up on a few carbs?'

'Of course,' agreed Simon. 'You should be making sure you are having enough calories to fuel your run. Just enjoy, okay?'

'But that doesn't include you, Duncan,' she said warningly. 'You know he still can't fit in the shirt I bought him for Christmas! And we go skiing in two weeks!' she told everyone. 'God knows what he's eating when I'm not there to keep an eye on him. At this rate I'll have to call that PA of yours again and set up a webcam on you.'

'She left,' said Duncan grimly.

'What, Issy did?' asked Marie. 'You never said. Why did she leave? I thought you said she was the best PA you ever had. Although, to look at her, you wouldn't think that was possible. Spider's web tattoos,' she announced. 'She was rough-looking, I can tell you.'

Duncan looked up and shook his head in despair.

'What?' said Marie. 'Well, she was, wasn't she? No idea why you gave her the job in the first place. You must have seen her hidden talents or something. Not surprised she screwed it up. Did you have to sack her?'

'No!' said Duncan. 'I never would have sacked her. She had a fall-out with another employee. Decided she couldn't work with her any more.'

'Catfight was it? Over a bloke?' said Marie. 'How predictable.'

Duncan raised his gaze slowly. He held Marie's stare, then slowly lifted his arm and selected the largest piece of French bread on the pile before deliberately putting it on his plate.

'Just that piece,' instructed Marie. 'And no butter. You know you have high cholesterol.'

'Wine, Tony?' said Simon, standing up, clearly detecting that distraction was required. 'It's a Merlot. That okay?'

'Depends where from,' he said, taking the bottle from Simon and scrutinising the label. After a few moments, he handed it back to Simon. 'That region does produce a reasonable Merlot,' he acknowledged, nodding to Simon to indicate he should pour some in to his glass.

Dickhead, thought Beth.

Simon moved round the back of Tony and pulled a face at Beth, causing her to giggle.

'Wine, Sarah?' he said. 'I know you really like this one.'

Simon carefully poured the red in to her glass.

'How?' asked Tony. 'Sarah doesn't normally drink red.'

The room went quiet.

'I asked how?' repeated Tony, staring at Simon and then his wife.

Beth watched as Sarah froze. She literally looked like a rabbit in the headlights. Her big eyes were bigger than ever. Her face drained of all colour. She opened her mouth and then closed it again.

'I, err…' She cleared her throat.

'Simon?' pushed Tony.

Simon looked in confusion between Tony and Sarah. Chris turned his steak over on the raclette stone.

'Didn't you tell him?' said Simon to Sarah.

'Tell him what?' roared Tony, standing up suddenly.

Beth stared in horror. This wasn't going to end well. What hadn't Sarah told Tony?

Simon shook his head. 'She just popped round for a chat, that's all,' Simon told Tony. 'Just the once, to talk about this job offer. The wine was open.' He turned to Sarah. 'Didn't you tell him you came round?'

Sarah shook her head. Totally mute.

'For fuck's sake,' shouted Tony. 'I'm sick of this. What the hell is going on? And don't tell me nothing. Don't treat me like an idiot. I've had an affair, remember? I can spot the signs a mile off.'

The room gasped. Beth wanted to leave, but she also wanted to stay. The sick feeling was back.

'Calm down, Tony,' said Sarah. 'Please. Nothing is going on. I promise you, but you have to calm down. Remember what happened last time.'

'You and her?' exclaimed Marie, directing her question at Simon.

'No!' roared Simon. 'You've got it all wrong. There's nothing going on. I swear it isn't.'

'Do you?' said Duncan. 'Do you really? Only Candice came to see me this afternoon and told me that you had another woman. But you had to keep quiet about it because she was married.'

Now it was time for the colour to drain from Simon's face. Beth had a curious urge to reach out to him and comfort him whilst also wanting to punch his lights out. Another woman – a married woman! So something *was* going on between him and Sarah. It had to be.

'No... I... No... that's not what...' Simon sat down, looking all around him at a loss.

'What do you mean, he has another woman?' Marie asked Duncan.

'You tell me,' said Duncan, turning on her. 'Is it you? All I bloody hear, day in, day out, is Simon this, Simon that. Are you training for a half-marathon or are you just back here shagging?'

Despite the fact she was being accused of an affair, Marie ignored her husband. Her eyes were fixed on Simon.

'Another woman?' she said again in shock.

'Perhaps he's got both of them on the go,' sneered Tony. 'Is that what's going on here? You stroll in to our lives and take your pick? Is that what you are up to? I never trusted you from day one.'

'Now, hang on a minute, guys,' said Chris, standing up after he'd extracted his steak and put it on his plate. 'You can't go throwing accusations around like this. I know Simon. He wouldn't do that. He's a good guy. They're wrong, aren't they, Simon? You tell them.'

Simon turned to look at Chris. He didn't reply. He didn't say anything. He just stared at Chris.

'Come on, lad,' Chris prompted. 'Tell them that they have got it all wrong and then we can all sit down because this steak isn't going to eat itself.'

Simon still didn't reply, just opened his mouth and closed it again.

Beth willed him to speak. To deny Tony's allegation. She couldn't bear the thought of it being true. She looked pleadingly at Simon.

'Guilty as charged, I reckon, don't you,' said Tony, taking a step towards Simon and towering over him. 'Who is it then?' he demanded. 'Sarah or Marie? Time to fess up, sonny. Either way *you* are a dead man.'

'Neither,' said Simon in anguish. 'Honestly.'

'Tony, you have to stop this,' said Sarah, getting up and putting a hand on his shoulder. 'You know what the doctor said. You *have* to calm down.'

'Bollocks,' said Tony, shrugging away her hand. 'Sod the doctor. I have to know,' he grunted at Simon.

'I told you. Neither,' repeated Simon.

'Tell me!' shouted Tony, grabbing Simon's hand.

There was a moment's eerie silence as Tony wrestled with Simon and then, right in front of everyone, Tony slammed Simon's hand down hard on the hot stone of the raclette and held it there.

Simon screamed in pain.

So did Sarah, Marie and Beth.

Duncan's hands flew to cover his face in shock.

Chris flew forward, hurling himself at Tony, trying to move his arm to release his grip on Simon's burning hand but to no avail.

'Tell me now!' said Tony, his face bright purple. Sweat dripping from his temples.

'It's Beth,' gulped Simon. 'But nothing has happened, I swear. She doesn't know. I've done nothing about it.'

There was a moment's delay before Tony released Simon's hand. Utter silence filled the room. Then he stepped back as Simon gasped in relief, stumbling backwards, staggering. Tears cascading down his cheeks.

'Get it under a tap,' cried Beth, leaping forwards and dragging him towards the sink. She grabbed his wrist and shoved it under the spout, putting the cold water on to maximum. *It's Beth* was coursing through her mind but was crowded out by the instinct to treat Simon's burn. She held his hand firm under the water and could hear his heavy breathing slowing down. She dared glance at him.

'Sorry,' he muttered.

'Beth!' said Marie behind them. 'I don't understand. How could it be Beth?'

Beth was suddenly aware of Sarah screaming at Tony.

'You absolute idiot,' she shouted. It sounded like she was crying. 'What have you done? How could you do such a thing?'

'Beth!' exclaimed Marie again.

'Is he all right?' said Duncan, coming up behind Beth.

'I'm not sure yet,' she replied. 'We need to do this for a while.'

'Is there anything I can do?' he asked.

Beth shook her head silently.

'I'm sorry,' he said to Simon.

Beth watched Simon nod and close his eyes in pain.

'I just don't get it,' said Marie. 'Beth!'

'I needed someone to talk to,' cried Sarah, still shouting at Tony. 'Because you wouldn't. That's all. Simon just listened. That's all, you absolute idiot. He just listened. Tony? Tony? Tony!'

Beth heard a thud behind her but didn't turn to look. She was concentrating on Simon's hand. But Simon suddenly ripped his arm away from her and was gone. She spun to see him crouching on the floor next to Tony. He was listening for his breath. He was taking his pulse.

'Tony!' screamed Sarah, flinging herself on the floor next to his collapsed body. 'Tony, get up! What's happening?'

Simon rearranged Tony's limbs, then leant forward and pressed his lips to his, breathing in to his mouth with three sharp breaths before performing compressions on his chest.

'What's happening?' screamed Sarah again.

It must be some kind of cardiac arrest, thought Beth, feeling her own heart suddenly leap up the scale. She ran towards Simon, automatically looking for what she could do to help, but as she did she realised that Simon was the right person for this. He was trained to perform in exactly this type of incident. It was, ironically, a godsend he was here.

She looked around her. Everyone was staring, white as a sheet, whilst Sarah continued to sob uncontrollably.

She went towards Sarah and put her arms around her, trying to calm her down. 'It could be a heart attack,' she whispered. 'But stay calm. He's in the right hands. Simon knows what to do.'

Sarah buried her head in her shoulder and shuddered uncontrollably. Duncan stared morbidly at Simon crouching over Tony. Beth was suddenly aware that Chris had disappeared. Had he left? Gone, after Simon's confession. But then the kitchen door opened and he appeared looking flushed.

'I… I… I've called an ambulance,' he said. 'They'll be here in ten minutes they reckon. How's he doing?' he asked Beth.

They looked at each other. He looked bleak. He looked in shock. 'He's in the right hands,' she repeated, although she knew the longer it lasted, the worse it could be.

'What should I do?' Chris asked her. She assumed he meant to help but he had the look of someone whose life had just collapsed and was lost.

'I hear a heartbeat,' said Simon, suddenly rearing up.

Sarah raised her head from Beth's chest. 'Really! Is he going to be okay?' she gasped.

'Hopefully.' Simon nodded wearily. 'Did you call an ambulance?' he said to Beth.

'Chris did,' she replied. 'It should be here any minute.'

'Right,' said Simon, sitting back on his heels and wiping his brow. 'We'll just have to sit tight until then. Nothing else we can do. Well done for calling them so quickly,' he said to Chris. He paused, his mouth still moving but nothing coming out. 'I'm sorry I…' he eventually began, tears starting to spill down his cheeks as he looked at Chris, then at Beth, then back at Chris. 'There is nothing going on, I swear,' he said. 'And Beth has done nothing to encourage me. It's just… I just… well, Candice was goading me and… and I admitted to her that I had fallen for someone and she wouldn't let it go and… and I was going to make this the last dinner party, my thank you to you all because I knew I had to walk away because if I spent any more time with you, Beth, I knew that I might do something that I might regret and I couldn't do that to you or to Chris and I know it's fucked up and I'm totally out of order, but I couldn't help myself so… so, like I said, I'd planned for this to be goodbye but… but…'

Beth stared at him open-mouthed. She couldn't believe what she was hearing. She'd thought she might have got it wrong before. That he'd actually said Sarah. But he hadn't. He had said Beth. Simon wanted her. All her life she had been waiting for someone to want her. Really want her. And Simon did. She couldn't take it in.

'Beth!' came Marie's shrill voice over the airwaves. 'I'm sorry, but I still don't get it. How can it be Beth?' Marie looked totally bewildered and it was nothing to do with the fact that Tony was lying on the floor barely breathing. 'No offence, Beth, but how?'

'Offence taken,' replied Beth.

'I just don't understand why someone like Simon would fall for Beth! I don't get it.'

Simon started to speak but he was interrupted.

'Get out!' shouted Chris.

Simon looked up abruptly, but Chris wasn't speaking to him.

'I said *get out*!' repeated Chris to Marie. 'You *cannot* speak to my wife like that.'

Marie stared back at him in shock but did not move.

'And let me tell you something, Marie,' he continued his face flaming red with emotion. '*I* get it. Of course I get it. Beth is… is amazing and do you want to know why? Because she is beautiful on the inside as well as the outside. Gorgeous, in fact. I wouldn't be surprised if half the men in Morbeck aren't lusting after her. She is the most beautiful person on the planet. And she's real and she doesn't have to fake it or add to it or put needles in her head. She's naturally beautiful. And I thank my lucky stars every single day that she is my wife. I still can't believe she said yes to me. That *I* got to marry the most beautiful woman in the world. So I am not surprised in the slightest that this day has arrived. That someone has spotted what I have known all along. That she is an absolute diamond. And I know I don't tell her that enough and how special she is, but it's in my head all of the time.'

He paused for a breath.

Beth had stopped breathing. She looked up at him in shock.

'Beth,' he said, taking her hand, 'I love you with all my heart and I always will. And I always have. You are it for me. You are everything. I always thought there might come a time when someone would want to sweep you off your feet. I knew marrying so young meant you might one day think that the grass is greener. That you would get itchy feet. Want to explore. And I can understand there are many men out there with so much more to offer than me but you have my heart, Beth, forever.'

It felt like no one was breathing.

'I'll go,' said Simon, standing up. 'I'll go and see if I can see the ambulance coming.'

'Hold on,' said Chris, reaching out and grabbing his arm. 'Do you want to go with him?' Chris asked Beth.

She stared back at him. Chris had never said anything like what he'd just said to her before. Never. Not even when they got married. But she'd always known. Always known he loved her unconditionally and relentlessly. And when he'd said those words, it felt like she was coming home after she'd been on an adventure. She was back where she was supposed to be. She'd enjoyed her trip. It had been exciting, thrilling, but also scary and disturbing. It was unpredictable and precarious, which had made her realise that she didn't want that. She couldn't live like that. She wanted safety and security. She wanted home. She realised that home was a good place. Home was actually where she wanted to be. And now home was even better because Chris had told her exactly what she needed to hear to make her realise what she had. He'd made her feel something. Feel love, genuine love, and that was all she really needed.

'I'm staying right here,' said Beth, reaching out and taking Chris's hand. 'You were right,' she said, looking up at Simon. She swallowed. 'I married a Caroline but a Caroline is exactly who I should have married.' She glanced over at Sarah and Marie and then looked back at him. 'I think there is a little bit of a Candice in you,' she added, 'and you were right, that doesn't suit me.'

Simon nodded. 'Well, he's a very lucky Caroline,' he said, then he walked out the door.

Epilogue

One Year Later

Dinner at Chris and Beth's Catered
for by a Michelin-Starred Chef

'So what are we having then?' asked Beth, wandering in to the kitchen.

'You wait and see,' said Chris. 'I'm learning loads. Paulo is a genius.'

'He's not getting in your way, is he?' Beth asked the highly attractive if slightly scary Portuguese chef that had landed from London three hours ago.

'No, no,' replied Paulo. 'He is a great assistant. Keen, enthusiastic.'

'We have created a new dip recipe,' said Chris excitedly. 'It has liquidised green stuff in it.'

'Wow,' replied Beth. 'You make it sound so appetising. Can I help at all?'

'No, love,' replied Chris. 'You're fine. Paulo has it all in hand. Can't have you ruining that dress of yours either, can we? You look amazing by the way. Doesn't she look great, Paulo?'

'Like a princess,' said Paulo, glancing up from his chopping board.

Beth swallowed. 'Thank you.' And she actually thought she did. She'd looked in the mirror, having had the luxury of over an hour to get ready, and thought, *do you know what, I look pretty good*. Maybe it wasn't just the fact she'd had an hour to get ready, maybe it was also that finally she was seeing herself through other eyes. Not hers. Not the joke of a colleague who said she was CUDDLY. No, she was finally seeing herself through Chris's eyes. And well, occasionally, maybe Simon's. But mostly Chris's.

'What time are they arriving again?' asked Chris.

'Any time now,' said Beth. 'The beds are all made up. I can't wait to see them. It's been far too long.'

'You got the hospital on speed dial?' asked Chris.

'Not funny,' said Beth. 'We wouldn't want to live through that again, would we?'

'You should have been at the last dinner party we had,' Chris said to Paulo. 'It's taken us a year to recover from that one.'

'It's why it's taken so long for us to organise this special night,' added Beth. 'I'm sorry we had such a delay, but we all needed time.'

'Sounds like it must have been quite an evening,' said Paulo.

'Life-changing,' nodded Chris.

The doorbell rang and Beth dived off down the hall the answer it, followed by Chris.

'So good to see you,' she gushed as she opened the door. 'It's been too long.'

'You too,' said Sarah, falling forwards. 'You look amazing,' she added. 'I told you that the Vera Wang was just your colour.'

Beth blushed. The thought of wearing designer clothes made her feel silly, but when Sarah had moved out of the farmhouse, she had insisted that Beth have some of her clothes that she thought would fit and flatter her. She was amazed to see what a difference a well-cut frock could make to the way she looked.

'Come on in, Chloe,' said Beth, giving Sarah's daughter a massive hug. 'It's great to see you too. Hasn't she grown, Chris?'

'She so has,' said Chris, embracing Sarah and Chloe. 'How's the big smoke then?'

'Good,' laughed Sarah, handing over a bottle of champagne. 'Work is hectic, you know. Especially now they've promoted me to head of buying. More travel and stuff, but I'm enjoying it. And now Mum has moved in with us, well, that's great. Her and Chloe are getting on like a house on fire. I think she's trying to make up for all the mistakes she made with me!'

'I'm so pleased for you,' said Beth. 'Genuinely.'

'I know,' replied Sarah. 'We miss him,' she said, tears suddenly coming to the corners of her eyes. 'Every day we miss him, but we're getting there.'

Beth leaned forward and embraced her friend. They stood there for several moments. A forty-year friendship flowing between them. When Tony had died of a second heart attack in hospital the night of the raclette dinner party it was Beth who had been by Sarah's side. Beth who had sat next to her and held her hand in the funeral car. Beth who had rung her every single day at seven in the morning for three months to help her through the early morning tears. The gulf that their apparently vastly contrasting lives had created had closed up immediately as pure love and friendship bonded them back together in Sarah's hours of need.

'I miss you too,' Sarah whispered in Beth's ear.

'And me,' replied Beth, pulling back and holding Sarah's face in her hands.

It was the doorbell ringing again that interrupted them.

'They're here!' said Beth. 'Everybody ready?'

'Can't wait for this,' said Sarah, gleefully wiping a tear from the corner of her eye.

'So good to see you,' said Duncan moments later, bursting in to the hall as they lined up to greet him. He headed straight for Sarah, embracing her in his arms.

'And you,' said Sarah. 'Really good to see you too.'

Duncan turned and beckoned towards a shy-looking woman with a spider tattoo on her elbow, standing by the door.

'This is Issy,' he said proudly. 'Issy, this is Sarah and Chris and Beth.'

'Thank you so much for inviting me,' she babbled. 'I... I... don't know what to say, because if I speak I know I'll fuck it up. Oh shit...'

'You are so very welcome,' said Beth, warming immediately to the girl they'd heard so much about.

'I know, but what about she who can't be mentioned. Shit, I'm sorry. Duncan told me not to mention Marie. Because she's your friend and that and...'

'Marie who?' said Chris, grinning openly at Issy

'So sorry, I'm not good with people I don't know,' she continued, 'and Duncan always talked so much about your legendary dinner parties and I've never been to a dinner party before, so I don't really know what to do, other than not mention Marie because Duncan told me to not mention Marie, but he didn't tell me anything else.'

'Don't worry about Marie,' said Beth. 'None of the rest of us do.'

'Oh,' said Issy.

'We haven't seen her since the last dinner party when...' said Chris.

'All hell let loose,' finished Beth.

Beth and Sarah glanced at each other. The memory of how Marie handled herself the night of the raclette dinner party flooding back. Her lack of concern for Tony as he lay on the floor grasping at life. Her lack of concern for Beth's feelings as she cried in wonder at the ridiculousness of Simon falling for Beth. Her lack of concern for her husband who bore witness to his wife's blatant pursuit of Simon right under his nose. Chris threw her out for her treatment of Beth and soon after Duncan threw her out for her treatment of him. But perhaps most shocking was the fact that Marie had not contacted Sarah once following Tony's death. An unforgiveable act that made it easy to strike her out of their lives.

'Please just be yourself,' Beth told Issy. 'That's the only rule at this dinner party.'

'But you shouldn't burn anyone's hand on a hot stone,' pointed out Chris.

'Or have a heart attack,' added Sarah, raising a watery smile.

'But you can declare your undying love,' added Chris, grinning at Beth. 'Speaking of which, I saw Simon today.'

The room went quiet. No one, other than Chris, who occasionally bumped in to him on his post round, had seen Simon since the last dinner party. Beth had deleted his number with a wistful smile on her face. Good whilst it lasted. Whatever it was. Time to make the most of what she had. And she had a lot.

'He's got a new girlfriend,' said Chris.

'Good,' said Beth enthusiastically. 'He needs a good woman.'

'Yeah,' replied Chris. 'He deserves a good woman. Said her name was Caroline. Said he used to go out with her when he was younger.'

'Caroline?' said Beth.

'Yeah, I think that was it. Caroline. I reckon he was proper in to her. He had that look in his eyes. He was really excited to tell me. Said he never should have left her in the first place.'

'Good for him.' Beth nodded.

'So,' said Chris, rubbing his hands together. 'It must be that time, guys. Anyone for some dips?'

A Letter from Tracy

Dear Reader,

I want to say a huge thank you for choosing to read *Dinner Party*. If you enjoyed it and want to keep up-to-date with all my latest releases, just sign up at the following link. Your email address will never be shared and you can unsubscribe at any time:

www.bookouture.com/tracy-bloom

I really hope you enjoyed *Dinner Party* and if you did I would be hugely grateful if you could write a review on your seller's website. I'd love to hear what you thought and it makes such a difference helping new readers to discover my books for the first time.

I would love to hear from you and you can get in touch on my Facebook page, via Twitter, Goodreads or my website.

Best wishes,
Tracy

 tracybloomwrites

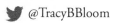 @TracyBBloom

 www.tracybloom.com

Acknowledgements

This book was inspired by the pleasure of sitting around a table whilst eating and chatting, so I'd like to start by thanking all those who I have enjoyed these special moments with. Of course, I have had many happy times with my mum and dad, brother Andrew and sister Helen at Hall Farm. The custard spitting was particularly memorable! I will also never forget the 'Christmas Dinner' in June and the airline dinner that never got off the ground in Leicester. Thank you, friends. I've always loved a murder mystery dinner party and we've had a few of those. My favourite guest, of course, being Phill's Herbacious Border, the shifty-looking gardener! And I really love an at-home Friday-night dinner, with my husband Bruce when the wine is drunk too quickly and the dip consumption is out of control. Happy times. Thank you everyone for sharing dinner with me and helping inspire this novel.

Of course other people get involved in this book publishing business, so a massive thanks to Madeleine Milburn, my agent, for lighting up the minute I mentioned the idea for this novel. Also Jenny Geras and Peta Nightingale at Bookouture for loving it too and providing great encouragement. I must also mention everyone who is kind enough to big up my books to the world, especially the irrepressible Kim Nash as well as all the book bloggers and reviewers who help get the message out there – much appreciated.

And finally I'll leave you with my fantasy dinner party guest list – perhaps you would care to send me yours. I'm going to go with my Gran Fan (sadly passed away many years ago, but I still dream about her gravy), Simon Cowell (I think he would give the golden buzzer to my gran's gravy and would have some great stories to share) and Frank Sinatra (because every good dinner party should end in a good old sing-song). Of course, I would have to feed them a dip and it would have to be spinach and artichoke. Here's the recipe in case you fancy making it for your dream dinner party.

Spinach and Artichoke Dip

INGREDIENTS

1 can (14 oz.) artichoke hearts, drained, finely chopped

1 pk. (10 oz.) frozen chopped spinach, thawed, well drained (or I tend to just boil a large bag of fresh spinach for a few minutes, drain it well and squeeze out any excess water and then chop)

3/4 cup grated Parmesan cheese

3/4 cup reduced-fat mayonnaise

1/2 cup shredded mozzarella cheese

1/2 tsp. garlic powder

METHOD:

- Heat oven to 350°F.
- Combine ingredients.
- Spoon in to 9-inch quiche dish or pie plate.
- Bake 20 min. or until heated through.

Made in the USA
Columbia, SC
30 November 2018